HUMANS, BEASTS, AND GHOSTS

∽

WEATHERHEAD BOOKS ON ASIA

Weatherhead East Asian Institute, Columbia University

HUMANS, BEASTS, AND GHOSTS

STORIES AND ESSAYS

Qian Zhongshu

EDITED, WITH AN INTRODUCTION, BY
Christopher G. Rea

With translations by
DENNIS T. HU
NATHAN K. MAO
YIRAN MAO
CHRISTOPHER G. REA
PHILIP F. WILLIAMS

Columbia University Press
NEW YORK

This publication has been supported by the Richard W. Weatherhead
Publication Fund of the Weatherhead East Asian Institute, Columbia University.

Columbia University Press
Publishers Since 1893

New York   Chichester, West Sussex
Copyright © 2011 Columbia University Press

Library of Congress Cataloging-in-Publication Data
Qian, Zhongshu, 1910–
Humans, beasts, and ghosts : stories and essays / Qian Zhongshu ; edited with an
introduction by Christopher G. Rea ; with translations by Dennis T. Hu . . . [et al.].
p. cm. — (Weatherhead books on Asia)
This book brings together the essay collection "Written in the margins of life (Xie zai ren
sheng bian shang)" and the short story collection "Human, beast, ghost (Ren shou gui)."
Includes bibliographical references.
ISBN 978-0-231-15274-7 (cloth : alk. paper)
ISBN 978-0-231-15275-4 (pbk. : alk. paper)
ISBN 978-0-231-52654-8 (e-book)
1. Qian, Zhongshu, 1910– —Translations into English. 2. Chinese essays—Translations
into English. 3. Short stories, Chinese—Translations into English. I. Rea, Christopher G.
II. Hu, Dennis T. III. Qian, Zhongshu, 1910– Xie zai ren sheng bian shang. English IV. Qian,
Zhongshu, 1910– Ren shou gui. English V. Title. VI. Title: Written in the margins of life.
VII. Title: Human, beast, ghost. VIII. Series.

PL2749.C8A2 2010
895.1′452—dc22

2010018856
∞
Columbia University Press books are printed on permanent and durable acid-free paper.
This book is printed on paper with recycled content.
Printed in the United States of America

References to Internet Web sites (URLs) were accurate at the time of writing. Neither the editor nor Columbia University Press is responsible for URLs that may have expired or changed
since the manuscript was prepared.

CONTENTS

❧

Human, Beast, Ghost

ACKNOWLEDGMENTS

～

This volume has been several years in the making, and I would like to thank the many individuals and institutions who have helped it reach completion. I began translating *Written in the Margins of Life* in Taipei in 2004 as a recreational adjunct to my doctoral dissertation research on comedic cultures of modern China. When publication became a possibility, I decided to make the essays more accessible by including notes to explain their numerous allusions and occasional instances of untranslatable wordplay. My thanks to Shang Wei and Liao Ping-hui, who early on illuminated several obscure terms and passages. I am also grateful to Philip F. Williams for his generous advice as this project was getting off the ground, and for contributing his masterful translation of "On Writers" to the volume.

I decided to combine *Margins* and *Human, Beast, Ghost* into a joint volume in order to offer readers a more comprehensive picture of Qian's early works. Three of the four stories in *Human* (all except "God's Dream") have been published previously in English translation, and I offer my sincere thanks to Dennis T. Hu, Yiran Mao, and Nathan K. Mao for sharing their translations. These translations have been revised both to match the 1983 Fujian renmin chubanshe edition and for overall stylistic consistency. Qian made many changes to both *Margins* and *Human* over the years, and I have preserved his more substantial alterations in the endnotes. My thanks to Michelle Cheng and Shannie Hsu at the University of British Columbia for their assistance in comparing editions, and to Bruce Fulton for his feedback on a portion of the manuscript.

At various stages of this project, I have relied on financial assistance from the graduate schools of arts and sciences of Columbia University and Harvard University, the Fulbright Foundation in Taiwan, the Chiang Ching-kuo Foundation for International Scholarly Exchange, the Whiting Foundation, and the Weatherhead East Asian Institute at Columbia University. To each my enduring thanks.

I am grateful to Jennifer Crewe, Mike Ashby, and two anonymous reviewers at Columbia University Press for their endorsement of this project and invaluable feedback on the manuscript. Any errors that remain are either mine or Qian Zhongshu's (you decide).

David Der-wei Wang has been a transformative figure in my life and an unparalleled mentor through graduate school and beyond.

This book is dedicated to the memory of Professor Pei-yi Wu, a teacher and friend to generations of Columbia graduate students.

My love, as always, to Mom, Dad, Sandy, Julie, and Peregrin.

Christopher Rea

HUMANS, BEASTS, AND GHOSTS

INTRODUCTION

Qian Zhongshu 錢鍾書 (1910–1998) was one of twentieth-century China's most brilliant writers. Born into a learned family, educated at one of the nation's best universities and later at Oxford and the Sorbonne, Qian came into his own as a creative writer during a period of chaos, producing most of his works between the early years of the Second Sino-Japanese War (1937–1945) and the Communist takeover in 1949.[1] Although he continued to write poems and essays intermittently throughout the remainder of his life, his career as a creative writer, like that of many of his contemporaries, was cut short by the outcome of the Chinese civil war. Over the course of that decade, however, Qian made several striking contributions to literary modernism that have yet to be fully appreciated, both within and beyond China.

Humans, Beasts, and Ghosts presents this startlingly original literary voice in the making. *Written in the Margins of Life* (*Xie zai rensheng bianshang* 寫在人生邊上, 1941) and *Human, Beast, Ghost* (*Ren shou gui* 人獸鬼, 1946), the two collections of essays and stories comprising this volume, together constitute the bulk of Qian's early creative prose.[2] Written primarily during wartime, after Qian had returned from three years of study in Europe, they offer iconoclastic commentary on one of the most tumultuous periods in modern Chinese history. As many of his contemporaries were rushing to answer the call for a "literature for national salvation," Qian instead published a collection of essays that appeared to be concerned more with literary squabbles than with military battles. Later in the war, he wrote four stories that eschewed the epic mode for psychological domestic drama or satirical fantasy. Yet in each essay, we find concerns more substantive than might be suggested by their sundry topics—the significance of windows versus doors or the failings of impressionist literary critics, for instance. His stories, too, transcend the topicality of current events. In Qian's essays and short fiction alike we find a sustained testing of the possibilities and limitations of language by a critically minded writer with an unparalleled linguistic repertoire and a spirit of fierce intellectual independence.

Fortunately, Qian has expressed his literary vision not through ponderous philosophizing or anguished moralizing but through a comedic prose style that yields maximum pleasure per paragraph. Indeed, the encyclopedic mode of satire that runs through these stories and essays, which I discuss later, is one of the interrupted trajectories of modern Chinese literature. While teaching at various universities before 1949, Qian had the freedom to display his wit through fiction, essays, poems, and reviews. The dogmatic politics of the Mao years (1949–1976), however, prevented the republication of these earlier works and redirected Qian's creative energies toward academic research. During that age of literary utilitarianism, satire became untenable (despite Mao's endorsement of the mode in a 1942 speech), and Qian worked in obscurity as a literary researcher and translator in government-sponsored academic research organizations. In the post-Mao period he was "rediscovered" in China thanks to the publication of his seminal work of literary criticism, *Limited Views: Essays on Ideas and Letters* (*Guan zhui bian* 管錐編, 1979–1980), and, in the early 1980s, the republication of much of his early fiction, prose, and criticism. China had unearthed a massive talent—one who joked at the time that his literary remains would have best remained buried. "Qian Studies" subsequently developed into a subfield in Chinese academia, and Qian Zhongshu became a household name in 1990 when his landmark novel *Fortress Besieged* (*Weicheng* 圍城, 1946–1947) was adapted into a television serial.

Famous though he is in China, Qian remains a relatively unknown writer in the English-speaking world, even though his acclaimed novel *Fortress Besieged* has been available in translation for thirty years. This neglect is due in part to the inaccessibility of the rest of Qian's creative oeuvre, only fragments of which have been published. *Humans, Beasts, and Ghosts* is thus intended to afford readers a more comprehensive portrait of this remarkable writer by bringing together translations of his early works. Since detailed overviews of Qian's life and works are already available in English, and since his early works have received little critical attention compared with *Fortress Besieged* and *Limited Views*, in this introduction I focus on the literary significance of the works contained in this volume.[3]

CIRCUMSTANCES OF AUTHORSHIP

In September 1938, Qian Zhongshu boarded the French steamer *Athos II* bound for China with his wife and daughter after three years of literary studies in Oxford and Paris. The Second Sino-Japanese War, now in its second year, had forcibly displaced many of China's schools of higher education, particularly those north of the Yangtze River. Three of China's top universities—Beijing, Qinghua, and Nankai—joined to form a new institution, Southwestern United University, and established a campus in Changsha, Hunan province. War pressures soon forced the school to relocate to Kunming, in the southwestern province of Yunnan. Qian, a Qinghua graduate, had been recruited that summer to teach in Southwestern United's Department of Foreign Languages, which he did from shortly after he landed in Hong Kong in October through the summer of 1939. During this time, he published a series of four essays in the Kunming literary journal *Criticism Today* (*Jinri pinglun* 今日評論) under the heading "Cold Room Jottings" (Lengwu suibi 冷屋隨筆). That summer, he rejoined his wife, Yang Jiang 楊絳 (b. 1911), who, with their daughter, had continued on the boat to Shanghai. A few months later, he departed again for the interior, this time to Lantian National Teacher's College, in the remote town of Baoqing, Hunan province, at the behest of his ailing father, who was on the faculty. During their separation, Yang collected ten of Qian's recent short works—one short story and nine essays—into a book she entitled *Written in the Margins of Life*. Qian wrote a preface to the collection, dated February 1939, which suggests that he had completed all ten pieces by then, but the volume was not published (by Shanghai's Kaiming shudian) until December 1941.[4] By that time, Qian had returned to Shanghai, now under complete Japanese occupation, where he stayed with Yang and their daughter through the end of the war.

Poshek Fu has characterized the moral environment in occupied Shanghai as presenting intellectuals like Qian and Yang a choice between passivity, resistance, and collaboration.[5] Qian Zhongshu's wartime activities would seem to place him within the first of these categories, as he largely eschewed wartime politics and focused on his own scholarly and creative works. This time of financial hardship and political peril turned out to be an extremely productive one for Qian. While teaching at the French Catholic Aurora Women's College in the French Concession, he continued work on a book of literary criticism that he had begun while teaching in the interior, *Discourses on Art* (*Tan yi lu* 談藝錄, 1948). He also wrote four pieces of short fiction, which were published after the war as *Human, Beast, Ghost*.[6] (I translate the title of the story collection in the singular, for reasons explained later.) Yang Jiang's success in Shanghai as a commercial playwright in 1943 is said to have inspired Qian to undertake his most ambitious creative project, *Fortress Besieged*, subsequently recognized as one of modern China's greatest novels.[7] *Fortress*, which took Qian two years to complete, was serialized for one year in the Shanghai literary magazine *Literary Renaissance* (*Wenyi fuxing* 文藝復興), beginning in February 1946, and published as a single volume in May 1947. In 1948, as the tide of the civil war was shifting in the Communists' favor, Qian reportedly turned down job offers from Oxford, Taiwan University, and the University of Hong Kong to remain in China.[8] A partially completed second novel, *The Heart of the Artichoke* (*Le Coeur d'artichaut* [*Baihe xin* 白合心]), begun after the war, was lost in transit when Qian moved to Beijing to take up a position in Qinghua University's Department of Foreign Languages in 1949. He was thirty-nine.

EARLY PROSE WRITINGS

The authorial persona that emerges from Qian's small body of pre-*Fortress* works is that of an intellectual aristocrat—an inheritor of a traditional Chinese scholarly legacy who has masterfully conjoined it with the vast territory of Western letters. These early writings are larded with an astonishing range of literary allusions and cultural references and—with the exception of the story "Souvenir" (Jinian 紀念)—written in an aloof, satirical style that reserves particular contempt for fellow intellectuals. Edward Gunn has characterized Qian's cutting satire, pessimistic remarks about humanity, and antihero protagonists as typifying an "antiromantic" trend in the literature of wartime Shanghai, which eschewed themes of self-realization for "individual failures caused by self-deception."[9] At the same time, Qian's early works seem less concerned with probing the individual psyche than with using individuals or "types" as focal points for linguistic play. *Written in the Margins of Life* and *Human, Beast, Ghost* offer a number of insights into Qian Zhongshu's worldview and literary style. I highlight three here.

Literary Cosmopolitanism

In these writing we encounter a temperament, vision, and expressive capacity that are decidedly cosmopolitan. Qian returns again and again to the seemingly narrow topics of literary and critical practice, but the scope of his inquiry is anything but provincial, as it targets the modes of perception that shape human experience. Unlike many of his contemporaries who used their familiarity with multiple languages and cultural traditions to reify the boundary between East and West and play one off against the other in dualistic fashion, Qian's writings created a multidimensional field in which languages and ideas interact in unexpected ways.

This phenomenon is most readily apparent in the stunning range of literary and cultural references that was to become a hallmark of Qian's discursive style. In the essay "On Happiness," for instance, the prophet Solomon, Stéphane Mallarmé, Su Dongpo, Wang Danlu, Novalis, Georges Rodenbach, and B. H. Brockes rub shoulders within the space of a paragraph. While such ostentatious displays of learning have dazzled many readers, they have also irritated others who have been unable to see past their superficial showiness. Qian would have been heartily amused, for instance, by a Western missionary's guide to modern Chinese literature published in 1948, in which the exasperated reviewer of *Fortress Besieged* complains that "the author cannot refrain from being pedantic i.e. giving unnecessary and irrelevant foreign slogans and maxims (German, Spanish, French, Italian, etc.), a fact which repels most readers. Anybody could have done that by referring to a dictionary."[10] In fact, Qian's comparisons are neither facile nor pointless, though they are certainly numerous.

These literary and cultural allusions deserve comment because in Qian's early works their onslaught is even more fast and furious. Besides showing off his much-remarked-on erudition, however, Qian's juxtaposition of ideas that may have no previous genealogical link also opens up an arena of contesting ideas without presupposing the superiority of one over another on account of its origins. This is an early iteration of Qian's unique brand of comparative literature—the close integration of literary and critical practice that defined his style as a creative writer and underpinned the structure of *Limited Views*. This literary approach seems to meld the traditional Chinese commentarial practice of juxtaposing relevant texts *sans* explanatory "connective tissue" with the spontaneity and contemplativeness of the "baroque style" of seventeenth-century European literature.[11] The result of this combination is particularly notable for two reasons. First, its intellectual egalitarianism was (and is) a rare thing in a Chinese literary field hampered by polar political tendencies to either elevate or denigrate the foreign. Second, it challenges both Chinese and non-Chinese writers and comparatists to be competent in many languages and cultures. Qian did not just bring foreign ideas into China but also created a literary practice whose range remains unmatched by writers working only in European languages.

In *Margins* and *Human*, Qian also expresses cosmopolitanism negatively by repeatedly castigating humans for their narrowness of vision. Qian saw this as a particular occupational hazard for the man of letters. In "Explaining Literary Blindness," he compares the worldview of linguists and philologists to "Gulliver in Brobdingnag gazing up at the jade-white bosom of the empress and seeing her hair follicles but not her skin," and to a fly "flying from one pinch of garbage to another" unaware of any world other than what it can see out of its tiny eye sockets. In "God's Dream," God's authorial vanity blinds him to the true nature of his creations, man and woman, who soon turn against him. In "Inspiration," a Swedish specialist in Chinese phonology refuses to interpret the meaning of a Chinese novel (translated into Esperanto) for his fellow Nobel Literature Prize committee members, telling them that "your inquiry just now lies in the area of Chinese semantics, which is quite outside my field of specialization. Whether the Chinese language contains meaning is a topic I should not blindly pass judgment on before I have obtained unimpeachable evidence." Deferring his colleagues' praise about his scholarly circumspection, the Sinologist "insist[s] that he was nowhere close to the [Nobel-winning] American ophthalmologist . . . [who] specialized only in the left eye, and did not treat any malfunction of the right." Qian later revived this theme in a self-deprecating sense by titling his critical masterwork *Limited Views*.

We see Qian's literary cosmopolitanism not only in his thematic concerns but also in his use of figurative language. The simile, for example, with its transformative powers of juxtaposition, was one of Qian's favorite linguistic devices for refining an idea. As Qian writes in *Limited Views*:

> The use of multiple similes to convey a single idea is a technique philosophers use in an attempt to prevent the reader from becoming fixated on a particular analogy and clinging to it rather than the idea. . . . A quick give-and-take enlivens the mind. When analogies and illustrations are presented *en masse*, each vying to be the most apt or alluring, the insights keep shifting and according themselves to different vehicles. In this way, each analogy gives way to the next and none lingers, the writing flows and does not dwell on a single notion, and the thought penetrates to all aspects of the subject and does not guard a single corner.[12]

This observation alerts us to a tension in Qian's prose between the multidirectional nature of figurative language and the singular truth posited by realism. Qian's further observation, made during a discussion about poetry, that "the abundant use of imagery and similes . . . is cumulative and convergent"[13] also aptly describes both his essays and his fiction. The extreme interpretation of Qian's language play would be that he was a postmodern writer whose relativist treatment of languages and ideas created a realm of floating signifiers.[14] Yet Qian at most skirted the bounds of the postmodern, because in playing with language's malleability he reaffirmed its value. However tenuous the link between signifier and signified, Qian appreciated that words have meaning and impact.

Qian's insistence on maintaining a critical breadth of vision testifies to his independence as a thinker, particularly his detachment from the intellectual and political imperatives of his day. Qian claims in the preface to *Margins* (discussed in the following section) that his book is simply a projection of individual sensibility, but we can nevertheless take "Cold Room Jottings," the title of the series in which four *Margins* essays first appeared, as indicating not just the frigidness of Qian's accommodations in wartime Kunming but also the critical ideal of dispassionate appraisal, which Qian believed could be best realized from a "marginal" position.[15] One of the hallmarks of the human, Qian argues in "Explaining Literary Blindness," is humans' possession of a "trans-subjective point of view": the ability "to divorce questions of right and wrong, authenticity and falsity from their own personal gain and loss, and separate questions of good and evil, beauty and ugliness from their individual likes and dislikes." Indeed, the self-possession that allowed him to complete these creative works during the material deprivations and political pressures of World War II may well have later helped him filter out the distractions of the Mao years to complete his monumental reappraisal of the Chinese literary canon.

Self-Marginalization

Another insight into Qian's attitude toward literary-critical practice can be found in the innocuous preface to *Written in the Margins of Life*. Positing life as "one big book," Qian proceeds to outline his view of how the book of life should be "read." Distancing himself from the establishment ("book critic") and its claims to authority, he celebrates the subjectivity of the individual response—the exclamation mark in the margins, the scribble between the lines. In doing so, Qian asserts his right to engage with his subject on his own terms without having to fit his thoughts and insights into a coherent grand narrative. He argues for the primacy of the discrete observation, waving aside the presumption that a critic must be consistent or systematic in his criticism.[16] The studiedly casual, even tongue-in-cheek, tone belies the great degree to which this critical philosophy influenced Qian's life and works.

Above all, it is a manifesto for independence. Reading emancipates new ideas, which are more easily attained and savored at a pace of leisurely browsing. While putting the world between two covers, as it were, Qian's bookish metaphor implies that life's inconsistencies and contradictions cannot be interpreted through a single idea. "Life-as-book" treats criticism of both life and literature as an ongoing dialogue, in which marginal scribblings expand the boundaries of the text itself. Furthermore, the metaphor advocates a mind-set open to free, wide-ranging language play. The posture invites the reader to lower his guard, to accept paradox and incongruity, and to join in the fun. As Qian tries to convince us at the end of "On Happiness," "contradictions are the price of wisdom."

The title theme of *Margins* was an enduring refrain in the careers of Qian Zhongshu and Yang Jiang alike. The title *Written in the Margins of Life* was first proposed by Yang, herself a noted dramatist, translator, short-story writer, novelist, and memoirist. Half a century later, when the publishing house Sanlian was preparing to issue *The Qian Zhongshu Collection*, she revived this theme by grouping many of Qian's other published essays under the title *In the Margins of the Margins of Life* (*Rensheng bianshang de bianshang* 人生邊上的邊上). In 2007, at age ninety-six, Yang published a book of reflections on death and the afterlife under the title *Arriving at the Margins of Life: Answering My Own Questions* (*Zou dao rensheng bianshang: Zi wen zi da* 走到人生邊上：自問自答). The title phrase, she wrote in her preface, had stuck in her mind and inspired her to write down her own answers to the questions that no one else could answer for her.

As much as he acquainted himself with the ideas of others, Qian Zhongshu, like Yang, searched for his own answers to life's big questions. In his personal life, as in his writing, Qian never courted popularity. During his years working for the Chinese Academy of Social Sciences, according to Yang's memoir, *We Three* (*Women sa* 我們仨, 2003), Qian attended the meetings he was obliged to attend but otherwise kept his head down and focused on his scholarship. He and Yang insisted that they "did not run with the herd" (*bu hequn* 不合群) and in later years publicly avowed hermitage to ward off the well-wishers who only interrupted their reading regimen. In one instance, Qian is said to have brushed off an interview request with the line, "If you enjoy eating an egg, why bother to seek out the hen that laid it?" Self-marginalization afforded Qian the mental space to indulge his personal interests, which lay primarily in the realm of ideas. This is to say that Qian chose to pursue knowledge in the open field of literature rather than in the relatively closed society in which he lived many of his adult years. Whether or not his chosen isolation might have limited his cosmopolitan vision in any way, Qian's inward turn indicates that he refused to be psychologically constrained by either the place or the time he happened to inhabit.

Encyclopedic Laughter

The essays and stories in this volume are propelled by a current of laughter. Fans of *Fortress Besieged* will find here a similarly dense concentration of inspired aphorisms, witticisms, similes, and wordplay. The very title of Qian's short-story collection *Human, Beast, Ghost*, for instance, is something of a word game. On the surface, the title simply groups the stories' protagonists into three categories. "God's Dream" features a divine being who becomes disappointed with his human creations and eventually hastens their deaths. Darkie, the title feline in "Cat," slinks into and out of the narrative of the longest story in the collection. The Writer, the protagonist in "Inspiration," turns himself into a ghost through inadvertent authorial suicide and descends to Hell to face judgment before King Yama, only to pull off an unexpected reincarnation. In "Souvenir," a pilot is martyred in battle after an affair with a lonely housewife, leaving her carrying his child. These stories exhibit a recurring focus on life, death, transmigration, and resurrection—in other words, of movement among these three categories.

Yet the title can also be interpreted as Qian's conflating or blurring the lines between these three categories. The God in "God's Dream" turns out to be all too human—even prehumanly infantile—while Aimo, in "Cat," is repeatedly likened to her pet. Qian may be implying that each of us is part human, beast, and ghost. Or, given the contempt for evolutionist thought on display in "God's Dream," "Reading *Aesop's Fables*," and "On Moral Instruction," "human, beast, ghost" may indeed posit mankind's devolution. In Qian's writings, we come to expect and enjoy such ambiguities. At the same time, the author alerts us that we are always on the cusp of falling prey to an authorial joke.

As this example suggests, Qian enjoys provoking laughter and reflection through playing with linguistic form. His familiar essays, for instance, frequently employ the structural device of contrasting necessity with surplus. In "Windows," the second piece in *Margins*, Qian writes, "For a room's inhabitant a door is a necessity, while a window is to some extent a luxury." In "On Laughter" he points out that "if we hold that laughter is an expression of humor, then laughter must be regarded as nothing more than a waste product or luxury good, since not all of mankind has a need to laugh." The loaded word "luxury" purposely misleads the reader to anticipate a moralizing attack on extravagance, but in fact it serves as the prologue to a paean to the aesthetic joys of the surplus, what the philosopher Zhuangzi called the "usefulness of uselessness."

Such inversions are a symptom of Qian's playful contrarianism, which itself can be taken as a type of self-marginalization. Distorting logic and common sense, these facetious riffs parody solemn discourse. Authorities are cited out of context, and quotations are misapplied in incongruous settings. By turning common wisdom on its head, Qian deconstructs logic and then reconstructs it in a recognizable but self-contradictory form. In doing so, he reveals how linguistic rules can lead one astray. Applying the same logic to two categories as seemingly parallel as the age of a man and the age of mankind results in absurdities such as the following chain of assertions in "Reading *Aesop's Fables*":

Looking at history in its entirety, antiquity corresponds to mankind's child-hood. Man began in infancy and, through several thousand years of advance-ment, slowly reached the modern age. The more ancient the era, the shorter man's history, while the later the era, the deeper his accumulated experience and the greater his age. Thus, we are actually our grandfathers' elders and the Three Dynasties of high antiquity cannot match the modern age in long standing. Our faith in and fondness for ancient things consequently takes on new meaning. Perhaps our admiration for antiquity is not necessarily esteem for our forebears but merely delight in children; not respect for age but the flaunting of age.

Qian thus does not stop at simply pointing out language's potential for engendering logical fallacies, but instead inverts and subverts linguistic forms to create them.

The critic C. T. Hsia once generously wrote that "to lampoon intellectuals is not Qian Zhongshu's central creative concern: it is rather to unfold the perennial drama of ordinary human beings in desperation, vainly seeking escape or attach-ment."[17] We see this broader scope of vision at work in dramatizations such as the relationship between Aimo, Jianhou, and Yigu in "Cat." It must be noted, however, that Qian was not above ad hominem attacks. Consider his fictional incarnation of Lin Yutang in the same story, which revolves around an imaginary upper-class social circle in Beiping. Even a partial excerpt gives a sense of the complexity of Qian's caricatures:

The man leaning back on the sofa with his legs crossed, smoking, was Yuan You-chun. . . . He believed that China's old civilization was best represented by play-things, petty cleverness, and hack entertainment writers. In this sense, his enter-prise was much like the Boxers' cause of "Supporting the Qing and Eliminating the Western:" he shelved high-minded Western religious theory and began to promote the style of intellectual hangers-on, such as Chen Meigong and Wang Baigu. Reading his writing always felt like eating a substitute—margarine on bread or MSG in soup. It was even closer to the "chop suey" served in overseas Chinese restaurants: only those who had never sampled authentic Chinese cui-sine could be tricked into thinking it was a real taste of China. . . . His pipe was famous. He mentioned it frequently in his articles, saying that his inspiration derived entirely from smoking, the same way Li Bai's poems were all the product of his drinking. Some suggested that he must be smoking not pipe tobacco but opium, since reading his articles made one yawn, as with the onset of a habitual craving, or want to sleep, as if one had taken an anesthetic. It was suggested that his works be sold not in bookstores but in drugstores as sleeping pills, since they were more effective than Luminal and Ortal but had no side effects.

Such "set pieces" are the mark of a particular encyclopedic mode of laughter known as Menippean satire, which derives its name from the Greek philosopher and Cynic Menippus. This classical European form differs from both plain satire and the novel in its intellectual orientation. Although definitions of the genre vary,[18] its salient features include a mixture of prose genres, often with verse mixed in; an erudite demeanor combined with a taste for derision; play with paradox; and a penchant for heaping, list making, and other forms of accumulation. The distinction between the novelist and the Menippean satirist, according to Northrop Frye, is that the former "sees evil and folly as social diseases, but the Menippean satirist sees them as diseases of the intellect." As such, he "deals less with people as such than with mental attitudes."[19] Goals of the Menippean satirist are to expose the inadequacies in others' thinking through dissection and analysis, and to demonstrate his own superior intellect. His most conspicuous technique is the repeated and exuberant display of learning.

Like many Menippean satirists, Qian operates not from a fixed position but within a fluid mode that makes him more difficult to pin down. W. Scott Blanchard writes that "the Menippean satirist—though nearly always an immensely learned author—poses uneasily between the role of sage and anti-intellectual iconoclast, a wise fool who is one of literature's most endearing pests. His attitude is . . . 'Mock away at system-makers.' "[20] Qian expresses his contempt for common sense parodically in mock encomia (a variety of Menippean satire) such as his praise of hypocrisy in "On Moral Instruction," of luxury goods in "Windows," and of hunger in "Eating," and, conversely, the Devil's endorsement of treaties over violence in "The Devil Pays a Nighttime Visit to Mr. Qian Zhongshu." His mode is interrogative and dialogic, rather than purely expository, so that the reader's happy insights may later be swept away,[21] as with the Yuan Youchun profile, quoted earlier, which ends disingenuously: "All this, of course, was said by people who envied him, so naturally none of it could be taken seriously."

The mode of Menippean laughter we see in these early works is one of the keys to the complexity, inconsistency, and comedy in Qian's literary vision. It provides us with a framework for interpreting his reliance on allusion, frequent inclusion of nonnarrative elements, and mirth-making attitude. In the passage from "Cat" quoted earlier, for example, the issue of fidelity between the fictional character and the satirized person is buried in a pastiche of images, compound similes, political and literary allusions, and medicinal and gastronomic references. Lin Yu-tang appears less as a target than as a pretext for authorial self-exhibition. This inversion of priorities works against the traditional expectation of continuous narrative progression in fiction. Like the back story of the cultural entrepreneur in "Inspiration" or numerous other examples, the profile of Yuan Youchun subordinates narrative to an accumulation of jokes.

ABOUT THIS TRANSLATION

The translations in this volume are based on the 1983 Fujian renmin chubanshe editions of *Written in the Margins of Life* and *Human, Beast, Ghost*, the last versions to which Qian made substantial alterations. These editions are preferable to those contained in Beijing Sanlian shudian's posthumously published *The Qian Zhongshu Collection* (*Qian Zhongshu ji* 錢鍾書集, 2001 [hereafter referred to as the 2001 edition]) because the latter introduces a number of editorial errors but is otherwise not substantially different from the 1983 edition.[22] The main text of this volume thus presents translations of the author's final versions of his early works.

Four of the translations included here have been published previously ("Cat," "On Writers," "Inspiration," and "Souvenir"); of these, the latter three translations were based on earlier editions and have been updated to match the 1983 editions. All other translations are my own and are not individually credited.

This book is designed to be at once accessible to the general reader and useful to the Qian Zhongshu scholar. Explanatory notes, often the bane of the literary translator, are absolutely essential for these works, which would otherwise be only partially comprehensible to any reader less familiar than the author with the Chinese and Western literary canons—that is to say, to all of us. To keep the main text uncluttered, however, the explanations of literary allusions; references to obscure people, places, and events; untranslatable plays on words; and the like are endnotes. Qian's original footnotes to "The Devil Pays a Nighttime Visit to Mr. Qian Zhongshu" have been preserved. This volume also includes Qian's prefaces to various editions of *Margins* and *Human*.

EDITIONS AND REVISIONS

My main goal with *Humans, Beasts, and Ghosts* is to share a pleasurable read. A subsidiary goal (and for a smaller audience) is to demonstrate how edition research (*banbenkao* 版本考)—a seemingly dry scholarly practice rarely encountered outside premodern fields—can enhance the pleasure of reading modern works. In addition to providing glosses and commentaries, endnotes identify places where Qian Zhongshu made significant cuts, additions, or alterations to his works. Qian tinkered with these pieces several times during the nearly six decades between their initial publications and his death, in 1998, leaving the two slim volumes with a rather complex revision history.[23] I have been able to consult many, but not all, extant editions. "On Writers," "Explaining Literary Blindness," "A Prejudice," and "On Laughter" were published individually, without titles, in the Kunming literary journal *Criticism Today* in 1939 before they were anthologized in *Margins* in 1941. "The Devil Pays a Nighttime Visit to Qian Zhongshu" is said to have first appeared in a literary supplement to *Zhongyang ribao* 中央日報,[24] although I have not seen this version. I have also been unable to consult the earliest editions of "Cat" and "Inspiration," which were first published in the literary journals *Wenyi fuxing* 文藝復興 (*Literary Renaissance* 1, no. 1 [January 1, 1945]) and *Xin yu* 新語 (*New Talk* 1, nos. 1–2 [October 1945]), respectively. Subsequently, the collections have usually been published in their entirety, sometimes together.

Most of Qian's revisions and self-edits are minor, and to mark all of them would result in thousands of additional notes that would be of limited use to most readers. In "Souvenir," the least-altered story in *Human, Beast, Ghost*, for instance, I count more than 250 differences between the 1946 and 1983 editions alone. My two selection criteria for notes have been the length of the change (usually one or more sentences) and its materiality (that is, significant alteration of the meaning of a passage). Philip F. Williams completed the edition comparison for "On Writers," one of the most heavily bowdlerized pieces in *Margins*. Typos, clarifications, and minor rephrasings I have left for true zealots to seek out on their own.

Many of these authorial interventions tighten the narrative flow of the original works by cutting out citations, allusions, and asides. All provide insight into how Qian regarded his own writings, constituting a type of self-critique. As much as Qian belittles his early works in his joint preface to the 1983 editions, he also tried to improve them. On the whole, Qian made minimal changes to his works between their first appearances in journals and their later collection in book form. (A list of editions is included in an appendix.) The most significant changes occur between the 1940s Kaiming editions (1941 for *Margins* and 1946 for *Human*) and the 1983 Fujian renmin editions, though I note some others as well. A few salient patterns of revision are worth discussing here.

In his joint preface to the 1983 Fujian editions, Qian, with characteristic understatement, claims to have "limit[ed] myself to only a few minor edits. As these books had pretty much already transformed into historical materials, I was not at liberty to make deletions and additions as I saw fit or to flat out rewrite them. But, as they were, after all, in my name, I still reserved some sovereign rights, so I took the liberty of making a few piecemeal cuts and minor enhancements."

The majority of these "piecemeal cuts" appear to be the elder Qian's reining in his younger self's enthusiasm for piling up allusions and doling out sarcastic abuse. In "Cat," for example, Qian cut the following italicized lines from his lengthy caricature of the japanophile Lu Bolin:

He never claimed to smoke pipe tobacco, but that was the only possible explanation for the color of his face. Not only did the black circles under his eyes seem to be the effect of smoke, but even their shape was like smoke, curling about and calling for deep thought. As for the dark redness of the tip of his nose, it could only be likened to that of steamed shrimps or crabs. *Otherwise, we'd have to say that the black circles under his eyes were marks of libertinism or insomnia, and that his red nose was a sign of hard drinking or constipation. Malicious speculation of this sort would be dishonest, however, and would furthermore contain too many hypotheses to accord with the scientific method.*

The elder Qian also excised numerous allusions that he felt were superfluous or redundant, effectively hiding the evidence for some of his claims. In the 1939 and 1941 editions of "On Laughter," for instance, he had originally followed his memorable line that Germans are "a sausage-making people who mistakenly believe that humor is like ground meat and can be wrapped up into tidy parcels of ready-made spiritual nourishment" with a pair of concrete examples: "For instance, the preface to Jean Paul Richter's [1763–1825] humorous novel *Quintus Fixlein* describes humor as an airtight, uniform worldview. Yet even the Germans appreciated that such a view would result in humor's annihilation: a paper on German humor presented at the September 13, 1846, Literary Forum (Blatter fur Literarische Unterhalttung [sic]) long ago criticized Richter for going against common sense." These lines disappear in the 1983 edition, and—from a literary point of view—for the better. The most extensive cuts of this sort are to "On Writers" and "Cat," though no piece went untouched. Later versions of the stories and essays on the whole tend to be slightly shorter.

Qian also corrects mistakes. In the 1939 and 1941 editions of "On Laughter," Qian identifies Rabelais as the first person to use laughter to distinguish man from beast, citing the latter's well-known claim that "rire est le propre de l'homme" (laughter is man's distinguishing feature). In the 1983 edition, he sets the clock on this insight back eighteen hundred years to Aristotle.

Qian's "minor enhancements" also contain occasional surprises. In the 1983 edition of "On Writers," for example, he inserts a line about Goethe's refusing to "roar battle cries" from his study—a sardonic reference to Lu Xun's 鲁迅 (1881–1936) short-story collection *Roaring Battle Cries* (*Na han* 呐喊, 1923). The revision is in line with the spirit of the essay as a whole, reiterating Qian's point that writers make inflated claims about the power of their products. Although the specific target was by then long dead, the allusion is clearly a swipe at one of modern Chinese literature's sacred cows.

It should also be noted that revision was not a linear process. Some lines from the 1946 edition of *Human, Beast, Ghost* disappear in the 1983 edition, only to reappear in the 2001 edition, for instance, suggesting that in making revisions in the 1990s Qian (or his editors) did not rely solely on his 1980s edits but also consulted the 1940s versions of the stories.

These and many more of the self-revisions documented in this volume make for a richer reading experience, imbuing each text with an internal dialogue. They show us how Qian's temperament and sensibilities changed over time, but perhaps more often reveal their constancy. If revision is an act of creation, these changes may indeed represent Qian's last true "creative writings," a set of artifacts worthy of further scholarly exploration. After all, Qian anticipated this authorial afterlife in 1941, remarking wryly in "Reading *Aesop's Fables*" that "great writers who were unable to provide for themselves while alive will have a whole group of people living off them after they die, such as relatives and friends writing sentimental reminiscences"—adding, forty years later, "and critics and scholars writing research theses."

REAPPRAISING QIAN ZHONGSHU

With *Humans, Beasts, and Ghosts*, the hope is to introduce Qian Zhongshu to new readers and, on the centenary of his birth, invite a broader reappraisal of an author who has often been hailed as a genius. Qian is very much a scholar's writer, and it is no surprise that his manifest learning overawes literary enthusiasts. Critics' tendency to put Qian on a pedestal was observed in the late 1970s by Theodore Huters, who cautioned: "The image being created of 'leading man of letters' and cultural giant, no matter how true, runs the danger of submerging that side of him that would have gleefully and pointedly lampooned such adulation had it happened to someone else."[25] Indeed, in the story "Inspiration," as elsewhere, Qian ruthlessly mocks the notion of genius by acclamation. His own opinions on the matter, however, have done nothing to undercut his ever-growing prestige.

In these early works, we see Qian making mistakes, recycling ideas,[26] and making repeated personal attacks on contemporaries such as Lin Yutang (or perhaps just the *idea* of Lin Yutang), with whom he may have had more in common than he cared to admit.[27] In the last regard, Qian may well have been influenced by the *zawen* 雜文 polemics popularized by Lu Xun in the late 1920s and 1930s, which valued rhetoric over truth. These works brim with the competitiveness, and even sexual anxiety, of a young man. Qian's harping on women's vanity (in "God's Dream," "Cat," and "Souvenir"), for instance, comes across less as democratic disgust for all hypocrisy and more as a personal prejudice against the female sex. (Notably, Qian cut a few unflattering comments about women from later editions.) In many cases, his attacks are a useful corrective that promotes tolerance; at other times, their ethos is the antithesis of live-and-let-live humanism. Qian, of course, never claimed to be a humanist, and he would point out that he anticipated charges of this sort in the preface to *Margins*, in which he allows that the "impressions" of a casual reader-writer like himself "may contradict one another or go overboard." To critique Qian by the standards of present-day morality is a dangerous, and likely misguided, proposition.

Nevertheless, the mean-spiritedness that sometimes creeps into Qian's prose is not easily dismissed as simply a man in his humor. Arch cynicism, which often accompanies Menippean satire, is not unlike the know-it-all pride that undoes the Creator in "God's Dream," and its pettiness somewhat limits the scope of Qian's literary vision. Such criticisms notwithstanding, the best measure of Qian's literary accomplishment, to me, is the rereadability of his works, which yield new insights and revelations with each perusal. As for Qian's politics, the true significance of his extreme individualism emerges only when read against the conformist cultural imperatives of both the wartime period in which he wrote and the Mao years that followed. In a repressive environment, the engaged and freethinking individual, however cynical, offers vastly more than the run-of-the-mill writer who time and again falls back on cliché, common sense, and the party line. Qian was not a political dissident in the traditional sense, but his composure, self-assuredness, and creativity enabled him to pioneer a uniquely comic model of literary cosmopolitanism within a nationalistic and deadly serious cultural climate.

In these early works, then, we find the paradoxes, quirks, enthusiasms, and partialities that have inspired both admiration and ambivalence among Qian's readers. Throughout, we are drawn into a dialogue with one of the most original and provocative literary minds of the twentieth century.

NOTES

1. If we take "On 'Vulgarity'" (Lun 'suqi' 論《俗氣, 1933) to be Qian's first piece of "creative prose," then his creative writing career began long before the Second Sino-Japanese War; however, his most productive period was from 1937, when he wrote "Discussing Friendship" (Tan jiaoyou 談交友, January 1937), to mid-1949, when he is said to have misplaced the partial manuscript of a second novel in progress, *Le Coeur d'artichaut* (Baihe xin 白合心 [*The Heart of the Artichoke*]). See Theodore Huters, *Qian Zhongshu*, World Authors 660 (Boston: Twayne, 1982), 8–9.

2. Qian also wrote poems and numerous critical essays during the 1930s and 1940s. Of his essays, "On 'Vulgarity,'" first published in *Dagong bao* 大公報 on November 4, 1933, and "Discussing Friendship" are closest to the informal style of *Margins*, blending literary criticism and philosophical ruminations. "Discussing Friendship" was written while Qian was at Oxford and first published in Zhu Guangqian's 朱光潛 (1897–1986) *Literary Magazine* (*Wenxue zazhi* 文學雜誌) in May 1937. These essays are collected in *In the Margins of the Margins of Life* (*Rensheng bianshang de bianshang* 人生邊上的邊上), in *The Qian Zhongshu Collection* (*Qian Zhongshu ji* 錢種書集) (Beijing: Sanlian shudian, 2002), 65–72, 73–81, respectively.

3. See the bibliography at the end of this volume. Qian's biographers, with the notable exception of Huters (*Qian Zhongshu*), mostly gloss over *Written in the Margins of Life*. *Human, Beast, Ghost* has garnered more scholarly attention but tends to be appraised primarily in evolutionistic terms as a proto–*Fortress Besieged*.

4. As Ma Guangyu notes, it is unclear exactly where and when Qian wrote these ten items, though the author himself states in his 1983 preface that he did not write them in Shanghai. Some scholars have claimed that some essays were written in England, though pieces with explicit allusions to conditions in the interior (for example, "Devil" and "Windows") suggest that they were written in Kunming. Kaiming shudian reprinted *Margins* three times after the war, in 1946, 1947, and 1948, around the time that *Human, Beast, Ghost* and *Fortress Besieged* were published. For a review of scholarship on *Margins* up to 1991, see Ma Guangyu 馬光裕, "*Xie zai rensheng bian shang* yanjiu zongshu" 《寫在人生邊上》研究綜述 (A Summary of Studies on *Written in the Margins of Life*), in *Qian Zhongshu yanjiu caiji* 錢鍾書研究采輯 (*Qian Zhongshu Studies*), ed. Lu Wenhu 陸文虎 (Beijing: Sanlian shudian, 1992), 1:268.

5. Poshek Fu, *Passivity, Resistance, and Collaboration: Intellectual Choices in Occupied Shanghai, 1937–1945* (Stanford, Calif.: Stanford University Press, 1993).

6. For a review of scholarship on *Human* up to 1991, see Ma Guangyu, "*Ren shou gui* yanjiu zongshu" 《人獸鬼》研究綜述 (A Summary of Studies on *Human, Beast, Ghost*), in *Qian Zhongshu yanjiu caiji*, 1:276–91.

7. C. T. Hsia, *A History of Modern Chinese Fiction*, 3rd ed. (Bloomington: Indiana University Press, 1999), 441.

8. "Qian Zhongshu nianbiao" 《錢鍾書年表》 (Qian Zhongshu Chronology), in *Qian Zhongshu Yang Jiang yanjiu ziliao* 錢鍾書楊絳研究資料 (*Research Materials on Qian Zhongshu and Yang Jiang*), ed. Tian Huilan 田蕙藍 et al. (Wuchang: Huazhong shifan daxue, 1997), 13. As Huters and others have noted, this was neither the first nor the last time that Qian passed up prestigious and remunerative offers from foreign universities.

9. Edward M. Gunn Jr., *Unwelcome Muse: Chinese Literature in Shanghai and Peking, 1937–1945* (New York: Columbia University Press, 1980), 9.

10. Jos. Schyns et al., *1500 Modern Chinese Novels and Plays* (1948; repr., Hong Kong: Lung Men Bookstore, 1966), 163.

11. Huters, *Qian Zhongshu*, 78–79, 70–95 passim.

12. Qian Zhongshu, *Limited Views: Essays on Ideas and Letters*, ed. and trans. Ronald Egan (Cambridge, Mass.: Harvard University Press, 1998), 137. See Egan's insightful analysis of Qian's practice of "striking a connection" (*datong* 打通) (15–22 passim).

13. Ibid., 138.

14. "God's Dream," in which the authorlike Creator dreams of inadvertently destroying his creations (man and woman) after discovering that they have stopped obeying his will, has inspired at least one productive reading along these lines, though it stops short of branding Qian a postmodernist. See Sheng-Tai Chang, "Reading Qian Zhongshu's 'God's Dream' as a Postmodern Text," *Chinese Literature: Essays, Articles, Reviews* 16 (1994): 93–110.

15. In a one-line preface to the series, which began in vol. 1, no. 3 of *Criticism Today* (*Jinri pinglun* 今日評論) (January 15, 1939), Qian explained: "'Cold' because the room I'm renting is freezing; 'jottings' because I let my pen wander freely. That's the truth, and that's my preface" (14). Zhang Wenjiang 張文江, one of Qian's biographers, hypothesizes that "cold" implies "to take a detached point of view" (literally, "to watch cold-eyed from the sidelines" [*lengyan pangguan* 冷眼旁觀]). See Zhang Wenjiang, *Wenhua kunlun* 文化崑崙：錢鍾書傳 (*Cultural Giant: A Biography of Qian Zhongshu*) (Taipei: Yeqiang, 1993), 56.

16. For more on the "discrete observation," see Ronald Egan, "Introduction," in Qian, *Limited Views*, 1–26.

17. Hsia, *History of Modern Chinese Fiction*, 437.

18. See, for example, Ingrid A. R. De Smet, *Menippean Satire and the Republic of Letters, 1581–1655* (Geneva: Droz, 1996); Howard D. Weinbrot, *Menippean Satire Reconsidered: From Antiquity to the Eighteenth Century* (Baltimore: Johns Hopkins University Press, 2005); and W. Scott Blanchard, *Scholars' Bedlam: Menippean Satire in the Renaissance* (London: Associated University Presses, 1995).

19. Northrop Frye, *Anatomy of Criticism: Four Essays* (Princeton, N.J.: Princeton University Press, 1971), 230–31, 309.

20. Blanchard, *Scholars' Bedlam*, 12.

21. For an insightful discussion of the "nonsense-making method" (*chedan fa* 扯蛋法) that Qian employs in *Margins*, see Huters, *Qian Zhongshu*, 79–95 passim.

22. The 2001 edition was published in traditional Chinese characters; in 2002, Sanlian published a simplified-character version of the collection, which corrected some, but not all, the errors introduced in the 2001 edition. Most subsequent reprints have been based on the 2002 edition.

23. For a detailed, if idiosyncratic, study of edition issues up to the 1990 Chinese Academy of Social Sciences edition of *Written in the Margins of Life*, see Wang Ziping 王子平, "'Xie zai rensheng bianshang' banben kao" 《寫在人生邊上》版本考 (Edition Research on *Written in the Margins of Life*), in *Liaodong Miusi zhi hun: Qian Zhongshu de wenxue shijie* 撩動繆斯之魂：錢鍾書的文學世界 (*Stirring the Muses: The Literary World of Qian Zhongshu*), ed. Xin Guangwei 辛廣韋 and Li Hongyan 李洪岩, 85–106, Qian Zhongshu yanjiu congshu 錢鍾書研究叢書 (Collected Studies on Qian Zhongshu) (Shijiazhuang: Hebei jiaoyu chubanshe, 1995).

24. Ibid., 86.

25. Huters, *Qian Zhongshu*, 155.

26. To note just a few brief examples of derivativeness: In "The Devil Pays a Nighttime Visit to Mr. Qian Zhongshu," the Devil remarks, "At art exhibitions I talk about connoisseurship and at banquets I talk about the culinary arts. But that's not all. Sometimes I instead talk politics with scientists and art with archaeologists; after all, they don't understand a word I say and I'm happy to let them pass off my phrases as their own." In "Reading *Aesop's Fables*" Qian repeats this pattern: "A bat pretends to be a crow when he encounters a crow and pretends to be a land animal when he encounters a land animal. Man, being much smarter than a bat, employs the bat's method conversely. . . . He parades refinement before soldiers and plays the hero to men of letters. Among the upper classes he is a poor and tough commoner, but among common people he becomes a condescending man of culture." In "God's Dream" God flashes a lightning smile from behind a cloud and issues thunderous laughter, repeating an allusion from "On Laughter." Liang Yuchun 梁遇春 (1906–1932) had also incorporated the old joke about Plato and the plucked chicken into one of his essays over a decade before Qian used it in "A Prejudice." See Liang Yuchun, "Zui zhong meng hua (yi)" 醉中夢話（一）(Drunken Dream Talk [1], 1927), in *Liang Yuchun sanwen ji* 梁遇春散文集 (*Collected Prose of Liang Yuchun*), ed. Qin Xianci 秦賢次 (Taipei: Hongfan shudian, 1979), 16.

27. Lin Yutang 林語堂 (1895–1976), founder of the humor magazine *Analects Fortnightly* (*Lunyu banyuekan* 論語半月刊, 1932–1937), was a prominent, bilingual intellectual in both China and the United States during the 1930s and 1940s. He appears as a satirical target in "On Laughter," "Cat" (as Yuan Youchun), and *Fortress Besieged* (which places his book *My Country and My People* on the bookshelf of a Westernized Shanghai businessman along such "other immortal classics" as the Bible and *Teach Yourself Photography*). "Cat" also contains caricatures of Zhou Zuoren, Shen Congwen, and Luo Longji, as noted in Huters, *Qian Zhongshu*, 113–14.

Written in the Margins of Life

A N D

Human, Beast, Ghost

Written in the Margins of Life AND Human, Beast, Ghost

പ

Since archaeologists began promoting tomb excavation, the withered bones of countless ancient dead people and other artifacts have been uncovered. Since modern literature became its own specialized field of research, the soon-to-wither or already-withered works of living writers have also been dug up and exposed. For some of us, our delight at having been dug up has caused us to overlook the danger of such exposure, since we don't realize that it is by leaving his works buried that the author preserves his undeserved reputation. Should the author himself take the lead in the excavation work, the loss might well outstrip the gains, and "digging one's own grave" will become a self-contradictory pun: to open the grave in which one's works are buried is also to dig one's authorial grave.

I wrote *Written in the Margins of Life* forty years ago and *Human, Beast, Ghost* thirty-six or thirty-seven years ago. Back then, I had yet to feel that my life was becoming increasingly cramped and marginalized, and my views on the difference between humans, beasts, and ghosts were uninformed and somewhat mechanical. After I finished writing *Fortress Besieged*, I made a few edits to those two volumes, but the edited versions then went missing, which goes to show that I'm not terribly fond of my old works. Four years ago, Comrade Chen Mengxiong, who specializes in digging up and opening literary graves, began selling me on the idea that the two books should be reprinted. He knew I didn't have copies of the books handy and he took pains to make copies of the originals and mail them to me. When it comes to writing, I could be said to be a bit of a loafer who has "forgotten his origins,"[1] because I'm too lazy to carefully preserve and collect my early publications. When an editorial committee was established for the Compendium of Shanghai Literature from the War Period, Comrades Zhu Wen and Yang Yousheng wanted the series to include these two books. I was confident that I had sufficient reasons to decline: *Written in the Margins of Life* was not written in Shanghai and *Human, Beast, Ghost* was not published during wartime, so to include them in this series would seem fraudulent. At that point, Comrade Ke Ling from the series editorial committee said to me: "If you don't allow these books to be reprinted domestically you're effectively allowing poorly edited 'pirated editions' to continue circulating overseas. That's irresponsible. The editorial committee has its own reasons for wanting to include these works in the series, so don't worry yourself on our behalf." He spoke convincingly and volubly, and as I've always gone along with my old friend's suggestions, there was nothing for me to do but to give my consent. I had to bother Comrade Mengxiong to furnish me another copy of the works, since I had long ago lost the copies he had mailed me earlier.

I bit the bullet and reread these two books, limiting myself to only a few minor edits. As these books had pretty much already transformed into historical materials, I was not at liberty to make deletions and additions as I saw fit or to flat out rewrite them. But, as they were, after all, in my name, I still reserved some sovereign rights, so I took the liberty of making a few piecemeal cuts and minor enhancements.

The format of the series called for each author to write a preface recounting his writing process and his works' circumstances of authorship. During the actual process of creative writing our imaginations are often pitifully deficient, but when we come to reminisce about it later—be it several days or several decades later and whether we are reminiscing about ourselves or others—our imaginations suddenly become shockingly, delightfully, even frighteningly fruitful. I am a man of tepid ambition and am not interested in indulging in such creative reminiscing, so I simply will not bother sharing any memories or recollections. As these two books are not worthy of each having their own preface, this one will do for both.

August 1982

WRITTEN IN THE
MARGINS OF LIFE

DEDICATION

To Jikang
JUNE 20, 1941

ACKNOWLEDGMENTS

Several of the essays in this collection appeared previously in publications edited or prepared by Messrs. Sun Dayu, Dai Wangshu, Shen Congwen, and Sun Yutang.

Messrs. Chen Linrui and Li Jianwu reviewed the entire book and provided unstinting assistance in its printing and publication.

Since the author is residing deep in the interior at the moment, Ms. Yang Jiang, in Shanghai, selected, edited, and arranged these essays into one volume.

The author hopes that these individuals will not begrudge his trifling expression of gratitude.

Life, it's been said, is one big book.

Should life indeed be so, most of us writers can only claim to be book critics. Possessing the book critic's skill, we need not read more than a few pages to churn out a pile of commentary and wrap up a book review in no time.

Yet, another type of person exists in this world. These people believe that the purpose of reading a book is not actually to write a criticism or an introduction. Possessing the casualness and nonchalance of spare-time diversion seekers,[1] they browse at their own leisurely pace. When an opinion strikes them, they jot down a few notes or write a question mark or exclamation mark in the blank margins of the book, akin to "eyebrow comments" in the top margins of old Chinese books or marginalia in foreign books. These piecemeal, spontaneous impressions do not constitute their verdict on the entire book, and having been written in passing they may contradict one another or go overboard. But the authors don't bother about this. After all, for them it's a diversion, unlike the book critic, who shoulders the weighty tasks of guiding the reader and chiding the author. Who has the ability and patience for such things?

If life is a big book, then the essays that follow can only be regarded as having been written in the margins of life. What a big book! It's hard to read all at once, and even if the margins have been written on, there's still plenty of blank space left.

February 18, 1939

THE DEVIL PAYS A NIGHTTIME VISIT
TO MR. QIAN ZHONGSHU

∽

"You and I should have met long ago," he said, taking the chair closest to the brazier. "I'm the Devil. You've been tempted and tested by me before."

"But you're a conscientious fellow!" A sympathetic smile crossed his face as he spoke. "Even though you've fallen into my traps before, you haven't recognized me. When you've succumbed to my temptations, you've only seen me as a lovable woman, a faithful friend, or a pursuable ideal. You've never been able to tell that it's me. Only those who have been able to resist my temptations, such as Jesus Christ, have recognized me for who I am. But we were destined to meet today. A family was holding a commemorative vegetarian banquet involving sacrifices to spirits and ghosts, and they invited me to sit in the place of honor.[1] I was tied up with that engagement for most of the evening and had a few too many drinks, so my vision got blurry, and while making my way back to my dark dwelling I entered your room by mistake. Electric lights in the interior provinces are a travesty—your house is as dark as Hell! But it's colder here than where I live. There, sulfuric fires burn from morning to night, which of course would be unthinkable for you here— I hear the price of coal has gone up again."

Recovering from my surprise, it occurred to me that I should fulfill my duty as host. I addressed my guest, "It's an honor to receive your midnight visit. You darken my humble dwelling![2] I only regret that I'm the only one here to receive you, and I apologize for not having prepared a better welcome! Are you cold? Excuse me a moment while I wake the servant to prepare tea and add coal to the fire."

"No need for that," he said, staying me with the utmost politeness. "I can only sit for a minute, and then I'll be on my way. Besides, let me tell you . . ." His expression became serious, yet intimate and sincere, like a patient reporting to his doctor that he is impotent, ". . . fire can't warm me up anyway. When I was young I wreaked havoc in Heaven by trying to usurp God's position. I didn't succeed, however, and ended up being cast down to suffer in the frozen depths of Hell*—much like how in your mortal realm the Russian tyrant exiled members of the Revolutionary Party to the Siberian tundra. The cold air has driven all the warmth in my body into my heart, making me cold-blooded amid the heat.[3] I once sat on a heated brick bed for three days and nights, but my bottom remained as cold as a pitch-black winter night . . ."

Surprised, I interrupted him, asking, "Didn't Barbey d'Aurevilly also once say—"

"Yes," he replied with a chuckle. "In the fifth story in *Les Diaboliques* he mentions my unwarmable bottom. This is why one abhors celebrity! As soon as you become famous you have no more secrets to speak of. All your private affairs get publicized by interviewers and reporters, and just like that you're deprived of your material for an autobiography or a confessional.[†] Should I decide to write an account of myself in the future, I'll have to make up some new facts."

"Wouldn't that run counter to the purpose of an autobiography?" I asked.

He laughed again. "I never imagined that your knowledge and insight would be as pedestrian as a newspaper editorial. This is the age of the new biographical literature. Writing biographies of others is also a type of self-expression, so there's no reason not to insert your own views or write about others as a way of showing yourself off. Conversely, autobiographers invariably don't have much of a 'self' to write about, so they gratify themselves by rendering a likeness that their own wife and child wouldn't recognize.[4] Or they ramble on about irrelevant matters, noting the friends they've made and recounting anecdotes about other people. So if you want to learn about a person, you should read biographies he's written of others, and if you want to learn about other people, you should read his autobiography. Autobiography is biography."

I couldn't help being impressed by this, and I inquired politely, "Would you permit me to quote that line of yours in the future?"

"Why not?" he replied. "Just be sure to use the formula 'as my friend so-and-so says.'"

I was delighted, and replied modestly. "You think too well of me! Am I worthy to be your friend?"

His response dashed my hopes. "It's not that *I* think well of *you* and am calling you my friend; it's that *you* are attending to *me* and claiming that I'm *your* friend.

---

* Book 1 of John Milton's *Paradise Lost* describes how the Devil was demoted for having rebelled and created a disturbance in Heaven. Canto 34 in Dante's *Inferno* says that the Devil suffers in ice.

† Garçon and Vinchon's *Le diable*, for example, collects a number of popular tales about the Devil.

When you quote the ancients in your writing, you should avoid using quotation marks to show that the words have been used before, but when you quote a contemporary, you always have to say 'my friend'—this is the only way to solicit friends."

Despite his frank talk, I plied him with a few more courtesies. "Many thanks for your excellent advice! I never expected you would also be such a writing expert too. You already surprised and impressed me just now with your mention of *Les Diaboliques*."

His reply was almost sympathetic. "No wonder other people say you can't escape your class consciousness. You think I'm unworthy to read books, don't you? I may be from the lowest stratum of society—Hell—but my aspirations have always aimed upward. I've done a fair amount of reading in my day, especially of popular magazines and brochures, and the like. That's why Goethe praised my spirit of progress and my ability to roll along with what the newspapers call the 'great wheel of the age.'* I knew you were a man who enjoys literature, so I mentioned a few famous literary works to demonstrate that I have similar interests and expertise. Conversely, had you been a prolific writer who opposed book reading, naturally I'd change my tune and tell you that I, too, considered it unnecessary to read books . . . yours excepted. Reading your books, after all, makes me feel that life is too short—how could I have the energy to read ancient tomes? I discuss inventions with scientists, archaeology with historians, and international affairs with politicians. At art exhibitions I talk about connoisseurship and at banquets I talk about the culinary arts. But that's not all. Sometimes I instead talk politics with scientists and art with archaeologists; after all, they don't understand a word I say and I'm happy to let them pass off my phrases as their own. When you play the zither to an ox, you don't need to pick a good tune! At tea parties I usually discuss cooking on the chance that the hostess will pick up on my comments and—who knows—perhaps invite me to taste her own cooking a few days later. Having muddled by like this for tens of thousands of years I've gained something of a reputation in this world. Dante praised me as a refined thinker and Goethe spoke of me as worldly and knowledgeable.† One should be proud to have attained my status! But not me. On

---

* In the "Witch's Kitchen" section in part 1 of Goethe's *Faust*, the witch blames the Devil for changing his form and the Devil replies that since world civilization constantly renews itself, he changes to keep up with it.

† In canto 27 in *The Inferno* the Devil calls himself a logician. In the "Study" section in part 1 of *Faust*, the Devil says that although he is not omniscient, he is quite experienced and knowledgeable.

the contrary, I've grown more and more humble, often reproaching myself that, 'I'm nothing but an underworld ghost!'* Like people who belittle themselves as 'country folk,' I worry that empty words are not enough to express my modesty, so I use my body as a symbol. A rich man's gigantic sack of a belly signifies that he has 'plenty in the bag,' while a thinker's bowed head and back arched into the shape of a question mark signifies his tendency to ask questions about everything. That's why . . ." As he spoke, he extended his right hoof for me to see the extremely high heel on his leather shoe, ". . . the shape of my legs is so incredibly inconvenient†—it symbolizes my modesty and 'inferiority.'[5] I invented foot binding and high heels because I sometimes need to conceal my deformities, especially when I transform into a woman."

I couldn't help asking, "Some people who have gazed upon your elegant countenance have said that the towering horns on your head look a bit like—"

"That's right," he cut in, "sometimes I take on the appearance of a bull.‡ This of course is also symbolic. Since bulls are often used for sacrifices, I manifest a spirit of 'Who will go to Hell if not me?' Furthermore, mortals love to 'blow their own bullhorn,' but a bull certainly can't blow itself—at least its biological structure won't permit it to do so. So, my bull shape is indeed a symbol of modesty. When it comes to false courtesy, I can't compete with you scholars and men of letters. The cocky ones, instead of refusing your flattery, will accept it as if you owed them a debt, regretting only that you didn't pay them back with interest. False modesty takes other forms too. Some will respond to your praise with protestations that they are embarrassed and unworthy, like a bribe-taking superior who, finding the bribe too small, returns it intact so that his subordinates will double it and send it again. Lender and superior alike maintain that praiseworthy people still exist in this world—at the very least they themselves. But my modesty could not be more sincere. In my view, if I have nothing to be proud of, how could other people be proud of me? Having always been cursed by others, I completely lack such vanity. However, although I'm not a writer, many literary works have come about because of me. On that score, I'm more like . . ." He spoke without a trace of embarrass-

---

* Both Samuel Taylor Coleridge's "The Devil's Thoughts" and Robert Southey's "The Devil's Walk" describe the Devil using politeness and modesty to cover up his pride.

† On the Devil's lame foot, see Alain-René Lesage's *Le diable boiteux* and Daniel Defoe's *The Political History of the Devil*, part 2, chap. 4.

‡ Regarding the Devil's frequent manifestation in the form of a bull, Psalms 106 in the Old Testament says that the heretics made a bull statue, which they worshipped. In later eras it was said that the Devil appeared in the form of a goat, which Defoe describes in detail.

ment—the nerve! The only color on his black face was reflected from the burning red coals in the brazier. ". . . a beautiful woman who doesn't actually write poems herself but inspires countless love-struck poets to use their broken hearts—no!— their broken throats to sing her praises. Byron and Shelley, for instance, both wrote poems inspired by me.* The packs of lies[6] one often finds in newspapers and magazines also owe to my influence."

"I'm impressed you have the energy," I remarked. "Newspapers around the globe are talking about nothing but war. At a time like this, shouldn't you be busy putting your destructive arts to work on massacres and invasions? How did you find the time in your busy schedule to come chat with me?"

"You mean to send me on my way, don't you?" he asked. "Well, I should be leaving. I forget that nighttime is when you mortals rest. We've chatted our fill today, but I still want to set you straight on a few things. You do me wrong by saying I'm involved in war. I have a peaceful disposition and absolutely oppose the use of military force. In my view, everything can be resolved with treaties. Just look, for instance, how civilized Dr. Faustus and I were when he swore a blood oath sealing the contract to sell me his soul![†] I used to be inclined to violence, but after my coup failed and I was expelled from Heaven I took my underlings' advice and accepted that a battle of wits is better than a battle of strength.[‡] Since then, I've substituted temptation for fighting. As you know, I'm in the soul business. God selects a portion of mankind's souls and the rest fall to me. Who could have guessed that during these past few decades business would be so light I'd be supping on underworld wind?[7] In the past, human souls could be divided into the good and the bad. God would keep the good souls, and I would buy and sell the bad ones. The mid-nineteenth century, however, suddenly saw a great transformation. Apart from a small minority, almost no humans had souls, and those who did were all good people who fell under God's domain. Soldiers have souls, for example, but their souls ascend directly to Heaven, so nothing is left for me. Modern psychologists promote 'soulless psychology,' a field that would never have emerged in ancient times, when everyone had souls. Now, even if there are a few souls left over from the ones God

---

* The preface to Southey's long poem "The Vision of Judgement" says that Byron and Shelley were both demonic poets.

† Christopher Marlowe's *The Tragical History of Doctor Faustus* records that Faustus pricked his arm and wrote the entire contract in blood.

‡ See *Paradise Lost*, book 2.

has selected, they're usually smelly and filthy. If they don't reek of laboratory medicine they're either covered in a layer of dust from old books or stink of money. I'm of a fastidious temperament, and I refuse to pick up leftovers from the rubbish heap. Bad people exist in the modern era too, of course, but they're so bad they have no personality or character; they're as inert as inorganic matter and as efficient as machines. Even poets disappoint me. They go on and on about baring their souls, but once they've finished baring them nothing is left over for me. You think I'm busy, but I'm so idle I'm going stir-crazy. I, too, am one of the unemployed—a sacrificial object of modern material and mechanized civilization. Plus, I'm burdened with heavy family responsibilities: I have seven million offspring to support.* I do still have social engagements, of course—someone of my level of prestige always does. Tonight I came from a dinner. In times like these I don't have to worry for lack of dinner invitations; I just find it depressing that people don't let one use one's talents to earn a meal."

He said no more. His loneliness filled the air, reducing the warmth of the brazier. I was about to ask him about my own soul when he abruptly stood up and announced he was off. Wishing me a good night, he said that we might have a chance to meet again. I opened the door and saw him out. The boundless darkness of the night awaited him in silence. He stepped outside and melted into it, like a raindrop returning to the sea.

---

* Johann Weyer's *De praestigiis daemonum* records that the number of little devils totals 7,405,926.

WINDOWS

❧

Spring has returned and we can start leaving our windows open. Spring comes in through the window, and when people indoors get restless they go out through the door. Yet outside springtime is too cheap! The sun shines everywhere, but it never seems as bright as the ray of sunlight that penetrates a dark room. Languid, sun-warmed breezes blow all about, but they, too, lack the vitality of a gust of air stirring up the gloomy indoors. Even the chirping of birds seems lackluster without the indoor silence as its foil. So we come to appreciate that spring should be seen set in a window, just as a painting is mounted in a frame.

At the same time, we realize that doors and windows signify different things. Doors, of course, were made for people to go in and out of. But windows, too, are sometimes used as entrances and exits. In novels, for instance, we read about thieves and lovers making clandestine rendezvous—both are fond of climbing through windows. We can thus be certain that the fundamental difference between windows and doors is not simply whether or not people go in and out of them.[1] Apropos of enjoying springtime, one might say that if one has a door one *can* go out, but with a window one doesn't *need* to go out. Windows bridge the lack of mutual understanding between nature and man, teasing in the wind and sun so that part of the room can share a bit of springtime. Instead of seeking spring outside we may sit and enjoy it where we are. Ancient poets like Tao Yuanming implicitly understood this essential quality of windows. One couplet in *The Return* [*Gui qu lai ci*] reads: "I lean on the southern window to express my pride / With just enough space for my knees, I find contentment."[2] Doesn't this amount to saying that even a tiny room can be livable, so long as one has a window to gaze out of? He also wrote: "In the leisure of the summer months, I recline under the northern window / Feeling the clear breeze, I imagine myself living in the age of Emperor Fuxi."[3] In other words, a single window that lets in a breeze can transform a tiny room into a paradise. Even though Tao Yuanming was from Chaisang[4] and had Mount Lu nearby, he didn't need to climb it to escape the summer heat. Thus, doors, which allow us to pursue things, signify desire, while windows, which allow us to dwell, signify enjoyment. This distinction applies not only to people living inside but also sometimes to visitors from outside. Whatever his request or inquiry might be, a visitor who knocks on and enters through the door is at most a guest who must await his host's every decision. Conversely, he who makes his way in through the window, whether to pilfer property or steal affections, has already decided to supplant you temporarily as the decision maker and not wait for your say-so. Musset's poetic drama *À quoi rêvent les jeunes filles* [*Such Stuff as Young Girls Dream Of*] has an apt phrase, the gist of which is basically that a father opens the door to welcome the material husband (*matériel époux*), but that the ideal lover (*idéal*) always enters and exits through the window.[5] Put another way, he who enters through the front door is the son-in-law in name only, because even if the father-in-law approves of him he has yet to capture the heart of the young lady herself. It is those who enter through the back window who are the true lovers to whom maidens surrender themselves body and soul. When entering through the front door, one must first be announced by the doorman, wait for the host to appear, and exchange a few pleasantries before explaining the purpose of one's visit. What a waste of thought and time compared to the delightful expediency of coming in through the back window! It's like using the index in the back of a book—a shortcut to learning that makes reading the main text from page one actually seem somewhat roundabout. This distinction, of course, is only relevant under normal social conditions. During extraordinary periods such as wartime one can scarcely talk about doors and windows when the room itself is in danger!

Every room in the world has a door, but some rooms are without windows. This indicates that windows represent a higher stage of human evolution than doors. For a room's inhabitant a door is a necessity, whereas a window is to some extent a luxury. The basic idea of a room is akin to that of a bird's nest or a beast's cave: one comes home for the night, closes the door, and is protected. When the wall has a window to let in light and air, however, it obviates the need to go outdoors during daytime and lets us live inside with the door closed. A room thus takes on an extra layer of meaning for human existence, since it is no longer simply a place to sleep or avoid the elements. Now, furnished and hung with paintings, it also becomes the stage upon which we think, work, play, and act out the tragicomedy of human existence. Whereas doors are entrances and exits for humans, windows may be said to be entrances and exits for Heaven. Rooms were originally designed to shelter man from nature's harm, but windows lured in a corner of the sky and tamed it for human use within the shelter, roping and domesticating it like a wild horse. Thenceforth, we were able to experience nature indoors. Instead of going out in search of light or a breath of fresh air, light and air could come to us. Windows thus represent one of man's victories over nature. This type of victory, however—like a woman's victory over a man—appears, on the surface, to be a retreat. When one opens a window, air and sunlight come in and occupy the space, but the occupiers end up being occupied by the space! We mentioned just now that a door is a necessity, but what constitutes necessity is not for man to decide. For example, one must eat when hungry and drink when thirsty. When someone knocks on the door, one is obliged to go open it. Who will it be? Perhaps it will be the youths a generation younger than you, described by Ibsen, who want to rush in. Perhaps, as De Quincey says in "On the Knocking at the Gate in Macbeth," the bright light of day wants to invade the world of evil and darkness. Perhaps the prodigal son has returned home, or perhaps someone has come to borrow money (or demand its repayment). The more unwilling you are to open the door for fear of who it might be, the greater your desire to open the door and find out who it is. Even the postman's daily knock fills you with apprehension and longing, since you both do and don't know want to know what news he brings. To open the door or not is out of your hands. But a window? Rising early in the morning, you need only pull aside the curtain to discover what greets you outside—snow, fog, rain, or sun—to decide whether or not to open the window. Windows, as I have said, are luxuries, and people choose to consume more or fewer luxuries depending on their circumstances.

I've often thought that windows are like a building's eyes. In *Explication of Names* [*Shi ming*], Liu Xi writes: "A window signifies wisdom. To peep out from inside is called intelligence." This matches the opening lines of Gottfried Keller's "Abendlied" [Evening Song]: "Eyes, my windows (*Fensterlein*), my fond delight / Giving me a lifetime's cherished light."[6] He, too, tells only half the story. As windows to the soul, eyes let us see the outside world and at the same time allow others to see our inner thoughts. Our eyes change with our thoughts, which is why Mencius believed that the best way to know a man is through his eyes.[7] Lovers in Maeterlinck's plays don't close their eyes when they kiss so that they can see how many kisses the other wants to elevate from heart to mouth. This is why when we converse with people wearing dark glasses we always feel we can't fathom their intentions, as if they were wearing a mask. According to Eckermann's record of his April 5, 1830, conversation with Goethe, the latter detested all people who wear glasses, since they could make out all the wrinkles on his face while he was dazzled by the reflection from their lenses and couldn't read their mood.[8] Windows let people on the outside look in while allowing people on the inside to look out, which is why people who live in busy places protect their privacy with curtains. In the evening, a visitor need only look for a light in the window to be able to guess whether or not the host is home; he need not open the door to ask. It's like reading someone's thoughts from his eyes before he opens his mouth. Closing the window, meanwhile, has the same effect as closing one's eyes. Dreams, like many things in this world, can be seen only with the eyes closed. Should the voices and action outside one's window grow too noisy, one may simply close the window to allow one's soul to wander freely and be able to ponder in peace and quiet. Sometimes, closing the window and closing the eyes are linked. Suppose you feel dissatisfied with the mediocre world outside your window; or perhaps you wish to return to your hometown to see your long-lost friends and family. Sleep will take you there, but before you shut your eyes and seek them in your dreams, you get up and close the window. It's only spring, after all, and the air is still chilly. Windows can't be left open all night.[9]

ON HAPPINESS

Flipping through a copy of Vigny's *Journal d'un poète*[1] I picked up at a secondhand bookshop, I happened across an interesting item. Vigny wrote that in French the juxtaposition of "good" and "hour" in the word for happiness (*bonheur*) testifies that the road to happiness is not an easy one, since happiness is but the plaything of an hour (*Si le bonheur n'était qu'une bonne demie!*). Considering similar expressions in Chinese, we see that their implications are equally profound and lasting. The presence of the character quick [*kuai*] in the words joy [*kuaihuo*] and happiness [*kuaile*], for instance, indicates the mutability of all delights with supreme clarity. So we say with a regretful sigh, "When joyful we find the night too short!"[2] For when a person is happy life passes too quickly, but as soon as he encounters difficulty or boredom, time seems to move painfully slowly, as if dragging a lame foot. The German word for tedium (*Langeweile*), translated literally, means "long while." In *Journey to the West*, the little monkeys tell Traveler Sun that "a day in Heaven lasts as long as a year on earth,"[3] a myth which, as it turns out, perfectly mirrors the human psyche: Heaven is a happier and more comfortable place than earth; therefore immortals live more quickly than humans, and a year on earth is equal to a single day in Heaven. To extend the analogy, since Hell is more painful than earth, life there must be even slower. Duan Chengshi writes in *Miscellaneous Morsels from Youyang*[4] that "three years with demons equals three days on earth." People who complain about the brevity of life really are the "quickest living" [happiest]; conversely, people who truly "live quickly" [that is, happily] can all be said to have come to a premature end, no matter what age they expire. In this light, being an immortal is not all it's cracked up to be either, since a person who lived a thirty-year lifespan in the mortal realm would be but a month-old child in Heaven. Nonetheless, there is an advantage to be gained yet through such "Heavenly reckoning." Dai Fu's *Broad Collection of Anomalies*,[5] for example, records that when Adjutant Cui captured a fox-demon and "sentenced him to five blows with the peach branch," Zhangsun Wuji complained that the fox-demon was being let off too lightly. To this Cui responded, "This is no mean punishment! Five blows in the spirit world is like five hundred in the mortal realm."[6] One can see from this that while it's well and good to flaunt one's old age or congratulate elders on their longevity on earth, punishments are best served in Heaven.

The expression "eternal happiness" is not merely so vague that it can never be realized; it's so absurd as to be completely untenable. That which passes quickly can never endure. To speak of "eternal happiness" is as self-contradictory as to talk about a square circle or static movement.[7] When we are happy life picks up speed and becomes slippery. Like Dr. Faustus, we call out in vain to time that vanishes in the blink of an eye: "Linger a while! So fair thou art!"[8] What's the point in that? If it's eternity you want, best look for it in pain. Leave the rest aside: a sleepless night, an afternoon date that never shows, or a tedious lecture will let one taste "eternal life" better than any religious faith. This is life's great irony: the things that refuse to depart quickly are invariably those one cherishes the least.

Happiness in life is like the sugar cube that entices the child to take his medicine, and even more so like the electric rabbit that lures dogs around the racetrack. For a few short minutes or days of happiness we endure a lifetime of suffering. We long for happiness to come, long for it to stay, and long for it to come again—these three phrases sum up the history of mankind's endeavors. As we pursue happiness or await its arrival, life slips by unnoticed. Perhaps we are no more than tickers counting the passage of time. Perhaps to live a lifetime is but to serve as a funerary object for the years of that lifetime without any prospect of happiness. But to the day we die we don't realize that we've been duped. We still harbor the ideal that after death there is a Heaven where—praise the Lord for that day!—we will finally enjoy eternal happiness. So you see, the lure of happiness is not merely like the electric rabbit or the sugar cube in making us endure life; it is also like bait on a fishhook in that it lets us die willingly. Put this way, life may be painful but it is not pessimistic, since it always harbors hope of future happiness. To pay our current debts we mortgage ourselves to future payments. For happiness, we are even willing to die a slow death.

John Stuart Mill likened "Socrates on the rack" to "a pig content."[9] If a pig can truly know joy, then a pig is little different than Socrates. While we don't know whether a pig can be as content as a human, we have abundant proof of how easily a human can be as happy as a pig. The most muddleheaded way to analyze happiness is to differentiate between the corporeal and the spiritual. All joy is spiritual, even when it's caused by the physical stimulation of the body. When a child is born, he drinks his fill of milk and obediently falls asleep not knowing what joy is, even though his body feels comfortable. The explanation for this phenomenon is that the child's mind and body are not yet differentiated and remain in an innocent, nebulous state. Should you feel happy taking a bath, looking at a flower, or eating a meal, it is not simply because the bath gets you clean, the flower blooms prettily, or the flavor of the food tickles your taste buds. In large part it is because your heart is unfettered and your soul is relaxed enough to focus on enjoying the corporeal sensation. Should you be unhappy, it will be like being at a farewell banquet: no matter how well the food was cooked, to you it will smell and taste like mud. At such times the soul is like the eyes of a sick patient that fear the sunlight or an open wound that fears contact with the air, even though air and sunlight are both good things. When one is happy, one becomes impervious to shame. Should you commit a crime but be genuinely happy, you will feel as carefree as people of morality and refinement, no matter whether your conscience is clean, nonexistent, or pitch-black.[10]

When we discover that happiness is determined by the spirit, human culture will take another step forward. Equally important to the acceptance of this principle will be the discovery that right and wrong and good and evil are determined by justice rather than violence. When we discover justice, no longer will any people in the world be able to be conquered solely by military force. When we discover that the spirit is the locus of all happiness, we will no longer be intimidated by the prospect of suffering and the dictatorship of the body will lessen. The alchemy of the spirit is able to transform corporeal suffering into the stuff of happiness. Thus, some people celebrate when their house burns down; some find happiness with just a bowl of rice and something to drink; and some carry on nonchalantly telling jokes through endless calamities. Thus, as we said before, though life may not be happy it can still be lived optimistically. Writers from Solomon, who wrote the Nevi'im, to Mallarmé, author of "Brise marine," for instance, all believed that the sufferings of civilized man were attributable to his physical fatigue.[11] Yet some people are able to make merry despite a bitter life and filter happiness out of their ailments as a sort of compensation for their loss of health. One of Su Dongpo's poems reads, "When you're sick you gain leisure, and that's not that bad / There is no better remedy than a mind at ease."[12] Similarly, Wang Danlu's A "New Tales of This Age" for Today[13] records that Mao Zhihuang was often ill, and that when people worried about this, Mao remarked, "The flavor of illness is fine indeed / But it is difficult to convey this to the healthy and restless!" In the sports-loving Western world we can find people with a similarly detached point of view. In Fragmente, the hypochondriac Novalis inaugurated something of a philosophy of illness, suggesting that illness was "a schoolmarm who teaches us how to rest."[14] Rodenbach's poetry anthology *Les vies encloses* includes a section dedicated to extolling illness as "cleansing of the soul (*épuration*)."[15] By adopting this point of view, people whose bodies are in good health and enjoy staying active will feel that ailments have their own distinctive flavor. The first time the stubborn eighteenth-century German poet B. H. Brockes fell ill he felt it was "an astonishing discovery" (*eine bewunderungswürdige Erfindung*).[16] What threat could life pose to such a man? This sort of happiness that transforms suffering into enjoyment is a great victory of mind over matter since it affords the soul its own autonomy. Then again, this may also be self-deception. A man who is able to maintain such an attitude is of course a great philosopher, but who knows—he may also be a great fool.

Yes, there is a contradiction here, but contradictions are the price of wisdom. This is life's big joke on philosophies of life.

ON LAUGHTER

Since humor literature came to be promoted, "selling laughter"[1] has become a profession for men of letters.[2] Humor is, of course, vented by means of laughter, but laughter does not necessarily indicate a sense of humor. Liu Jizhuang's *Guangyang Notes* states, "The donkey's bray sounds like crying; the horse's whinny sounds like laughter."[3] Yet the horse is not celebrated as a great humorist—likely because he has a long face. In truth, most people's laughter is akin to the horse's whinny and cannot be considered humorous.

Aristotle appears to have been the first person to use humor to distinguish man and beast.[4] In *The History of Animals* [*sic*] he states, "Man is the only animal able to laugh." The gist of the modern genius W. S. Blunt's sonnet "Laughter and Death" is that the natural world of birds and beasts has a fitting sound to express every emotion—joy, anger, love, and fear—but lacks only laughter to denote humorousness.[5] Nevertheless, if we hold that laughter is an expression of humor, then laughter must be regarded as nothing more than a waste product or luxury good, since not all of mankind has a need to laugh. The cries of birds and beasts would be sufficient to convey the average man's emotions: when angry he roars like a lion; when sad he howls like an ape; when arguing he croaks like a frog; when he encounters his enemy he barks like a dog that's seen its shadow; and when he spies his lover he starts cooing like a turtledove. How many people who truly possess a sense of humor, we may well ask, need laughter to express it? Moreover, the Creator distributed the ability to laugh evenly throughout humanity—every person's face can smile and throat emit laughter.[6] To have this inborn talent but not use it would be a pity indeed. Thus, most people laugh not because they are humorous, but in fact because they have the capacity to laugh and use laughter to cover up their lack of a sense of humor. Thus, laughter gradually lost its former purpose: what originally signified an abundance of humor slowly became a cover for a dearth of humor.

Hence, we have the idiot's dull-witted laugh, the blind man's naughty and mischievous laugh—as well as the recent vogue of "humor literature."

A smile is the quickest and most fluid of expressions, spreading from the eyes to the corners of the mouth. "The Eastern Wasteland" section of Dongfang Shuo's *The Classic of the Divine and the Strange* records that when Duke Dongwang lost in a game of dice, "Heaven smiled at him."[7] Zhang Hua's annotation that lightning is Heaven smiling was truly inspired. According to Lady Holland's *A Memoir of the Reverend Sidney Smith*, Sidney Smith once remarked that "lightning is Heaven's wit." The smile could indeed be said to be lightning on the human face: the eyes suddenly light up and the teeth flash through parted lips. Just as lightning cannot be captured and substituted for the sun and moon that hang on high and shine upon all, neither can a smile be turned into a fixed, collective expression. As a promoted product, humor is inescapably artificial. Such a mechanical smile is akin only to the bared teeth of a skull—not nearly as agile as in a living person. In *Le rire*, Henri Bergson writes that everything laughable arises from something flexible becoming stiff and awkward, from the "mechanical encrusted on the living" (*le mécanique plaque sur le vivant*).[8] This is why repetitive, monotonous speech patterns and movements, such as stuttering, clichés, and children's mimicry of adults provoke laughter. Old people tend to be funnier than young people because they can't move as nimbly and are full of ossified habits. Humor cannot be promoted for the same reason. The moment it is promoted, the natural turns into affect, and the mercurial transforms into rigidity. Such humor is itself fodder for humor; such laughter is itself laughable. A man with a genuine sense of humor possesses a particular type of understanding. He laughs merrily, smiles calmly, and breathes a breath of fresh air into life's dreariness. Perhaps only hundreds of years and tens of thousands of miles hence will he find a kindred spirit, standing on the opposite bank of time and space, who smiles back. A large crowd of people choosing the same moment to open their mouths and relax their throats in a merry group laugh is the type of chain reaction that can only be generated by some vulgar traveling vaudeville show. If promoting domestic goods results in more bogus brands, humor is even less suited to mass production. Instead of generating humorists, the promotion of humor has multiplied only the number of clowns playing with brush and ink. The clown's social status, of course, rises dramatically as he muddles his way from the theatrical stage to the literary stage under the banner of humor. Nevertheless, humor's quality deteriorates when the clown turns it into a bogus brand, and most literary art of this sort must be regarded as little more than "entertainment art." A clown can make us laugh, to be sure, but he is completely unlike a person with a genuine sense of humor. When a person endowed with a genuine sense of humor laughs, we laugh with him, while a clown feigning humorousness is laughable, and we laugh at him. The clown makes us laugh not because he possesses a sense of humor, but because we ourselves do.

Thus, humor is at most a sensibility. It most certainly cannot be branded as a doctrine, and it is even less well suited to being a profession. We must recall that the original Latin meaning of *humor* is "fluid." Put another way, humor, like woman in the eyes of Jia Baoyu, is made of water.[9] To turn humor into a doctrine or a means of livelihood is to congeal a liquid into a solid, to transform a living thing into an artifact. When someone possessed of a genuine sense of humor starts selling laughter as his means of livelihood—Mark Twain, for instance—his works will no longer be worth reading. Since the end of the eighteenth century, Germans have loved to discourse on humor, but the more they've said, the less relevant the discussion has been to its ostensible topic. This is because the Germans are a sausage-making people who mistakenly believe that humor is like ground meat and can be wrapped up into tidy parcels of ready-made spiritual nourishment.[10] Humor lessens life's seriousness and by no means takes itself seriously. True humor can laugh at itself. It not only has a humorous view of human life, it has a humorous view of humor itself. Promoting humor as a slogan or a standard is a gesture bereft of humor. This is not humor but its earnest avocation, laughter pried from a solemn countenance. Again, we are reminded of the horse's whinny! It may indeed sound like laughter, but the horse's face is still without a trace of a smile, and is as long as that of a surviving friend of the deceased at a memorial gathering, or of a master of the advanced sort at the lecture podium.[11]

Generally speaking, people have one of two motivations for pretending to be something they're not. Some do so out of respect, such as an uncouth person who respects art and collects antiques in order to pose as a man of culture and refinement. Some do so for profit, like the scoundrel who passes himself off as an upright man by invoking religion and morality. Humor, presumably, is usually appropriated for one of these two purposes. In the long run, however, bogus goods cannot pass as the real thing. Westerners call bright and uplifting laughter "silvery laughter."[12] Fake humor gives forth the dull clunk of a leaden slug and can only be considered leaden laughter. Then again, it could be that "silvery laughter" means to profit from selling laughter or to laugh for silver, akin to the old saying "in books there are roomfuls of gold."[13] I'll stop here for the time being and leave this sampling for the reference of lexicographers.

EATING

"Eating rice"[1] is sometimes just like getting married. What is in name the most important thing often ends up being just a subsidiary consideration. When properly "eating rice" we in fact eat vegetable and meat dishes, just as when someone pursues the daughter of a rich old man, his primary object is not the girl! This type of lateral shift in perception involves a roundabout and rather complicated worldview. Savoring flavors rather than satisfying hunger becomes the real purpose of "eating rice" for us. The tongue replaces the belly as the ultimate or highest arbiter. Nevertheless, we persist in camouflaging enjoyment as need. We do not say we are "eating vegetable and meat dishes" but rather say we are "eating rice."[2] It is like when we study philosophy or art, we always claim that the truth or beauty we find in them has utility. Things that have utility may, of course, be used by people for their benefit, and so be preserved and protected. Things without utility, conversely, find ways of using people to cover up or construct apologies for them so that they can avoid being discarded. Plato's *Republic* divides the nation into three levels of people corresponding to the three components of the soul. The desires of the senses—hunger and thirst, eating and drinking—are the soul's basest components, akin to the commoners or the masses in a political organization. The clever politician knows how to do just enough to satisfy the masses while dressing up his ambition as the will and welfare of the masses. Inviting a guest to a meal at a restaurant on the pretext of eating is an excuse the tongue makes to the stomach, as if to say, "Don't complain, there's something in it for you too! I do the work and you get the credit—what do I still owe you?" In fact, Heaven knows—a belly shrunken from hunger knows even better—that if filling the stomach is one's sole purpose, tree bark and grass roots differ little from chicken, duck, fish, and pork! Who could have imagined that the humble biological processes of digestion and excretion would necessitate so much political maneuvering?

The Roman poet Persius[3] once exclaimed that the belly was the "Master of Arts and Dispenser of Genius" (*Magister artisingeni que largitor venter* [*sic*]). Rabelais elaborated on this point in detail. Volume three [*sic*] of *Gargantua and Pantagruel* contains a chapter in praise of the belly, which it esteems as mankind's true master, the originator and promoter of all manners of human knowledge and vocation. It goes so far as to say that the flying of birds, the running of animals, the swimming of fishes, the creeping of insects, and the hustle and bustle of all living things are "all for their innards" (*et tout pour la tripe*).[4] All of man's creations and activities (including essay writing) indicate not only the richness of the brain but also the emptiness of the stomach. A full stomach is good for nothing, and it turns the brain to jelly, making it good only for dreaming silly dreams. These two have an unwritten agreement, as powerfully evidenced by the postlunch siesta. We unfairly despise hunger, saying it produces only beggars, thieves, prostitutes, and the like, while forgetting that it has also inspired thought, skill, and the political and economic theory that "when there is food, it is for all to share." In an earlier time, the German poet B. H. Brockes wrote a poetic encomium likening God to "a great chef" (*der gross Speisemeister* [*sic*]) who cooks food for all of humanity to eat, but this view inescapably betrays some religious childishness.[5] The people who provide the food we eat are certainly not our true masters. No point in being that kind of God! Only those who have others to cook for them have the ability to control our actions. The master of the house, for instance, is not in fact the father who earns money to support the family but the newly weaned child sitting and eating contentedly. This fact, needless to say, goes unappreciated in childhood and is one that fathers would surely be unwilling to concede. Rabelais has a good point. Think about it: if the belly—to which we make offerings of tea and food from dawn to dusk—is not God, then what is it? In the final analysis, however, it is a lowly thing that only has the capacity to ingest and lacks enjoyment and appreciation. This is where life becomes complicated. On the one hand, there are people looking for food to fill their bellies, while on the other there are people who have food but lack appetite. The worldview of the first type of person might be called rice eating, while that of the second might well be called dish eating. The first type of person works, produces, and creates in exchange for food to eat. The second type uses the fruits of the first type's activities to strengthen his disposition and whet his appetite, to help him eat and expand his eating capacity. Thus, it is not enough for us to have music when we eat—we must have "beauties" and "lovelies" to press us with wine.[6] When we want to be even more refined we throw parties to pass the season or admire calligraphy and famous paintings at banquets. Even when admiring flowers or going on excursions to the mountains, we are treating famous scenic spots as accompaniments to our meal. Naturally, we insist that the dishes be the very finest. In an environment of such material abundance, the tongue imitates the body: once exceedingly wanton, it now becomes chaste and upright. Many things that it was used to eating it now absolutely refuses to allow to enter its mouth, as if eating them would sully its purity. One would expect that, being so meticulous, the tongue would eat less, but in fact it eats more. If the belly were the decision maker, it would have the propriety to stop when full. But the tongue wantonly selects the choicest and fattiest morsels for the greedy and reckless mouth. The stomach is consequently left to bear the burden and can only envy the mouth, while the tongue, as Lu Zhishen put it, "feels birdy bland."[7] Retribution for excessive greed! From this perspective, the dish-eating worldview seems a bit improper.

Tasty food is still to be celebrated, however. Man has thrown this world into confusion. Friction and conflict are everywhere. Only two harmonious things can be said to be man-made: music and cooking. A good dish of food is like a piece of music—a flavor of consistently varied and harmonious proportion whose opposing elements complement and complete each other, forming a composite in which they can be distinguished but not separated. The most pedestrian and superficial of examples include white-boiled crab and vinegar or roast duck and sweet sauce. Examples from Western cuisine include roast pork and apple sauce, or marinated cod and lemon slices. These things, which originally had nothing to do with the other, were fated to come together like matches made in Heaven or such well-paired couples as a beautiful woman and a talented scholar or a sow and a leprous boar.[8] Once united, they can never be torn asunder. Some flavors have what Leibniz's philosophy calls "preestablished harmony" (*harmonia praestabilita*).[9] Others have preestablished incompatibility, such as pepper with boiled shrimp or crab, or sweet and sour sauce with stir-fried beef or lamb. Similarly, in ancient music the *shang* and *jue* tones are mutually inconsonant and *zheng* and *yu* do not match.[10] As Confucius understood long ago, the principles of music accord with those of cooking. *The Analects* record that when Confucius was in the state of Qi and heard the Shao he "did not know the taste of meat for three months."[11] Unfortunately, although the old gentleman exhibited a fair degree of culinary expertise in the "Xiang dang" chapter, before he had grasped the essence of the Way of Eating, he deviated from these two types of harmony toward music. In discussing how to cultivate mind and body in the *Doctrine of the Mean*, for example, he tries to develop the musical personality merely by saying that "when emotions are stirred and each exist in measured proportion, there ensues what might be called a state of Harmony."[12] This truly is the talk of someone who appreciates music but doesn't know the taste of meat. In our opinion, the perfect personality—"my Dao," which "threads things together by a single means" to rule the perfect nation—not only needs to be as harmonious as music but should also elevate cooking to a harmonious ideal. On this point, rather than follow Confucius, we extol the forgotten Yi Yin, China's first philosopher-chef. In his eyes, the human world could be likened to a kitchen where food is cooked. In the "Basic Flavors" chapter of *Master Lü's Spring and Autumn Annals*, Yi Yin's discussion of the best way to flavor soup turns the greatest philosophy of governance into a mouthwatering cookbook. This idea seeped through political consciousness in ancient China, so that beginning with the chapter "On Fate" in the *Book of Documents*, being a prime minister was always likened to "stirring porridge in a pot." Laozi also said that "governing the state is like cooking a small fish."[13] Mencius praised Yi Yin as "the capable sage" and Liu Xiahui as "the harmonious sage," but here the order of the bamboo slips may have gotten mixed up.[14] In fact, Liu Xiahui, who did nothing when naked women came before him, should be considered laissez-faire, while it is Yi Yin who deserves to be called "harmonious"—a "harmony," of course, still imbued with connotations of cooking and balancing the five flavors.

Eating also has a number of social uses, such as forging interpersonal connections, talking business, and the like. This, in short, means "treating someone to a meal." Although the various types of social eating are complex, in essence they are extremely simple. To feed someone who already has food to eat is to "treat someone to a meal." To have food of one's own but eat off someone else instead is to "bestow the honor of your presence." These are the subtleties of social intercourse. Conversely, to feed someone who has nothing to eat is to "give a handout." And should you have nothing to eat and go eat off someone else, what was "bestowing the honor of your presence" suddenly becomes "losing face." This is charity, not social intercourse. As for how many guests you host or the proportion of men and women at the meal, we'll leave such questions for another day. That said, the endlessly fascinating *Almanach des gourmands*[15] contains a witty remark that must be raised here. Besides exploring eating, this precious and remarkable book also discusses the problem of treating others to a meal at one point in its eight volumes. It says, roughly, that after being treated to a meal, the number of days one should refrain from saying bad things about our host behind his back should be proportional to the quality of the food. Thus, to remain upstanding, one should treat others to eat as often as possible and make sure they eat well, so as to increase friends' goodwill and lessen enemies' slander. I introduce this array of opinions with utmost sincerity to all friends who would not become foes, and to all foes who would become friends. As for myself, while respectfully anticipating your invitations I firmly adhere to Zhu Bajie's words to the little demons who serve the king of the Southern Mountain: "Don't fight over me. Be patient and I'll eat with each of you, one house at a time."[16]

READING *AESOP'S FABLES*

Younger people can probably be divided into two categories. In the first are those who are many years younger than us, whom we not only tolerate but even delight in and seek to protect. We can flaunt our age at them and our relative seniority only adds to our dignity. In the second are those just slightly younger than us. These people invite only our loathing and envy. As they have already lost a sense of respect for their elders, our age fails to elicit their pity for the old and infirm. Not only can we not flaunt our age at them, but our advanced years actually work to our disadvantage and we strive to emulate their youth. These two attitudes can be seen everywhere. A woman approaching thirty, for instance, may still be willing to speak well of the features of an eighteen- or nineteen-year-old girl, but she will mercilessly criticize those of a young woman of twenty-three or twenty-four. For this reason, grown-ups always dote on little kids, whereas between big and little kids frequent conflict is unavoidable. Any human relationship that touches on issues of age and generational seniority can validate this analysis.

Looking at history in its entirety, antiquity corresponds to mankind's childhood. Man began in infancy and, through several thousand years of advancement, slowly reached the modern age. The more ancient the era, the shorter man's history, while the later the era, the deeper his accumulated experience and the greater his age. Thus, we are actually our grandfathers' elders and the Three Dynasties[1] of high antiquity cannot match the modern age in long standing. Our faith in and fondness for ancient things consequently takes on new meaning. Perhaps our admiration for antiquity is not necessarily esteem for our forebears but merely delight in children; not respect for age but the flaunting of age. No old fogey is willing to acknowledge his stubbornness and decrepitude. Likewise, we believe the value and quality of everything in the modern age to be more advanced than that of antiquity.

These revelations came to me as I happened to be flipping through *Aesop's Fables*. That's right—*Aesop's Fables* is well worth reading. At the very least, it offers us three types of consolation. First, it is an ancient book, so reading it can increase our pride in modern civilization. Second, it is reading material for children, so reading it enhances our sense that we are grown-ups and have surpassed such childish notions. As for the third sort of consolation, this book is pretty much entirely about animals—just think how long it takes an animal to evolve into a human! As we read about the doings and sayings of so many bats, foxes, and the like, we get the distinct impression of visiting a poor friend after gaining fame and fortune, or of returning to our hometown having made good. Still, poor friends need our help and children deserve our guidance, so when we read *Aesop's Fables* we also sense that it has a number of superficial views that require correction.

Take the story of the bat, for example. A bat pretends to be a crow when he encounters a crow and pretends to be a land animal when he encounters a land animal. Man, being much smarter than a bat, employs the bat's method conversely. Among crows he will pretend to be a land animal to show that he is down-to-earth, while among land animals he pretends to be a crow to show that he transcends worldly matters. He parades refinement before soldiers and plays the hero to men of letters. Among the upper classes he is a poor and tough commoner, but among common people he becomes a condescending man of culture. Of course, this is not bat, this is just—human.

The story of the ant and the cricket:[2] When winter arrives, the ant takes out his winter rice to dry in the sun. Half dead with hunger, the cricket asks to borrow some food and the ant replies: "You're the one who sang the summer away and now you're going hungry—serves you right!" This story shouldn't end here. According to the Platonic dialogue *Phaedrus*, when the cricket evolves he turns into a poet.[3] We can deduce from this that a person who sits by and watches a poet suffer poverty and hunger, not deigning to lend him money, was undoubtedly an ant in his former life. The cricket himself turns into ant food after he dies. Similarly, great writers who were unable to provide for themselves while alive will have a whole group of people living off them after they die, such as relatives and friends writing sentimental reminiscences and critics and scholars writing research theses.[4]

The story of the dog and his shadow: A dog holding a piece of meat in his mouth sees his shadow in the water while crossing a bridge. Thinking it's another dog holding a piece of meat, he drops the meat in his own mouth and fights with the reflection, trying to snatch the meat the reflection is holding. As a result, he loses the meat in his own mouth. This fable cautions against greed, but today we can apply it another way. It's been said that everyone needs a mirror in which to look frequently at one's own reflection and know what one is. However, those with self-knowledge don't need to look in the mirror, and looking in the mirror is of no use to those who lack it. For this meat-holding dog, for instance, looking in the mirror actually hurt him by provoking him to throw a fit and futilely attack his own reflection with vicious barking. One can see from this that some creatures are best off not looking at themselves in the mirror.[5]

The story of the astronomer: While looking up at the constellations, an astronomer loses his footing, falls down a well, and cries "Help!" Neighbors who hear him sigh, "Why did he only look up and ignore what's on the ground!" Always looking up and not watching one's feet sometimes results in a fall down a well and sometimes a fall from office or a fall from power. After falling, however, one should never admit that one fell due to carelessness. Instead, one should claim to be carrying out a planned investigation or working with one's subordinates. This astrologer, for instance, had a splendid excuse—looking at the sky from the bottom of a well.[6] It's true: even after we have fallen, our eyes still look upward.

The story of the crow: God wants to choose the most beautiful bird to be the king of the birds. The crow covers his entire body and tail in peacock feathers and goes before God as a candidate. Sure enough, God picks him. The other birds are furious and tear out the inserted feathers, revealing his original crow likeness. This goes to show that those with long hair are not necessarily artists. By the same token, bald people are, of course, not necessarily scholars or thinkers—what could emerge from a head that has produced nary a sprout? Nor does the parable stop here. After the crow has had his borrowed feathers pulled out and his original form exposed, his shame turns to anger and he proposes that everyone else might as well pull out all their own feathers so that when all are naked they can see how a real peacock, swan, or other bird differs from a crow. This method of covering up one's own embarrassment is one that man, at least, uses frequently.

The story of the cow and the frog: A mother frog inhales as much air as she can and asks her baby frog, "Is a cow as big as me?" The baby frog responds: "Don't swell up so much or your belly might burst!" What an idiotic mother frog! She shouldn't compete with a cow on size—she should compete on delicateness. Thus, each of our defects has its upside: stinginess we call frugality, stupidity we call honesty, unscrupulousness we call finesse, and lack of talent we call virtue. Thus, no woman on earth considers herself completely unlovely, nor does any man think himself inferior to others in every respect. This way there is something for everyone, and peace and harmony reign as a matter of course.

The story of the old woman and the hen: An old woman raises a hen who lays one egg a day. The greedy old woman wants her hen to lay two eggs a day, so she feeds her twice as much. From then on, as the hen eats more and more she gets fatter and fatter and stops laying eggs—so the injunction is against greed. But Aesop got it wrong! He should have said: fat people are always stingy.

The story of the fox and the grapes: A fox sees a vine full of ripe grapes, but no matter what he tries he can't get them into his mouth. All he can do is give up and console himself by saying, "Those grapes are probably still sour. I'm better off not eating them anyway!" Had he eaten them, he still would have said, "Just as I expected: these grapes are sour." If he were a fox with high standards, he would have told himself this because reality is always "insufficiently ideal." If he were a fox who is easy to please, he would have said this to others because by telling a sob story he could prevent others from coming to share the spoils.[7]

The story of the donkey and the wolf: A donkey encounters a wolf and pretends that his hoof is hurt, saying to the wolf: "There's a thorn in my hoof. Please pull it out so it won't prick your tongue when you eat me." The wolf believes him, and while he is focused on looking for the thorn the donkey kicks him in the head and escapes. The wolf sighs: "Heaven intended me to be a butcher who sends others to their graves; why be a physician who cures illnesses?" This is funny in a childish way, of course—he doesn't know that a doctor is also a type of butcher.

These few examples demonstrate that *Aesop's Fables* is not suitable reading material for today's children. In *Émile*, book 2, Rousseau opposes children's reading fables because he claims that fables have bad intentions. He cites the example of the fox who tricks a piece of meat from the mouth of a crow and says that children who read this story will envy the crafty fox instead of sympathizing with the cheated crow. If this is the case, doesn't it prove that children have bad intentions to begin with? Whether or not children should read fables depends entirely on the kind of world and social environment that we grown-ups create for children to grow up in and inhabit. Rousseau believes that fables are detrimental because they make unsophisticated children complicated and deprive them of their innocence. I believe that fables are detrimental because they make unsophisticated children even more simpleminded and childish. Fables lead them to believe that in human affairs the distinction between right and wrong and the consequences of good and evil are as fair and clear-cut as in the animal kingdom. As a result, when these children grow up they will be tricked and rebuffed at every turn. The essential difference between Rousseau and me is that he is a primitivist who advocates a return to antiquity, while I am a man who believes in progress—though not like the fly in the fable who sits on the axle of the cart wheel, buzzing, "It's all my power that's moving this cart along."

ON MORAL INSTRUCTION

We dislike filth, so we profess to cherish purity. Consequently, those obsessed with hygiene would prefer not to bathe than to have to borrow someone else's bathing implements. Distinguishing between dirty and clean becomes a way of differentiating self from other. A person who considers himself clean will always despise others as filthy, even going so far as to believe that his own dirtiness is preferable to others' cleanliness. Though he may reek of sweat and bad breath, he will disdain to borrow a toothbrush or towel that someone else has used.[1] We can see from this that "love of cleanliness" is really narcissism. The idiom "preserve one's purity" carries a profound psychological observation.[2] In truth, worldly distinctions between right and wrong, good and bad, deviant and upright, and so on sometimes boil down to the difference between self and other. This is no different from the dirtiness or cleanliness of the body. Thus, if you want to pass yourself off as a good person, the first thing to do is to call everyone else a scoundrel, and if you want to pass yourself off as being of upstanding moral character, the first order of business is to adopt a stern demeanor and condemn others as immoral hypocrites. Having written to this point, we are reminded of the she-ghost's reply to the fox-fairy in *Liaozhai*: "You say I'm inhuman, but are you human?"[3]

I've long found it curious that the world has so many people undertaking to serve as mankind's moral guide, and publishing essays every day to chide him. "That animal called man"[4] cannot be completely written off, since a few are still capable of self-sacrifice. More puzzling to me is that with such an abundance of moral guides mankind still has not improved much. This is of course like asking why it is that with so many skillful and attentive doctors in active practice mankind still suffers from illness. For although the doctor cures illness, he hopes at the same time that more people will get sick, the better to get a sweet price for his bitter medicine. By saving other people's lives he saves his own, since patients must eat medicine in order for him to eat food. It is thus completely unsurprising that human nature has not improved despite the existence of such leaders. What's real food for thought is that people undertake the responsibility of instructing and guiding mankind despite the incorrigibility of human nature. Mankind may be impervious to moral instruction, but didactic essays about the current state of affairs fill a need even if they have no practical value. It's akin to how we feel compelled to send for a doctor and take medicine when we get sick, even though doing so may not cure the illness. If man really was a quick study and no longer needed moral instruction, wouldn't all those people die of idleness? Thus, they write about everything from the individual's responsibilities in life to the attitude of the critic, their words flowing as volubly as an outdoor sermon. Their essays may not be worth a dime, but at least the ink and paper didn't cost them a penny.[5]

Middle age and moral instruction appear to be intimately correlated. We can appreciate this curious fact just by looking at authors. Upon reaching forty or so, many men of letters suddenly task themselves with saving the world. Everything and everyone around them they curse and seek to put right. Well-known British examples include Matthew Arnold, John Ruskin, William Morris, T. S. Eliot[6] (who is still living), and J. M. Murry. Even the aesthete Oscar Wilde had a change of heart on his deathbed and preached socialism. We can find more examples among our friends, should we be so inclined. The goals of such an honorable transformation are of course as pure as fresh-fallen snow: to rescue the world and educate mankind. Yet pure goals may well have complicated motives. Bellowing with the force of righteousness may be a cover-up for declining literary creativity, despair and frustration with life, a way of exploring a career change, or middle-aged envy toward one's peers or juniors. When a middle-aged woman can no longer hide her loss of good looks with makeup, for instance, she naturally cuts down on socializing and willingly settles into the role of the proper housewife. What's more, she will not abide the bizarre and sexy way that young women dress. Jules Janin called Balzac the Columbus who discovered forty-year-old women. Forty-year-old men, apparently, are still waiting to be discovered. Sages like Confucius didn't really understand the particular nature of middle-aged people. As a result, the "Ji Family" chapter in *The Analects* records only three prohibitions in life: youthful lust, fighting in one's prime, and old age covetousness—forgetting middle-aged moralizing. Of course, there are also those who enjoy preaching from an early age. At most this reveals that they were middle-aged at birth and should be congratulated on having reached ninety or one hundred when they turn sixty.

Just as one person's idea of personal finance is simply to borrow money without repaying it, so another's moral philosophy is to chide others even though he himself lacks moral character. Ancient books tell us that a "good man" is one who "doesn't give better than he can take," but this is an inescapably shallow view. A man who is truly good will give without taking and instruct others without ever accepting their instruction. This is what is known as "the spirit of self-sacrifice."

One could say that the change from an artistic philosophy of life to a moralizing philosophy of life is the product of a new phase in life. Yet the beginning of each new phase also marks the end of another. For instance, to a man with a job, breakfast is the beginning of the day, and once he has eaten his fill he can go to work. But to a member of the leisure class who spends his whole night playing cards and dancing, breakfast is just the conclusion of the previous night, and once he has eaten his fill he is ready to sleep. The onset of moral instruction may well mark the death of literary creation, but here I have no intention of passing judgment on the relative merits of each, since that depends completely on the individual.[7] Some people's literary works essentially constitute preaching with a mask on, but this is inferior to flat out moralizing. Conversely, some people's moralizing can make something out of nothing and pass off fiction as fact and thus can be dubbed "creation" as justifiably as poetry, fiction, rumors, and lies.

The simpleminded might object that an immoral person who goes around chiding others is a hypocrite. To this we reply: what's wrong with hypocrisy?[8] Compared to true morality, hypocrisy is even more difficult to accomplish and therefore all the more estimable. A moral person offering moral instruction is unremarkable, but to lack morals and instruct others takes real skill. A man of learning can teach, but his learning is self-evident. To teach others despite being ignorant is like doing business without capital—a veritable art. A true moralist promoting morality, like a shopkeeper advertising his inventory of goods, cannot avoid self-promotion. It is only when someone absolutely lacking in morals talks of morality that we can understand the true meaning of selflessness, and the delight he takes in speaking of man's goodness further attests to morality's greatness. We might take this one step further and say that a truly moral person who trumpets morality will in fact see his original morality gradually erode. La Rochefoucauld writes in *Maximes supprimées*: "The moralists, and Sénèque above all, have not done away with men's crimes through their precepts; all they have done is use them to build up their own pride."[9] Should you think that other people are bad and in need of your instruction, you cannot help but adopt a certain posture. You will say at first that other people lack ideals, and then gradually begin to think yourself an ideal character and force others to emulate you. Should you lord your learning and talent over other people, your pride will not cause you to forfeit your learning. Should you lord your poverty and lowliness over other people, your pride will not make you rich and noble. Morality and pride, however, cannot coexist. The greatest evils and cruelties in the world—and no evil is greater than cruelty—are mostly the work of people with genuine moral ideals. When the immoral man commits a crime he knows it's a crime, but when the truly moral man hurts others he maintains that it is the price of morality. God sometimes punishes mankind with a famine year, sometimes with pestilence or war, and sometimes by producing a moralist who harbors ideals too lofty to be attained by ordinary mortals. Accompanying these are a confidence and zeal that are in direct proportion to his ideals, which merge into an unself-conscious pride. Christian philosophy holds pride to be one of the seven cardinal sins. Volume three of Wang Yangming's *Chuanxi lu* says, "Life's greatest affliction lies in one word: 'pride.' Self-pride is the chief of all evils."[10] Put this way, genuine morality can be considered the early stage of evil. Conversely, hypocrites who promote morality actually tend to turn fiction into reality, transform habit into second nature, and truly improve moral conduct. Flirting can turn into love; imitation leads to innovation; mingling with men of letters and posing as a lover of culture can cultivate expert appreciation; and numerous real goods start as bogus brands. Thus, hypocrisy can be said to be an apprenticeship for genuine morality. However, whether phony or genuine, goodness will be repaid in kind. Genuine morality may ascend to the halls of Heaven after death, but living hypocrisy ascends to the lecture hall. What a relief!

Thus, those least worthy to offer moral instruction are most likely to become moralists, and the bigger the hypocrite the more he ought to attack hypocrisy. Hypocrisy's defining characteristic could be said to be shamelessness combined with an eagerness to preserve face. According to the words Prince Hamlet used to curse his fiancée, women's use of makeup represents a concern with face combined with shamelessness:[11] "God has given you one face, but you make yourself another."[12] Hypocrisy, too, is a cosmetic art . . .[13]

Having written this far, I'm suddenly struck by a thought. Isn't this essay filled with moral chiding? Have not I, too, reached middle age—walked half of life's road! Words written in black and white cannot be retracted. Might as well make up some nonsense and wrap things up.

A PREJUDICE

❧

Prejudice can be said to be a vacation from thinking.[1] For the unthinking man it is a daily necessity, while for the thinking man it is a Sunday amusement. If we were unable to harbor prejudices and always had to be objective, fair, upright, and serious, it would be like building a house with a living room but no bedroom, or being obliged to strike photogenic poses in front of the bathroom mirror. In canto 27 of Dante's *Inferno*, the Devil is quoted as remarking: "Maybe thou didst not consider that I was a logician!"[2] From this one can see that Hell was made for the reasonable sort, and that in the current age it is completely unnecessary to focus one's words and deeds solely on the pursuit of rationality. Of course, "correctness" and "common sense" are basically also prejudices. The fundamentals of biology hold that the position of the human heart is not actually in the center, but slightly to one side—and, most fashionable of all, it inclines slightly to the left. It appears that the ancients' referring to the deviant path as the "left path" has some scientific basis. That said, many opinions nevertheless retain what the Zen sect calls "inclination to the central and upright"—academic theories, for example. Only jottings in the margins of life,[3] love letters written in the throes of passion, and the like are honest-to-goodness, out-and-out prejudices.

The world is too vast. We face it squarely with our eyes wide open, but our field of vision is still pitifully narrow. When a dog has its eyes fixed on a meaty bone, does it ever notice the other dog at its side? What we commonly refer to as prejudice is best likened to using one eye to take aim at a target. Some people actually believe this is the way to see the true core of things. Plato, for instance, defined mankind as "a featherless biped." Objective in the extreme! But according to Diogenes Laertius's *Lives of Eminent Philosophers* (volume 6, chapter 2), Plato found himself being cross-examined by a man carrying a plucked chicken. The fool in Beaumarchais' *Le Mariage de Figaro* declares that "man is that animal which drinks without thirst and is lustful year-round." We know perfectly well that this is the jest of a wine-loving, womanizing clown, but we must still admit that this novel theory exposes a fundamental part of human nature. The characters 'partial' [*pian*] and 'stimulate' [*ji*] that make up the word 'extreme' [*pianji*] are related to begin with, since our views become especially partial when we are stimulated. Perhaps we could say that "man is the animal that makes noise whether day or night, winter or summer." And why not, after all?

Birds twitter in spring, crickets chirp in autumn, and mosquitoes gather before thunderstorms in the summer.[4] At night insects awake and birds sleep. Not every day sees wind and rain. The dog does not bark unless someone comes, nor does the hen cluck unless it has laid. Man is alone in that, whenever and wherever he is, he makes noise with speech, movement, and machinery. Even when he is alone in a room without someone to banter with, he can turn on the phonograph or listen to the wireless. Even while sleeping he emits thunderous snores. Speech is more than mere sound, of course. But when speech is not worth listening to, or should we not care to listen to it, or if we cannot hear it clearly due to distance or obstruction, the words lose their edges and contours and turn into a ball of undulating racket that is as meaningless as a chicken's clucking or a dog's barking. Such is the so-called "piping of man!"[5] It ruins sleep, shatters thought, and induces neurasthenia.

This world is, after all, ruled by humans. The human voice overcomes all. The myriad voices of Mother Nature combined cannot stand up to the hubbub of two people talking at the same time, at least as it sounds to the ears of a third person. The famous line in Tang Zixi's poem "Drunken Sleep" [Zui mian], "the mountains are as still as in ancient times," no doubt refers to the age of high antiquity, before humans appeared.[6] Otherwise, the mountain would have a monk living on top, tourists arriving at its base, and restaurants and tea shops open for business midway up its slopes. Tranquillity would be impossible. The piping of man is a mortal wound to silence, while the piping of Heaven can melt into one with silence. The sounds of wind and waves are to silence as the wind is to the air and the waves to the sea. These are but two examples. Each day at the east's first light we awaken from our dreams, still groggy, to the sound of innumerable birds welcoming the dawn. At this time, before night has completely disappeared, silence still lingers, harboring unfinished dreams. The chirping of countless sparrows adds to a cacophony that seems ready to peck through the silence. The call of the magpie, clear and sharp as a pair of scissors, and of the stork, slow and grating as a saw, both try to cut a hole in the silence with each cry. But the silence seems too plentiful, too fluid and elastic. No sooner has its surface been broken by a birdcall then silence fills back in. Nor does the rooster's ringing, melodious morning report leave any trace. Gradually, we forget that the twittering of birds is breaking the silence, as if silence had already absorbed and digested the bird chirps and turned them into a sort of silence with sound. At such a moment, the mere sound of a neighbor's crying child, the coughing of a person sleeping upstairs, or the footsteps of an early-morning walker outside is enough to make the silence, like nighttime mist encountering morning sunlight, break apart and scatter completely. Once the piping of man begins and humans resume their affairs, don't hope for any more peace and quiet. When, late some weary night or deep in meditation, one suddenly hears the racket of the piping of man, even the most compassionate humanist might momentarily be seized with murderous thoughts and lament that he can't shut the person up so as to keep his ears free of worldly discord and preserve his peace of mind. Birds, beasts, wind, waves, and all the other pipings of Heaven can peacefully coexist with silence, as the ancient poets who appreciated the true nature of things realized long ago. In the *Book of Odes*, the line "As if at ease, the horses neighed / Long and slow fluttered the pennants and banners"[7] is subsequently glossed as "noise without clamor." Evidently, if a horse whinnies but no man shouts, it won't create a din. *Family Instructions of Master Yan* also points out that Wang Ji's famous line "Cicadas chirp, the grove turns quieter still / Birds sing, the mountain grows more remote" precisely captures the sense of "noise without clamor."[8] The chirping of insects and singing of birds actually add to the stillness. Shelley's poem "To Jane: A Recollection" [*sic*] describes the woodpecker by saying that when the bird pecks the mountain grows more remote.[9] Samuel Taylor Coleridge's poem "The Æolian Harp" reads: "The stilly murmur of the distant Sea / Tells us of silence." Should this sea be a sea of people, the poet would assuredly go deaf and suffer a headache. Thus, though we often liken the din of human voices to "the calls of crows and sparrows," this is a misrepresentation that displays a certain degree of bias toward humanity. For us to always liken the sound of a group of women chatting and laughing to "orioles trilling and swallows twittering," however, is tantamount to an insult to the bird kingdom.

Silence is not the complete absence of sound. The complete absence of sound is death, not silence. That's why Dante said that in Hell even the sun "in silence rests" (*dove il sole tace*).[10] Silence can be likened to auditory transparency, just as effulgence can be said to be visual quietude. Silence lets people hear noises they wouldn't ordinarily hear. It lets philosophers hear the "still small voice" of the conscience and enables poets to hear faint sounds such as the stealthy onset of dusk or the sprouting of grasses.[11] The more noise one hears, the harder it becomes to hear clearly. Humans alone are fond of making such a racket, so much so that when a group of people gathers together without making noise it seems unnatural. The five minutes of silence before the start of a meeting, or long-lost relatives or friends meeting again and holding hands wordlessly are but two examples. This type of silence is like pregnancy—full of latent sound waiting to be emitted.

The piping of man is also frightening in one respect. Traffic may be noisy, but it occurs on the same plane as you, so it only disrupts your immediate environment. Only man will target his racket at your head from above. Let's say, for example, that you live one floor below an upstairs neighbor. Leave the rest aside: the sound of a few footsteps will be enough to make you feel that someone is stomping on your head like Concubine Zhao in *Dream of the Red Chamber*. When you can't tolerate it any longer, you will be seized by two great desires. First, you will hope that you, living downstairs, will transform into what *The Classic of Mountains and Seas* calls "a commoner who punishes Heaven,"[12] with your head growing on your torso. This way, your head will be unlikely to bear the brunt[13] of being trampled upon by your upstairs neighbors' shoes. Second, you will hope that your neighbor will transform into something like a Christian angel, with a body that stops at the waist and two wings growing out of its back that obviate the need for legs and feet.[14] Your intentions are so benevolent. You don't wish your upstairs neighbor to suffer Sun Bin's fate of having his feet chopped off, even though your neighbor has given no consideration to your head or to your being what Rodenbach called "a soul hurt by clamor."[15]

Noise and heat, silence and cold are mutually interconnected. This is why in the wretched darkness of Hell even the sun imparts a feeling of desolation. This is also why a cacophony of human voices can turn a cold room into a hot pot, making one's entire body fidgety. Schopenhauer has a good point when he says, in section 278 [*sic*] of *Parerga und Paralipomena*, that a thinker should be deaf.[16] If he isn't deaf, he will hear sounds, and if those sounds are noisy, he'll have a hard time keeping his mind collected, with the result that prejudice will take the place of impartiality. At this point—having forgotten that you too are a noise-making animal; that you too have stomped on the heads of people living downstairs; and that your own bawling has prevented people next door from thinking or sleeping—you will find yourself even more impervious to others' complaints that your prejudices are too ingrained. As you add this new prejudice, you make another note in the margins of life.[17]

EXPLAINING LITERARY BLINDNESS

Finding a literary turn of phrase in a nonliterary book is like going through old clothing and suddenly discovering a dollar bill or spare change in a pocket.[1] Even though it was yours to begin with, you still feel unexpectedly delighted. One autumn three years ago, for example, I happened to be flipping through Nicolai Hartmann's masterpiece, *Ethik*, when I came across a curious item. Its gist is that there exists a certain type of person who can't tell good from bad or distinguish good from evil, the same way a color-blind person can't tell green from red or black from white, and that this person can be said to be suffering from "value blindness" (*Wertblindheit*). I found this metaphor to be simultaneously delightful and novel, never thinking that I would be quoting it today. Of course, borrowing a great methodological philosopher (and a German besides) for the opening of a casual essay seems like overkill—using antiaircraft guns to exterminate mosquitoes.[2] However, if one doesn't make a mountain of out a molehill, will anyone pay attention? That's why when we open up a small shop or school we always find a way to invite the local headman to attend the ceremony, and when we publish a short book we beg a celebrity to grace its cover with his calligraphy.[3]

Value blindness is characterized by a lack of aesthetic sensibility, the complete inability to appreciate works of literature and art. Following the example of color blindness, we might well dub this symptom "literary blindness." On this point, Su Dongpo and I are in complete agreement. When Dongpo passed the examination but Li Fangshu did not, Dongpo wrote a poem bidding him farewell, which reads: "Having followed you for so long I have reason to doubt the elegance of my literary style / In the past we talked casually of ancient battlefields / Now, what passes before my eyes makes me confuse the five colors of the sunlight."[4] You see, he long ago compared failing to appreciate literature to being unable to differentiate colors. Odd though it may seem, those who make literature their profession appear to suffer from literary blindness even more acutely. Indeed, when it comes to the merits of poetry and prose, many literary scholars are utterly unappreciative and undiscriminating, but we need only expand our field of vision to realize that such a commonplace shouldn't raise an eyebrow. Reading literary books without being able to savor them is perfectly analogous to the imperial age when the people guarding the rear palace and spending entire days mingling among a bevy of women were court eunuchs—they had the opportunity but lacked the means! Perfection is an unreasonable demand, and enemies inevitably cross paths; if it were otherwise, how could there be the farce of life?

This expression "literary blindness" is too perfect; we should demand it from the educators of the masses. Literate people, after all, may yet be literature-blind. For example, no one on earth knows more characters than the linguist, but some experts on writing and language can never avoid fouling the air and suffering from cloudy vision when they read literary works. A linguist once remarked: "All literary criticism is rubbish. Only the shape, meaning, and tone of each character have any foundation." Having had the privilege of hearing such brilliant views, we cannot help thinking of Gulliver in Brobdingnag gazing up at the jade-white bosom of the empress and seeing her hair follicles but not her skin. Should a fly be able to read characters—and I think it could, as evidenced in the *Records of Fujian* of the *Book of the Jin*—should a fly be able to read characters, I say, its view of literature would certainly be the same as that of a linguist.[5] With such tiny eye sockets, its vision presumably would not be terribly far-reaching. Reading poetry or prose it would see only individual characters, and looking at people it would see only individual hair follicles. I must admit that the worldview of the fly is rich with poetic meaning. Apart from Blake himself, the fly, too, may be credited with the breadth of mind "to see a world in a grain of sand / And a heaven in a wild flower."[6] It can find a treasure island in a pile of meaty bones, and when flying from one pinch of garbage to another it appreciates the joy of a long-distance Eurasian flight. So long as it does not believe that no paradise exists beyond meaty bones or that no world exists beyond garbage, we should not hesitate to let this little creature buzz contentedly to itself. Exegetical studies and phonology are extremely useful and interesting fields. Our only fear is that these scholars' brains are relics from the "plain study"[7] period of the Qing dynasty, and that they are convinced that no learning exists beyond their own field, or that literary research involves nothing more than the examination and correction of characters and so forth. The high-handedness of plain study scholars is a fearsome thing. Sainte-Beuve points out in volume six of *Nouveaux Lundis* that learning how to read but not how to appreciate literature and instead devoting one's efforts to philological work is akin to failing in one's pursuit of a young lady and having to resort to her maid as a substitute.[8] Unfortunately, a maid is the one sort of person you should not provoke, because as soon as you show her favor she will want to outdo the priceless young lady. How many maids in the world would not want to emulate Aroma from *Dream of the Red Chamber*?[9]

Color-blind people never become art critics, but people with a blindness for literature sometimes do air their views on literature and do so, moreover, with particular verve and passion. What then is produced is a type of impressionistic literary criticism, which is also sometimes referred to as "self-expressive" or "creative" literary criticism. Of course, artistic connoisseurship can never be completely free from impressions. But exactly how such impressionistic criticism can be construed as "self expression" is something I do not understand. Common sense would have it that the literary work in question is what gives rise to the impressions in the eyes of the critic. One cannot say that the critic is expressing his own inner self. The impressions are what the work has engendered in him and cannot count as examples of his self-expression. At any rate, when these "impressionistic and creative critics" hold forth on literature, things get really lively! Probably because these persons are so lacking in aesthetic sensibility, their writing is especially colorful. Could it be that this is an example of what psychoanalysts call the "compensatory effect"? I dare not say. These critics will alternately cry out in anger, shout wildly, or even refrain from uttering a single word—thus entering the realm of "the sublime that transcends language." They do no analysis—who has the patience? They offer no judgments—that's too pedantic. Inspiration, Purity, Truth, Life—they misuse every word. Misusing big words is like not begrudging petty change, which indicates the boldness of their literary style. They're not short on "impressions"—they have a whole string of worn-out and rotting metaphors. One may write an essay discussing Shelley, but you will find little Shelley in his essay. All you'll find is a lengthy paragraph describing searing flames, a long section depicting the howling west wind, and an even bigger pile of carefree flying skylarks. These three nondescript things are said to be Shelley. But wherefore? It would be a miracle if the wind didn't blow out the fire or the fire roast the skylarks. So, every time you come across a line like "His life is a beautiful poem," you know that what inevitably follows is not a beautiful poem, but prose. Calling such literary and artistic connoisseurship "creative" or "impressionistic" criticism is still not quite apt. We might attempt a little alchemy and change one character in each. "Creative" [*chuangzao*] becomes "fabricated" [*niezao*], in the sense of having a dream while "pinching" [*nie*] one's nose[10] and "making things up" [*zao*] out of one's head. As for the "impressionists" [*yinxiang pai*]—we of course still remember the story of the four blind men feeling [*mo*] the white elephant [*xiang*]—they can be changed to "elephant feelers" [*moxiang pai*]. What do you think? This fits the literature-blind even better.

How do fabricationists distinguish value when they basically repudiate artistic appreciation? Anything that matches their honorable tastes is good, and anything that does not is trash. Here we see even more clearly that literary blindness is a type of value blindness. A rich and fashionable lady once told the great painter James McNeill Whistler: "I don't know much about art, but I know what I like."[11] Whistler bowed and responded politely, "My dear madam, your view on this matter is the same as that of a wild beast." Indeed, the difference between civilized humans and savage beasts is that humans possess a transsubjective point of view. For this reason, humans are able to divorce questions of right and wrong, authenticity and falsity from their own personal gain and loss, and separate questions of good and evil, beauty and ugliness from their individual likes and dislikes. Man is not, in fact, inextricably bound to daily life. Rather, he does his utmost to escape his human body and criticize himself. This is how he knows truth beyond pragmatism; learning beyond teaching and submitting manuscripts for publication; and art beyond posters of movie stars.[12] Though he cherishes life, he also understands the value of sacrificing oneself for one's country or religion. Being born of humankind, he will inevitably do stupid things and make mistakes, eat forbidden fruit and love unworthy things.[13] Yet his mind will stay balanced and he will not confound right and wrong or blur good and bad in order to protect himself. He understands that the things he has to do may not be those he likes to do. This division of the self, this fork between knowing and doing, results in tragedy during times of crisis and satire in times of repose. Only birds and beasts are born with their thoughts and actions united as one, oblivious to any higher ideal than their own personal sensual desires. Evolving from monkey to man was hard enough. To now confuse value with one's own predilections and become a beast in human form is really a bit of an injustice to Darwin.[14]

There is no need here to mention people who hate literature. Those with a thorn in their eye are bound to be blind. Even so, though their eyes may have problems, their noses are extremely acute, since they often say they detest the stench of literary men. "Those to whom Heaven gave feet it deprived of horns, and those to whom it gave wings it deprived of teeth." As for the fairness of the Creator, we can only sing His endless praises.

ON WRITERS

The writer is commendable for his modesty: while knowing how to get ahead in the world, he refrains from hankering after social position and eschews complacency with his lot.[1] In truth, the writer's own view of himself is sometimes more scornful than that of the ordinary outsider looking on. He finds it singularly annoying that he is a writer and goes to great lengths and with considerable expenditure of words, labor, time, and paper to prove how unwilling and dissatisfied he is to be a writer. In an age like the present, could this not be considered the mark of "a hero who has taken note of the contemporary situation"?

It stands to reason that the concept of "writer" ought to refer to anyone who writes books, pens articles, or submits manuscripts for publication. In actual practice, however, the use of the term "writer" is limited to authors working in such genres as poetry, the familiar essay, fiction, and playscripts. That is to say, the term refers precisely to what the ancients called a belletrist, a "useless writer," or someone who "once a writer, had no prospects worth noting." As to the avoidance of such empty writing, specialists who have mastered subjects of substance in the social and natural sciences look askance at the very idea of being considered useless writers [*wenren*]—even though they may have written a flood of voluminous tracts, and in spite of the fact that they cannot quite measure up to the usefulness of military officers [*wuren*].[2] Perhaps this looking askance at the very idea of being considered a writer derives from a correct self-assessment on their part, since writing black characters down on white paper does not necessarily make the finished product a literary composition.

We can probably divide this idea of usefulness into two categories. The first would be the utilization of waste, such as the burning of cow dung in place of firewood, or something on the order of Tao Kan's insistence that wood chips and bamboo stubs were both too useful to be casually discarded.[3] The second would involve things that we have no choice but to use each day, such as toothbrushes and privies—things to which we feel a strong attachment akin to Wang Ziyou's regard for bamboo: "One cannot get by for a single day without this esteemed companion."[4] Among the things in this world that have such a multitude of uses, it is only writers who have been crowned with the lofty title of sheer uselessness. Isn't it a pity that writers have been reduced to sighing over their inferiority to such humble things as a wood chip, a bamboo stub, a toothbrush, and a privy?

If we turn instead to useful persons [*youyong renwu*], we might as well give them a title that will serve to distinguish them from writers. We might call them "servants" [*yongren*], for example. The two characters in the term "servant" are an abbreviation of the four characters in "useful persons," making it an apt counterpart to the two-character term "writer." A word so pithy and broad ranging should not be monopolized by amahs, maids, and private rickshawmen. Furthermore, this term has two other advantages. First, it is replete with the spirit of democratic equality, in which experts and advisers employ the same title as that used for their attendants and menservants, with whom they line up directly alongside. Second, it avoids running counter to the principle of China's total Westernization. In America, there is a president who is said to have called himself the "public servant of the citizenry," that is to say, a servant at everybody's beck and call. In Rome, the Pope calls himself the "menial of menials," or the "servant of servants" (*servus servorum*). In the French Revolution, all the revolutionary party members called their servants "brother servant" (*frères servants*). Now the "president" is a ruler, the "Pope" is Father (*Papa*), and the "frère servant" is one's brother; since in Europe and America all these terms are used in connection with "servant," it is only proper that China should follow suit.[5]

Servants look down upon writers; this has been the case since ancient times[6] and is not at all some news snippet gleaned from this morning's newspaper. For example, Sima Qian's "Annals of the Han Emperor Gaozu" records that "the Han emperor disliked literature." The "Biography of Lu Jia" goes on to explain the situation with a quote from Gaozu himself: "I have won the empire on horseback; why should I pay homage to the *Classic of Odes* and the *Classic of Documents*?"[7] Full of candor and outspokenness, this famous dictum can rightly be considered a sagely imperial decree from a founding emperor. Among the plethora of expressions and myriad words used by opponents of literature from ancient times up to the present day, it all boils down to these two lines. During the War of Resistance to Japan, reading those lines about staying "on horseback" seems all the more envigorating and vivid. When it comes to Plato's exclusion of poets and writers from his ideal society in *The Republic*, how could a long-winded fellow like him adopt such a trenchant and vigorous tone as Gaozu's?[8] Plato's writings are rich in poetical feeling, and Emperor Gaozu once experienced a spell of poetic inspiration during which he composed his "Ode to the Great Wind" in an impromptu recitation. Despite all this, a loathing for literature was shared by them both—and all the more so among those primates who are so vulgar as to be "wholesome."

Théophile Gautier's *Records of Eccentrics* (*Les Grotesques*) has recounted how wealthy merchants have been susceptible to a strange sickness known as "poesophobia" (*poésophobie*).[9] This sickness manifests itself in a rather singular manner. The story goes that a man of wealth one day happened to open his son's desk drawer, there espying a sheaf of writing paper covered with words. These papers were neither account registers nor debt ledgers—and while the first letter in each line was capitalized, the last letter for some reason stopped short of the right margin. After careful investigation, the father discovered that these papers were manuscript drafts of poetry. His heart seethed with fury, and he proceeded to fly into a rage. He sorely lamented the ill fortune that had struck his family in producing such a disobedient and unworthy son. A rapid progression to insanity ensued.

Actually, this kind of sickness has been noted for its high degree of infectiousness. At such times, it can spread as an epidemic, just like cholera during the summertime or influenza in winter. As to a prescription, it is said that one does exist: commit to the flames a diverse assemblage of literature both ancient and modern, native and foreign, then swallow the remaining ashes. According to what people say, as long as the potion has been properly concocted, the upshot naturally is that the noxious humors within one's chest will be dispelled and the thorn in one's side removed; from this time on, moreover, the nation will be strong and its citizenry secure, government will be honest and its policies enlightened, and prosperity will reign with martial vigor in the ascendant![10] As to the magnificent theories in this mold by celebrated figures of modern times, they have long since achieved extremely broad circulation in leading periodicals of all types—and since everyone has gotten thoroughly acquainted with them, there is no need to belabor the point further.

Literature must be destroyed, but there is actually no harm in rewarding writers—rewarding those who turn away from the profession of writing. Pope would often speak in metrical rhythms (lisp in numbers), and Bai Juyi was able at birth to distinguish one character from another: incurable though they may be, born writers of this sort all in all amount to but a small minority in their profession.[11] Ordinary writers, in all frankness, do not actually relish literature, nor are they particularly talented at writing it. In their diversions with literature, they resemble those young women of good family in old novels who become prostitutes, it is said, due to circumstances beyond their control and the lack of any viable alternative. As long as there was an opportunity to escape from this fiery hell, not one of these talents in the making would hesitate to abandon his books and throw away his pens, switch professions, and turn over a new leaf. Literature is a profession of ill fortune and gloomy spirits, where prospects are among the bleakest anywhere, hunger and cold dog one's steps, and sickness is one's constant companion.[12] We have all heard of "literati beggars" [*wengai*], but there has not ever been a term for scholars manqués in other disciplines, such as "scientist beggar," "engineer beggar," "lawyer beggar," or "business-executive beggar." As for the most foolish and stupid of people, were it not for the fact that they had no other path to follow, they certainly would not have been willing to churn out any poetry, fiction, or whatnot. Because of this, it is not only the ordinary bystander who feels contempt for literature and writers; even writers themselves are plagued with an inferiority complex, for they are utterly deficient in either a belief in literature or a reverence for it. For example, the bona fide writer Yang Xiong once proclaimed, in his *Rules of Composition*, "To the carving of insects or the engraving of seals, the stout man does not put his hand."[13] Obviously, he would rather be a stout fellow than a writer.[14] Because of this, we have noticed a peculiar phenomenon: in general, scholars unanimously strike a bold pose and an imposing manner, lavishing praise upon their particular special field and declaring that they believe in it 120 percent. Harboring ulterior motives, writers alone meet rudeness with an obsequious smile and endure unending shame; even if they occasionally indulge in braggadocio during discussions of the literature of "national crisis," "propaganda weaponry," and so on, the effect is nothing more than pounding a waterlogged leather drum, with only muffled sounds audible from the most vigorous drumbeating.

Goethe was once reviled for not having written patriotic poetry, and thus in his *Conversations with Eckermann* (*Gespraceche* [*sic*] *mit Eckermann*) complained bitterly that he had not been a soldier, nor had ever gone to the front line—how could he have roared battle cries or written martial songs while seated in his study (*Kriegslieder schreiben und in Zimmer siteenl* [*sic*])?[15] Yet under present-day circumstances favorable to the creation of heroes, a minority of writers are able to discourse on military strategy, hold forth on political theory, and send their reports up to the leadership; failing that, they appoint themselves instructors of the populace, upon whom they bestow their advice. Such skillful and artistic persons should not and will not just bury their talents in literature. As long as there are opportunities for them to make a change, they can abandon literature and the arts without further ado and make their living some other way.[16]

In his "Defence of Poetry," Shelley argues that poets are the legislators (Legislator) of mankind. Carlisle, in his essay "The Worship of Heroes," claims that writers can be considered heroes. The sole desire of these present-day writers of special mettle is to assume the mantle of a hero, and they hope to become legislators or something else along those lines. If they were to go so far as to style themselves heroes or legislators, they could not avoid seeming megalomaniacal. Yet as far as the desire to be a legislator or hero goes, this is nothing other than the will to get ahead in the world. The will to get ahead in the world is something that ought to be rewarded. A person who has the will to get ahead in the world feels dissatisfaction or shame for his position in real life. In understanding shame one approaches the embodiment of courage. Courage is to be rewarded, and how much more so during an age such as this!

In brief, we should destroy literature and yet reward writers—reward them for ceasing to be writers, for having nothing to do with literature.

Translated by Philip F. Williams

NOTES

AUTHOR'S PREFACE

1. Qian is punning here on the dual meanings of *ben* 本—"origins" and "book"—suggesting that since he forgot about the original copies of his books (*yuanben*) that Chen Mengxiong had sent him, he could be said to have "forgotten his origins" (*wangben*).

PREFACE

1. The 1941 edition reads: "They possess the laziness—that is, nonchalance—of the man of culture, so they browse . . ." Changed in the 1983 edition.

THE DEVIL PAYS A NIGHTTIME VISIT TO MR. QIAN ZHONGSHU

1. A banquet consisting of vegetarian dishes and a ritual sacrifice to the spirit of the departed are traditional features of Chinese memorial events and commemorations held on the hundredth day after or on a later anniversary of a family member's death.

2. A pun on the idiom "luster lent to a humble house" (*pengbi zenghui* 蓬蓽增輝), a polite expression said by a host in thanks for a guest's visit.

3. The phrase *re zhong lengxue* 熱中冷血 means "to keep one's cool."

4. The 1941 edition reads: "Whenever they wanted to write an autobiography they would find they had no 'self' to write about, so they gratify themselves by rendering an ideal likeness that they wouldn't recognize even if they saw it in the mirror." Changed in the 1983 edition.

5. Literally, "sprained foot," here used punningly.

6. A punning use of the idiom "a chain of ghost talk" (*guihua lianpian* 鬼話連篇)—that is, a pack of lies or nonsense.

7. A play on the common expression "to be drinking the northwest wind" (*he xibei feng* 喝西北風)—that is, to have nothing to eat.

WINDOWS

1. In the 1941 edition, Qian refers to "difference in worldview" (*yuzhou guan* 宇宙觀) rather than "fundamental difference." Changed in the 1983 edition.

2. Tao Yuanming 陶淵明 (Tao Qian 陶潛 [365–427]) is one of the most famous pre-Tang poets, whose eremitic lifestyle and poems about idyllic pastoral life earned him the epithet "Poet of the Fields."

3. Emperor Xi (Fuxi shangren 羲皇上人 or Fu Xi shi 伏羲氏) is one of the legendary Three Emperors of high antiquity (the others being Yao 堯 and Shun 舜), who taught the people how to fish and hunt and presided over one of the golden ages of early Chinese civilization.

4. The name of an old county in what is now Jiangxi province. In the 1941 edition, Qian identifies Tao's hometown as Pengze 彭澤 county, which is in the same region.

5. Alfred de Musset (1810–1857) was a French playwright, novelist, and poet. The passage from his play *À quoi rêvent les jeunes filles* (1832), alluded to here, reads:

C'est dans les nuits d'été, sur une mince échelle,
Une épée à la main, un manteau sur les yeux,
Qu'une enfant de quinze ans rêve ses amoureux.
Avant de se montrer, il faut leur apparaître.
Le père ouvre la porte au matériel époux,
Mais toujours l'idéal entre par la fenêtre.

[Lovers, to any lass not yet sixteen,
Climb up a ladder on a summer night,
Sword in their hand, cloak veiling them from sight;
You must appear, rather than just be seen.
Dad lets a fleshy bridegroom in the door,
But through the window comes the fair ideal.]

Translation from *Twelve Plays by Alfred de Musset*, trans. Francine Giguère, E. H. Blackmore, and A. H. Blackmore (Lewiston, N.Y.: Mellen Press, 2001), 36.

6. Gottfried Keller (1819–1890) was a German poet. The first stanza of his poem "Abendlied" reads, in the German original and in English translation:

Augen, meine lieben Fensterlein,
Gebt mir schon so lange holden Schein,
Lasset freundlich Bild um Bild herein
Einmal werdet ihr verdunkelt sein!

[Eyes, my windows, my fond delight,
Giving me a lifetime's cherished light,
Letting pictures in, so kind, so right,
Darkness lies in wait for you, and night.]

Translation adapted from Robert M. Browning, ed., *German Poetry from 1750 to 1900* (New York: Continuum, 1984), 249.

7. The 1941 edition reads: ". . . which is why Huang Shangu said that the eyes move when the heart is moved and Mencius . . ." Cut in the 1983 edition. Huang Shangu 黃山谷 (Huang Tingjian 黃庭堅 [1045–1105]) was a Northern Song poet and calligrapher. The quoted phrase is attributed to him in the anonymous Song dynasty work *Daoshan Clear Talk* (*Daoshan qinghua* 道山清話).

8. In his entry for April 5, 1830, Johann Peter Eckermann (1792–1854) quotes Johann Wolfgang von Goethe (1749–1832) as saying:

It always seems to me as if I am to serve strangers as an object for strict examination, and as if with their armed glances they would penetrate my most secret thoughts and spy out every wrinkle of my old face. But while they thus endeavor to make acquaintance, they destroy all fair equality between us, as they prevent me from compensating myself by making theirs. For what do I gain from a man into whose eyes I cannot look when he is speaking, and the mirror of whose soul is veiled by glasses that dazzle me?"

Conversations of Goethe with Johann Peter Eckermann, trans. John Oxenford, ed. J. K. Moorhead (Cambridge, Mass.: Da Capo Press, 1998), 368.

9. The 1941 edition reads: ". . . left open all day." Changed in the 1983 edition.

ON HAPPINESS

1. Alfred de Vigny (1797–1863), a Romantic poet and dramatist, rose to literary prominence following the French Revolution and was in his later years elected to the Académie française. His highly regarded *Journal* was published posthumously in 1867.

2. The second half of this parallel couplet reads: "When lonely we lament that it's too long" (*jimo hen geng chang* 寂寞恨更長). The locus classicus of this idiom is found in act 3 of Luo Guanzhong's 羅貫中 (ca. 1330–ca. 1400) *zaju* 雜劇 play *The Wind-Cloud Meeting* (*Fengyun hui* 風雲會), an edition of which may be found in *Xuxiu siku quanshu* 續修四庫全書 (Shanghai: Shanghai guji chubanshe, 2002), 1763:193.

3. *Journey to the West*, chap. 4.

4. *Miscellaneous Morsels from Youyang* (*Youyang zazu* 酉陽襍俎) is a major Tang dynasty (618–907) collection of "tales of the strange" (*zhiguai* 志怪) and other miscellany compiled in the mid-ninth century by the literatus Duan Chengshi 段成式 (ca. 803–863). Divided into thirty *juan* (twenty in the original work; ten in an encore), the work contains over twelve hundred entries, including stories about supernatural creatures, legends about bandits and knight-errants, and notes on pharmacopeia and natural phenomena.

5. *Broad Collection of Anomalies* (*Guangyi ji* 廣異記) is a twenty-*juan* collection of *zhiguai* stories from the mid-Tang dynasty. Approximately 280 items from this work are reproduced in the *Extensive Records of the Taiping Era* (*Taiping guangji* 太平廣記), an important Song dynasty (960–1279) collection of about seven thousand stories selected from over three hundred books published between the Han (206 B.C.E.–220 C.E.) and Song dynasties.

6. In the story, which is also found in the *Taiping guangji*, a five-hundred-year-old male fox-demon is possessing the duke's daughter. The duke summons Adjutant Cui, who punishes the

demon by beating him with a peach branch, which reduces the demon's supernatural powers to the point where he can become human. The demon repents, becomes human, and ends up marrying the duke's daughter.

7. The 1941 edition reads: ". . . a square circle, static movement, or the thinking masses." Cut in the 1983 edition.

8. The line is drawn from Johann Wolfgang von Goethe's (1749–1832) *Faust*, part 1 (first published in 1808). A translation by Bayard Taylor is available at http://www.gutenberg.org/dirs/ etext02/faust10.txt. In the 1941 edition, Qian refers to blink-of-an-eye time as *Augenblick*.

9. John Stuart Mill (1773–1836), *Utilitarianism*, chap. 2. The quoted phrases appear in English in the 1941 edition.

10. In the 1941 edition, these two sentences read: "Should you kill someone for money but be genuinely happy, your state of mind will be more tranquil than that of an ascetic moralist. Thus, having a clean conscience and having no conscience at all are effectively the same."

11. Nevi'im (Prophets [Xianzhi shu 先知書]) is the second of three major parts of the Hebrew Bible (Tanakh), the other two being the Torah (Teachings) and Ketuvim (Writings). The story of Solomon is found in 1 Kings 1–2. It is unclear why Qian credits Solomon as being its author. Stéphane Mallarmé (1842–1898) was a major symbolist poet and critic of fin-de-siècle Paris. The earliest manuscript of the poem "Brise marine" is dated 1865.

12. Su Dongpo 蘇東坡 is the sobriquet of Su Shi 蘇軾 (1037–1101), a major poet of the Song dynasty. The couplet is from the poem "Touring the Patriarchal Stupa Monastery While Ill" (Bing zhong you Zutayuan 病中遊祖塔院).

13. Danlu 丹麓 is the style name (*zi* 字) of Wang Zhuo 王晫 (b. 1636), an early Qing dynasty *biji* writer from what is now Hangzhou. *A "New Tales of This Age" for Today* (Jin Shi shuo 今世説) is a collection of anecdotes about prominent men of letters from Wang's time, modeled after the great fifth-century work *New Tales of This Age* (Shi shuo xin yu 世説新語). The line from *Jin Shi shuo* appears in the "Sayings" (Yanyu 言語) section of *juan 2*.

14. Novalis is the pen name of Friedrich Leopold von Hardenberg (1772–1801), a philosopher and author of the early German Romantic movement. Like Qian, he was a man of encyclopedic learning who exhibited an appreciation of the fragment as a form of literature and criticism. The 1941 edition reproduces Novalis's line about the schoolmarm: "Ein Erzieherin zur Ruhe."

15. The Belgian symbolist poet and novelist Georges Rodenbach (1855–1898) published eight collections of poetry and four novels during his lifetime. The reference to *épuration* can be found in the opening poem in part 4 ("Les Malades aux fenêtres") of *Les Vies encloses* (1896), which was published near the end of his life.

16. Barthold Heinrich Brockes (1680–1747) was a member of the Hamburg senate and one of the first German poets to include religious interpretations of natural phenomena in his poetry.

ON LAUGHTER

1. The term *maixiao* 賣笑, usually translated as "selling smiles," has pejorative connotations of insincerity and is most often associated with courtesans, prostitutes, and singsong girls, the last who may clarify to clients that "I sell smiles but not my body" (*maixiao bu maishen* 賣笑不賣身).

2. The earliest version of this essay appeared in the series "Cold Room Jottings" (Lengwu suibi

冷屋隨筆) published in the Kunming literary magazine *Criticism Today* (*Jinri pinglun* 今日評論)
1, no. 22 (May 24, 1939). The title phrase *shuoxiao* 說笑 carries two additional meanings besides
"On Laughter": (1) telling jokes or funny stories, and, most literally, (2) talking and laughing.

3. Jizhuang 繼莊 is the style name (*zi* 字) of Liu Xianting 劉獻廷 (1648–1695), a scholar from
the early Qing dynasty. *Guangyang zaji* 廣陽雜記 is an important collection of "jottings" (*biji*
筆記) spanning various historical, legal, administrative, geographical, agricultural, medical, and
artistic topics.

4. In the 1939 "Cold Room Jottings" and 1941 Kaiming editions of this essay, Qian credits this
claim to Rabelais: "Rabelais appears to have been the first to use laughter to distinguish man from
beast. In the opening chapter of *Gargantua et Pantagruel* he writes, 'rire est le propre de l'homme'
[laughter is man's distinguishing feature]." Changed in the 1983 edition. Aristotle's claim in fact
appears in a different book: *On the Parts of Animals* (*De Partibus Animalium*, ca. 350 B.C.E.), 3.10.
A translation by William Ogle is available at http://ebooks.adelaide.edu.au/a/Aristotle/parts/
book3.html.

5. Wilfrid Scawen Blunt's (1840–1922) sonnet "Laughter and Death" reads:

> There is no laughter in the natural world
> Of beast or fish or bird, though no sad doubt
> Of their futurity to them unfurled
> Has dared to check the mirth-compelling shout.
> The lion roars his solemn thunder out
> To the sleeping woods. The eagle screams her cry.
> Even the lark must strain a serious throat
> To hurl his blest defiance at the sky.
> Fear, anger, jealousy, have found a voice.
> Love's pain or rapture the brute bosoms swell.
> Nature has symbols for her nobler joys,
> Her nobler sorrows. Who had dared foretell
> That only man, by some sad mockery,
> Should learn to laugh who learns that he must die?

6. In the 1939 and 1941 editions, Qian is more physiologically specific and mentions the "muscles" of the face and throat.

7. Dongfang Shuo 東方朔 (154–93 B.C.E.) was a famous Han dynasty (206 B.C.E.–220 C.E.)
courtier and wit. "The Eastern Wastelands" is the first of nine sections in *The Classic of the Divine
and the Strange* (*Shenyi jing* 神異經), a short work about marvels and wonders. Duke Dongwang,
for instance, is described as being "ten feet tall, white-haired, shaped like a man with a bird's face
and a tiger's tail."

8. *Laughter: An Essay on the Meaning of the Comic*, Cloudesley Brereton and Fred Rothwell's
authorized translation of Henri Bergson's (1859–1941) *Le Rire*, is available at http://www.guten-
berg.org/dirs/etext03/laemc10.txt.

9. In the 1939 and 1941 editions of this essay, Qian does not cite Jia Baoyu 賈寶玉 but instead
writes: "Put another way, humor, like woman, is made of water." Changed in the 1983 edition. The
first mention of Jia Baoyu's theory on woman's "watery" nature appears in chap. 2 of the classic

novel *Dream of the Red Chamber*. See Cao Xueqin, *The Story of the Stone*, vol. 1, *The Golden Days*, trans. David Hawkes (London: Penguin, 1973), 76.

10. The 1939 and 1941 editions of this essay include the following German example here: "For instance, the preface to Jean Paul Richter's [1763–1825] humorous novel *Quintus Fixlein* describes humor as an airtight, uniform worldview. Yet even the Germans appreciated that such a view would result in humor's annihilation: a paper on German humor presented at the September 13, 1846, Literary Forum (Blatter fur Literarische Unterhalttung [*sic*]) long ago criticized Richter for going against common sense."

11. The use of the term *dashi* 大師 (master) is a clear stab at Lin Yutang 林語堂 (1895–1976), founder of the humor magazine *Analects Fortnightly* (*Lunyu banyuekan* 論語半月刊), who at the time was popularly celebrated as the "Master of Humor" (*youmo dashi* 幽默大師). The 1939 and 1941 editions read: ". . . a master of the advanced sort who is a leader of youth."

12. "Silvery laughter" usually refers to laughter with a melodious, rippling quality. Here, Qian ironically imbues the term with a profit motive.

13. "In books there are roomfuls of gold" and "In books there are jade-white beauties" (*shu zhong ziyou huangjin wu, shu zhong ziyou yan ru yu* 書中自有黃金屋 / 書中自有顏如玉) are two lines from "Encouragement for Study" (Li xue pian 勵學篇, or "A Poem to Encourage Study" [Quan xue shi 勸學詩]), a poem by Zhen Zong 真宗 (968–1022), the third emperor of the Song dynasty. Taken together, they formed a cliché that was used to exhort young scholars to study for the civil service examination in imperial China, the implication being that success in scholarship would lead to a government position and thus wealth and women.

EATING

1. *Chi fan* 吃飯 (eating rice), a generic Chinese term for eating a meal, is used in this essay in its most literal sense.

2. A similar quibble about "eating rice" versus "eating dishes" appears in a comedy of manners written in 1943 by Qian's wife, Yang Jiang. See Yang Jiang 楊絳, *Chengxin ruyi* 稱心如意 (*As Your Heart Desires*), in *Yang Jiang zuopin jingxuan: xiao shuo, xiju* 楊絳作品精選：小說，戲劇 (*Selected Works by Yang Jiang: Stories and Plays*) (Beijing: Renmin wenxue chubanshe, 2004), 188.

3. Aulus Persius Flaccus (ca. 32–ca. 62) was a Roman poet and satirist. The translation is from François Rabelais, *Gargantua and Pantagruel*, trans. M. A. Screech (New York: Penguin, 2006), 831–34. Qian does not refer to Persius by name in the 1941 or 1983 editions, but just as "a Roman poet." In the 1941 edition, the quote in Latin appears as "Venter laritor ingeni."

4. The correct citation is *Pantagruel*, book 4, chap. 57. Screech notes in his introduction to this chapter, "In the Prologue to his *Satires*, Persius calls the Belly the world's 'Master of Arts and Dispenser of Genius.' All the earthly arts, crafts and accomplishments of men and beasts derive from him. Rabelais develops that theme" (Rabelais, *Gargantua and Pantagruel*, 831). The original French text appears only in the 1941 edition.

5. Barthold Heinrich Brockes (1680–1747).

6. In the 1941 edition, we need only "women" (*nüren* 女人) to press us with wine, not "beauties" (*jiaren* 佳人) and "lovelies" (*liren* 麗人).

7. Lu Zhishen 魯智深, the dog-meat-loving "Flowery Monk," is one of the bandit-heroes of *The Water Margin* (*Shuihu zhuan* 水滸傳), also known as *The Marshes of Mount Liang*, a popular

novel from the Ming dynasty (1368–1644). After becoming a monk, Lu promptly breaks his vows to abstain from meat and wine and goes on a drunken rampage. This mildly vulgar colloquial expression (the *niao* 鳥 in *dan chu niao lai* 淡出鳥來 can also be interpreted as "penis" [*diao*]), which appears in chap. 4, is alternatively rendered as "This bloody horrible taste in my mouth!" in Shi Nai'an, *The Broken Seals: Part One of "The Marshes of Mount Liang*," trans. John Dent-Young and Alex Dent-Young (Hong Kong: Chinese University Press, 1994), 95. In the 1941 edition, Qian attributes this phrase to another *Water Margin* bandit, Li Kui.

8. Literally, "leprous elephant" (*laixiang* 癩象). Pigs (*shi* 豕) and elephants (*xiang* 象) occupied the same imaginative category in ancient China, hence the incorporation of the former character into the latter. In this context, the linking of "leper" and "elephant" seems to suggest that a boar can hardly be elevated to the status of an elephant; thus "leper elephant" is an inferior or a denigrated version of an elephant. Thanks to Shang Wei 商偉 for this interpretation.

9. Gottfried Wilhelm Leibniz's (1646–1716) notion of preestablished harmony is a theory of causation holding that all entities have been designed by God to "harmonize" with one another. As entities (including mind, body, and other substances) have only a causal relationship with themselves, they do not actually physically affect one another, and their "interactions" merely realize a pattern preestablished by God. The original term appears only in the 1941 edition.

10. *Shang* 商, *jue* 角, *zheng* 徵, and *yu* 羽 are four of the five tones in the traditional Chinese tonal scale.

11. Shao 韶 is the name of the music of Shun 舜, one of the legendary rulers of Chinese antiquity. The effect of music on Confucius is recorded in *The Analects*, book 7, chap. 13.

12. Adapted from James Legge's translation of *The Doctrine of the Mean*, chap. 1, line 4, which reads in full: "While there are no stirrings of pleasure, anger, sorrow, or joy, the mind may be said to be in the state of EQUILIBRIUM. When those feelings have been stirred, and they act in their due degree, there ensues what may be called the state of HARMONY. This EQUILIBRIUM is the great root *from which grow all the human actings* in the world, and this HARMONY is the universal path *which they should all pursue*" (*The Four Books* [Shanghai: Chinese Book Company, 1930], 350 [emphasis in original]).

13. That is, requiring a sensitive hand.

14. Before the invention of paper, the Chinese wrote on vertical strips of bamboo, which were then tied together into books. When unearthed from tombs hundreds or thousands of years later, the bamboo strips often would be out of order because the strings holding them together had rotted away.

15. Alexandre-Balthasar-Laurent Grimod de La Reynière's (1758–1838) eight-volume *Almanach des gourmands* (*The Gourmand's Almanac*) was published between 1803 and 1812.

16. Zhu Bajie 豬八戒, one of Monkey's traveling companions in *Journey to the West*, is an anthropomorphic pig who personifies human corporeal desires, particularly gluttony.

READING *AESOP'S* FABLES

1. The Three Dynasties are the Xia (ca. 2070–ca. 1600 B.C.E.), Shang (ca. 1600–1046 B.C.E.), and Zhou (1122–256 B.C.E.). While recorded in the *Records of the Grand Historian* (second–first century B.C.E.), the Xia dynasty is considered by some scholars to be semimythical, and its dates are subject to debate.

2. The fable is better known today as "The Ant and the Grasshopper," though in the Greek original and subsequent Latin version the grasshopper is a cicada. (Qian uses the term *cuzhi* 促織, which refers to the *xishuai* 蟋蟀 [cricket].)

3. Qian uses the term *jinhua* 進化 (evolve), but the story in fact concerns transmigration, and of a Muse-poet turning into an insect rather than vice versa. Translators differ as to whether this insect is a cicada or a grasshopper. In one English translation of *Phaedrus* (360 B.C.E.), Socrates tells Phaedrus:

> A lover of music like yourself ought surely to have heard the story of the grasshoppers, who are said to have been human beings in an age before the Muses. And when the Muses came and song appeared they were ravished with delight; and singing always, never thought of eating and drinking, until at last in their forgetfulness they died. And now they live again in the grasshoppers; and this is the return which the Muses make to them—they neither hunger, nor thirst, but from the hour of their birth are always singing, and never eating or drinking; and when they die they go and inform the Muses in heaven who honors them on earth.

Plato, *Phaedrus*, trans. Benjamin Jowett, *The Internet Classics Archive*, http://classics.mit.edu/Plato/phaedrus.html. For an analysis of this passage, which has cicadas instead of grasshoppers, see Rory B. Egan, "Cicada in Ancient Greece," *Cultural Entomology Digest* 3 (1994), http://www.insects.org/ced3/cicada_ancgrcult.html.

4. The 1983 edition added the clause "and critics and scholars writing research theses."

5. The 1941 edition reads: "Dogs and their ilk have no business looking in a mirror!"

6. The Chinese idiom "looking at the sky from the bottom of a well" refers to someone with a narrow field of vision. Qian touches on this theme frequently in his criticism of contemporary critics, his references to his own learning, and his observations about humans' limited capacity for wisdom and knowledge. The title of Qian's critical magnum opus, *Limited Views: Essays on Ideas and Letters* (*Guanzhuibian* 管錐編 [literally, *The Tube and Awl Collection*]), for example, "alludes to the ancient saying 'using a tube to scan the sky or an awl to measure the depth of the earth'" (*zhuizhi guankui* 錐指管窺)—a hyperbolically modest self-appraisal of Qian's breadth of knowledge (Ronald Egan, "Introduction," in Qian Zhongshu, *Limited Views: Essays on Ideas and Letters*, trans. Ronald Egan [Cambridge, Mass.: Harvard University Press, 1998], 14).

7. The 1941 edition reads: "If he were an enterprising fox he would say this to himself—akin to the common saying 'Other people's wives always seem preferable.' If he were a conservative fox, he would say this to others—those who cling most strongly to their position are invariably those who are complaining that things are not up to snuff and threatening to resign." Changed in the 1983 edition.

ON MORAL INSTRUCTION

1. The 1939 and 1941 editions have an additional sentence here: "Of course, unless you're the sort to share your lover, you'd never share your towel or toothbrush with friends." Cut in the 1983 edition.

2. The idiom "to preserve one's purity" (*jieshen zihao* 潔身自好) is usually taken to mean to preserve one's moral integrity by isolating oneself from evil influences.

3. The *Liaozhai zhiyi* 聊齋誌異, translated by John Minford as *Strange Tales from a Chinese Studio* (London: Penguin, 2006), was written by the Shandong literatus Pu Songling (1640–1715). It is considered the preeminent collection of ghost stories from imperial China and is, in Minford's opinion, "the supreme work of fiction in the classical Chinese language" (i).

4. A phrase from Jonathan Swift's (1667–1745) letter to Alexander Pope (1668–1744) of September 29, 1725: "Principally I hate and detest that animal called man; although I heartily love John, Peter, Thomas, and so forth."

5. The 1939 and 1941 editions have additional sentences here: "Like Dante, they're halfway across the bridge of life, but they have no way to pen a *Divine Comedy*: they seem to be too old to start love affairs or take up arms to defend their nation, but too young to become vegetarian Buddhist monks; they'd write literature but seem to have exhausted their talent; they'd become researchers but unfortunately they lack the training. By this point, what can they do but pen moralizing essays?" Cut in the 1983 edition.

6. Here Qian humorously transliterates T. S. Eliot's name as "Loves profit and despises morality" (Aili e'de 愛利惡德).

7. The 1939 and 1941 editions have an additional sentence here: "Even I don't necessarily consider literary creation any more valuable than moralizing." Cut in the 1983 edition.

8. The 1939 and 1941 editions have an additional sentence here: "The vituperative revulsion that many people express toward hypocrisy can only be likened to the reaction of a monkey looking in the mirror who doesn't recognize his own ugly reflection." Cut in the 1983 edition.

9. "Maxims Withdrawn by the Author" is the final section in François de La Rochefoucauld's (1613–1680) *Réflexions ou sentences et maximes morales* (1665). The French title appears in Qian's original essay. The English translation is adapted from La Rochefoucauld, *Maxims*, trans. Leonard Tancock (London: Penguin, 1982), 118. Tancock's translation refers to "philosophers" and "Seneca"; Qian's text specifies "moralists" (*daoxuejia* 道學家) and "Sénéque" [*sic*]. As Qian specifies in the 1939, 1941, and 2001 editions (but not in the 1983 edition), the quote appears in section 589.

10. Wang Yangming 王陽明 (1472–1528) was one of the most prominent neo-Confucian philosophers of the Ming dynasty. This line can be found in Wang Yangming, *Chuanxi lu* 傳習錄, annot. Ye Jun 葉鈞 (Taipei: Taiwan shangwu yinshuguan, 1965), 274.

11. Literally, "not wanting face," a pun on the literal meaning of the expression.

12. Hamlet's actual line is "God / has given you one face, and you make yourselves / another" (*Hamlet*, act 3, scene 1).

13. The 1939 and 1941 editions read: "That said, cosmology, like all arts, is subject to a wide-ranging hierarchy. As the preface to the Roman poet Martial put it: 'Some are extremely good, some are extremely bad, and some are extremely mediocre.'" Changed in the 1983 edition.

A PREJUDICE

1. The earliest version of this essay appeared as the third installment of the series "Cold Room Jottings" (Lengwu suibi 冷屋隨筆), *Criticism Today* (*Jinri pinglun* 今日評論) 1, no. 14 (April 2, 1939).

2. Lines 121–23 of canto 27: "O me dolente! come mi riscossi / Quando mi prese, dicendomi; Forse / Tu non pensavi ch'io loico fossi!" ["O wretched me! How I started when he seized me, saying to me: 'Maybe thou didst not consider that I was a logician!'"] (Dante Alighieri, *Divine Comedy: The Inferno*, trans. John A. Carlyle [New York: Harper, 1851], 289–90).

3. The 1939 "Cold Room Jottings" version of this sentence refers to "jottings in a cold room"; all subsequent versions read "jottings in the margins of life."

4. A reference to the saying "When mosquitoes are numerous, thunderstorms begin" (*wen duo leiyu xia* 蚊多雷雨下).

5. The translation is based on Burton Watson's rendering of *tianlai* 天籟 (piping of Heaven), in *Chuang Tzu: Basic Writings*, trans. Burton Watson (New York: Columbia University Press, 1969), 31–45.

6. Tang Geng 唐庚 (Tang Zixi 唐子西 [1070–1120]) was a poet of the Northern Song dynasty.

7. The couplet appears in part 2, book 3, poem 5 of *The Book of Poems*. The translation is adapted from James Legge's version, in *The Chinese Classics*, vol. 4, *The She King* (Hong Kong: Hong Kong University Press, 1960), 290.

8. *Family Instructions of Master Yan* (*Yanshi jia xun* 顏氏家訓), written by Yan Zhitui 顏之推 (531–591) in the last years of his life, is a seven-volume classic from the Northern and Southern dynasties (386–589) covering a wide range of topics, from ethics and morality to writing, art, Buddhism, phonology, and historiography. The line quoted is from the Southern dynasty poet Wang Ji's 王籍 (dates unknown) poem "Entering Ruoye Stream" (Ru Ruoye xi 入若耶溪).

9. Qian uses the poem title as given, which should be "To Jane—The Recollection." The sentence about Shelley does not appear in the 1939 "Cold Room Jottings" version but appears in all subsequent versions.

10. Dante, *Inferno*, canto 1, "Parafrasi."

11. In the 1939 and 1941 editions of this essay, this sentence contains more specific attributions: "It let Thomas Carlyle [Kalai'er 卡萊爾] hear the 'still small voice' in his heart, and let Annette von Droste-Hülshoff detect the faint sound of grass growing." The expression "still small voice" has a long history in Western religion and philosophy, tracing back to the Bible (1 Kings 19:11–12). Its first use referring specifically to the conscience appears in the poet William Cowper's (1731–1800) *The Task* (1784): "The STILL SMALL VOICE is wanted. He must speak, / Whose word leaps forth at once to its effect; / Who calls for things that are not, and they come" (*The Task* [New York: Carter, 1878], 199). Carlyle mentions a "small still voice" in a letter to Matthew Allen of October 8, 1820: "The mob [is an] obtuse animal, and if amid this flourish of royal drums and trumpets, intermingled with the universal crash of weavers' treadles and a boundless hurlyburly, the 'small still voice' should fail to attract much notice, you must not be disheartened" (*The Carlyle Letters Online*, http://carlyleletters.dukejournals.org/cgi/content/full/1/1/lt-18201008-TC-MAL-01?#FN6).

12. *The Classic of Mountains and Seas* (*Shanhai jing* 山海經, third century B.C.E.–second century C.E.) tells stories of 204 mythical creatures from eighteen regions in the early Chinese cosmological landscape. See *The Classic of Mountains and Seas*, trans. Anne Birrell (London: Penguin, 1999). The "commoner who punishes Heaven" (*xingtian zhi min* 刑天之民), also known as "Form Sky" (*xingtian* 形天), is distinguished physically by having a face on his chest and stomach and no head.

13. *Shou dang qi chong* 首當其衝 is an idiom meaning "to bear the brunt" or "to be the first to

suffer disaster." Here, Qian plays on the double meaning of *shou* (first, head), so that the phrase also means "to be struck on the head."

14. The 1939 and 1941 editions read: "Second, you will hope that your neighbor will transform into the ideal primary school student of Lamb's memoir *The Christ's Hospital of Five and Thirty Years Ago*, with a body that stops at the waist and two wings growing out of its back, so that he can fly around and not need legs and feet for walking."

15. Sun Bin 孫臏 (ca. 380–316 B.C.E.) was a military strategist from the state of Qi 齊 who lived during the Warring States period (403–221 B.C.E.). He is thought to have been a descendant of Suntzu, the author of *The Art of War* (*Sunzi bingfa* 孫子兵法). Although a brilliant strategist, he was betrayed by a minister in the kingdom of Wei, which resulted in Sun's mutilation by having his legs cut off at the knees. Despite this ignominy, Sun went on to serve two sovereigns of his home state of Qi who launched successful military campaigns against Wei. The story of Sun Bin can be found in *Sun Bin: The Art of Warfare: A Translation of the Classic Chinese Work of Philosophy and Strategy*, trans. D. C. Lau and Roger T. Ames (Albany: State University of New York Press, 2003), 4–16. The 1939 "Cold Room Jottings" version of this sentence ends at "no consideration to your head"; all subsequent versions include the Rodenbach reference.

16. The actual section is 378, in chap. 30, "On Din and Noise." See Arthur Schopenhauer (1788–1860), *Parerga and Paralipomena: Short Philosophical Essays*, trans. E. F. J. Payne (Oxford: Clarendon Press, 1974), 2:642–45.

17. The 1941 edition ends: "you jot down another essay" (*you xiele yi pian suibi* 又寫了一篇隨筆); all subsequent versions contain the current ending. In the penultimate sentence, the clause ". . . and that your own bawling has prevented people next door from thinking or sleeping" was first added in the 1983 edition.

EXPLAINING LITERARY BLINDNESS

1. The earliest version of this essay appeared as the second installment of the series "Cold Room Jottings" (Lengwu suibi 冷屋隨筆), *Criticism Today* (*Jinri pinglun* 今日評論) 1, no. 6 (February 5, 1939).

2. In editions previous to that of 1983, this line referred to "shooing" rather than "exterminating" mosquitoes.

3. In the 1939 and 1941 editions, the final clause in this sentence reads: "and when teachers ask for a raise, they make it seem like a mere ten or twenty dollars would influence the course of human culture."

4. Su Shi, "I and Li Zhi Fangshu Have Known Each Other for Ages; Now I Have Passed the Examinations but Li Has Not, and I Feel Deep Regret, So I Have Written a Poem to See Him Off" (Yu yu Li Zhi Fangshu xiangzhi jiu yi, linggong jushi, er Li bu dedi, kui shen, zuoshi songzhi 余與李廌方叔相知久矣，領貢舉事，而李不得第，愧甚，作詩送之), in *Su Shi shiji* 蘇軾詩集 (*Collected Poems of Su Shi*), annot. Wang Wengao 王文誥, punct. Kong Fanli 孔凡禮, Zhongguo gudian wenxue jiben congshu 中國古典文學基本叢書 (The Basics of Classical Chinese Literature: A Collection) (Beijing: Zhonghua, 1982), 5:1568–70.

5. *Jinshu* 晉書, *juan* 113, *zaiji* 13. In the 1939 and 1941 editions, Qian elaborates: ". . . and I think it could, since the *Records of Fujian* of the *Book of the Jin* mentions that Fujian was drafting a secret

decree and kept the door closed so that no one would know, when a sole fly that had been hovering above his brush suddenly turned into a boy in black and leaked the contents of the decree to the outside. This is perfect evidence, and moreover it appears in a standard history, so its veracity is unshakable." Shortened in the 1983 edition.

6. William Blake (1757–1827), "Auguries of Innocence."

7. Exegetical studies and phonology were two disciplines pursued by *puxue* 朴學 (literally, "plain study") scholars during the Qing dynasty. The *puxue* movement advocated rigorous evidentiary and textual research into the Confucian classics, at the expense, Qian suggests, of true aesthetic and philosophical understanding.

8. The multiple tomes of French literary historian Charles-Augustin Sainte-Beuve's (1804–1869) *Nouveaux Lundis* were published between 1863 and 1870.

9. Aroma (Hua Xiren 花襲人), the favorite maid of Jia Baoyu in the novel *Dream of the Red Chamber*, goes on to become the highest-ranking courtesan in the Jia family.

10. To "have a dream while pinching one's nose" (*nie bizi zuo meng* 捏鼻子作夢) means to indulge in impossible fantasizing (since as soon as one falls asleep, one can no longer continue pinching one's nose). For an explanation of the expression, see Wang Zhongxian 汪仲賢 (text) and Xu Xiaoxia 許曉霞 (illus.), *Shanghai suyu tushuo* 上海俗語圖説 (*Shanghai Slang Illustrated and Explained*) (Shanghai: Shanghai shehui chubanshe, 1935), 570–72 (entry no. 232).

11. Qian's translation of this apocryphal statement literally reads: "I don't know what's good, but I know what I like."

12. The 1941 edition reads: ". . . sublime art beyond gazing at fashionable women." Changed in the 1983 edition.

13. The 1941 edition reads: "unworthy women."

14. The 1941 edition reads: ". . . a bit of an injustice to Traveler Sun!"

ON WRITERS

1. The earliest version of this essay appeared as the first installment of the series "Cold Room Jottings" (Lengwu suibi 冷屋隨筆), *Criticism Today* (*Jinri pinglun* 今日評論) 1, vol. 3 (January 15, 1939).

2. Qian here uses a different meaning of the word for "writer" (*wenren* 文人) than that found in the title of the essay. The second use of *wenren* refers to literati in traditional China who took the government examinations that served as the gateway to coveted postings in the civil service. The less prestigious route of advancement to wealth and power was rising in the military (*wu* 武) ranks. The suggestion seems to be that during the modern age, when utility reigns supreme, the traditional respect for *wen* 文 rather than *wu* has been inverted, since modern scientists stuck in between these two categories of the governing elite seem to aspire to the usefulness of the *wu* officials rather than to the *wen* officials' role as cultural stewards.

3. Tao Kan 陶侃 (259–334) was a Six Dynasties era official whose frugality was legendary. See *Jinshu* 晉書, chap. 66.

4. *Shishuo xinyu* 世説新語, "Rendan" 任誕. For an English translation of the relevant story, see Liu I-ch'ing, *Shih-shuo Hsin-yu: A New Account of Tales of the World*, trans. Richard B. Mather (Minneapolis: University of Minnesota Press, 1976), 388.

5. The terms that Qian employs for "ruler" (*jun* 君), "father" (*fu* 父), and "elder brother" (*xiong* 兄) denote fundamental Confucian categories of traditional China's social hierarchy.

6. The author is toying here with the third-century poet Cao Pi's well-known dictum: "Literary men disparage one another; it has always been that way."

7. *Shiji* 史記, "Biography of Lu Jia" (Lu Jia liezhuan 陸賈列傳).

8. The 1941 edition has additional sentences here: "As the poem by Chen Shiyi [陳石遺 (1856–1937), who worked in the education section of the Qing government and later taught at Xiamen University in the late 1920s] puts it, 'Those adept in literature / Will never high rank secure; / How could men in the seat of command / Waste their time on mere words?' This explains why Gaozu was capable of realizing his goal to become emperor, whereas Plato could gratify his political yearnings merely by dreaming about the reign of 'philosopher-kings,' devising in vain his plans (*Republic*) and blueprints (*Laws*) for founding the nation. From this, one can see not only that writers are despicable wretches unworthy of rapid advancement in the official world, but that even those worthies who are opposed to literature seem to come up with excessively long writings and an overabundance of discussion—they lack the dignity of someone sparing in words but high in position." Cut in the 1983 edition.

9. Théophile Gautier's (1811–1872) *Les Grotesques* (1844) is a work of literary criticism in praise of "grotesques" and formerly unpopular poets like François Villon (ca. 1431–1463).

10. The 1941 edition has an additional sentence here: "That is why the ancient Roman church father Tertullian, in his *On Idolatry* (*De idolatria*), argues that if the Great Teaching is to be manifested in all its glory and a realm of divine bliss is to be realized on earth, literature must first be uprooted."

11. Alexander Pope (1688–1744) epitomizes English poetry of the Augustan age. The Tang dynasty poet Bai Juyi (772–846) is the subject of an apocryphal legend about his ability to read Chinese characters at birth.

12. The 1941 edition has an additional sentence here: "Wang Shizhen's [王世貞 (1526–1590)] essay 'Nine Fates of Literature' [Wenzhang jiuming 文章九命] long ago provided an exhaustive account of how writers since ancient times have been subject to myriad calamities and misfortunes." Wang's essay discusses nine faults that plagued the writing of poetry from the pre-Qin period to the Song dynasty.

13. *Fayan* 法言, "Wuzi pian" 吾子篇. Here, Yang Xiong 楊雄 (53 B.C.E.–18 C.E.) belittles his own earlier aesthetic orientation. The original phrase is *diaochong zhuanke, zhuangfu bu wei* 雕蟲篆刻, 壯夫不為.

14. The 1941 edition has additional sentences here: "When J. G. Lockhart wrote a biography of his father-in-law, he noted that Sir Walter Scott deeply regretted that he was able only to record the martial feats of great heroes but was himself incapable of bringing any astounding accomplishments to fruition. Hugo's poem 'My Childhood Days' (Mon enfance) articulates the same sentiment. When even persons of this sort bewail their fate and regret having become writers, one can well surmise how dim a view others take of them." The 1939 "Cold Room Jottings" version does not contain the Hugo sentence.

15. This sentence contains a sardonic reference to Lu Xun's 魯迅 (1881–1936) somewhat melodramatically titled short-story anthology *Roaring Battle Cries* (*Nahan* 吶喊, 1923). The phrase "how could he have roared battle cries or written martial songs while seated in his study (*Krieg-*

slieder schreiben und in Zimmer siteenl [*sic*])" does not appear in the 1939 "Cold Room Jottings" version.

16. In the 1939 "Cold Room Jottings" version, this sentence refers to "we" and "us" instead of "they" and "them." The 1941 edition has additional sentences here: "In Browning's ideal world, a baker could write poetry, and a hog butcher could paint at his easel. In our ideal world, nobody would bother about literature or the arts; the poet would become a baker, and the painter would take up the trade of the hog butcher—and if there are useful occupations that offer even more fame and fortune than the trades of baker and butcher, they would naturally be all the more palatable."

HUMAN, BEAST, GHOST

FIRST PREFACE TO THE 1946 KAIMING EDITION

Should this manuscript not end up lost or burned and one day happen to be published, a preface is unavoidable.

Labor-saving devices are becoming more advanced every day, and there are always people more than happy to identify themselves as the original model for a particular character in a novel or play as an effortless way to promote themselves. To preempt those who would assume a false identity in this manner, let me declare categorically that the characters and events in this book are completely fictitious. Not only are the humans within its pages good, law-abiding citizens, but its beasts are domesticated pets, and even its ghosts are not those homeless spirits that roam about unchecked. All live strictly within the confines of this volume and will never step outside its covers. Should someone claim to be one of the humans, beasts, or ghosts who appear in this collection, it would be tantamount to saying that a character, who is purely a product of my imagination, has walked off the page, taken on blood and flesh, soul and vitality, assumed that person's likeness, and now moves about freely in the real world. I'm afraid that since man was first molded out of clay we have yet to see another such miracle of creation, and I dare not dream that my artistry has reached such heights. I must thus refute any such claims in advance and respectfully thank those who would so flatter me.

April 1, 1944

SECOND PREFACE TO THE 1946 KAIMING EDITION

∝

This manuscript was originally put together on my behalf by Ms. Yang Jiang during the chaos and strife of wartime. "Inspiration" was previously published in the first and second issues of *New Talk* [*Xin yu*], edited by Messrs. Fu Lei and Zhou Xuliang. "Cat" was previously published in the first issue of *Literary Renaissance* [*Wenyi fuxing*], edited by Messrs. Zheng Zhenduo and Li Jianwu. The publication of this book was made possible by the efforts of Mr. Xu Tiaofu. To all I would like to offer my thanks.

January 3, 1946

GOD'S DREAM

~

At that time, our world had been trained into utter obedience by scientists, philosophers, and politicians. Every day, it revitalized and improved itself according to the laws of creationism, evolutionism, accretionism, eugenics, and the "New Life Movement."[1] Today's way of life supplanted yesterday's through natural selection, and culture became more refined from morning to afternoon. Life and civilization underwent a thousand transformations in the blink of an eye. The changes came so fast that History had no time to record them all, and even Prophecy couldn't keep up. At that time, the course of human life was measured in "steps." Instead of saying "another year has passed," we said "another step forward has been taken." Instead of saying "die of old age," we said "pedestrians halt." Instead of saying "lament so-and-so's passing," we said "run a hundred steps and laugh at someone who has run only fifty"—laugh because he didn't succeed in running forward a few more steps.[2] When a man and woman joined in marriage, well-wishers at the gathering spoke of the lovebirds "flying together," but not "nesting together."[3] Only a few sticks-in-the-mud still insisted on expressing the wish that the bridal couple might "keep each other warm for five minutes"—roughly akin to our blessing, "May you spend a century growing old together"—knowing full well the impossibility of that empty phrase. Yet this beautiful world of progress had one shortcoming: it rendered every history of a near century, every half-century "cultural self-criticism," every diary, biochronology, autobiography, "A Certain Percentage of My Life,"[4] and other such epitaphs utterly useless. As luck would have it, people at that time were just too plain busy to read. And the authors of such reading material? Fortunately for them, they had long ago hastened to reincarnate themselves in the early twentieth century, where they were born, wrote, had their works read (or go unread), and were forgotten.

The Law of Evolution holds that what comes later is superior to what precedes it. Out of Time and Space evolved inorganic objects, which then evolved into animals and plants. Out of the inanimate plants evolved woman, who is placid but able to root one in place with her nagging. Out of the rambunctious animal kingdom evolved man, who is rough and risk taking. Man and woman created children, and children brought forth dolls. Thus, though God, who is supreme and peerless, should by rights be the final product of evolution, producing a God is easier said than done. Has any great man throughout history deigned to be born before spending ten months in his mother's womb? Take, for instance, the Yellow Emperor, whose four hundred million descendants are now cruelly slaughtering one another. He burdened his mother with a full twenty months of pregnancy. Lao-tzu, the Right Supreme Moral Paragon, likewise lived in his mother's belly for eighty years before dropping to the ground with a wail—an "old son" [*lao tzu*] indeed![5] Thus, by the time the powers of evolution finally created a God, the human race had vanished from this world eons ago. Perhaps that was because they "flew together" but didn't "nest together"—even evolutionists couldn't wait that long. As a result, this world of material abundance was also empty, like the head of a simpleton expanded to the nth degree.

The night was deepening. The ancient darkness gently enveloped the aging world like heavy eyelids over weary eyes. The powers of evolution pushed God out from the nothingness. Entering time and space, he began to sense his own existence. At this moment, the testimonies of theologians and mystics and the prayers of lovers, soldiers, peasants, and the poor since time immemorial finally had a Lord. But, these various signs of devotion were like a letter from home to a vagabond or parents' aspirations for a child who has passed away—God was completely oblivious to them. He opened his eyes and saw nothing. The silence surrounding him was limitless, unfathomable. Instincts bequeathed by the extinct human race half awoke in God. He felt frightened like a child and wanted to cry, but the stillness, long unbroken by the human voice, had coalesced into glue that prevented sound from floating about within it. God realized that the stillness around him and the fear in his heart had incubated in this darkness, and this realization made him loathe darkness and long for light, which he had yet to see or know by name. Moment by moment, this desire grew stronger. After an indeterminate interval of time, the darkness suddenly thinned slightly and the pressure of the night lessened, revealing faint contours of high mountains and deep valleys. His eyes began to serve their purpose and were rewarded with things to see. God was astounded at the stupendous power of his own will. He had wanted it to not be dark, he reflected, and, tactfully, the darkness withdrew. But this was not enough! In the past, his gaze had met with nothing. Now, wherever his eyes rested, they were obliged with something emerging from the darkness. Yet again, God's subconscious seemed to rumble with the strains and echoes of mankind's earlier elegies to the Omnipotent Creator.

God's temperament was also human. Aware of his own powers, he liked to wield them arbitrarily. He wanted to banish darkness once and for all to see whether or not it would obey his order. Hey! Sure enough, the east quickly turned from gray to white and from white to a fiery red as the sun came out. God was delighted with the thought that this was his doing—that this had come about on his command. Reflexively, he closed his eyes against the blinding glare of the sun. At the same time, he thought, "This fellow's not to be trifled with! We can do without him for the time being." And, curiously, in a trice everything vanished before his eyes. All he could see was darkness, which gave off round flashes of red. By this point, God had no more doubts about his own capacities and powers. Anyone could do away with the light by closing one's eyes, but it was his eyes that had generated light in the first place. Not convinced? Just open your eyes. Look, isn't that the sun? Aren't those mountains and, over there, water? Each thing obediently and respectfully presented itself to his gaze. Long ago, a rooster swaggered before his hen and crowed loudly and smugly at the sun because it dared not show its face before his morning report. God, who was immeasurably greater than a rooster, at this moment was actually thinking along quite similar lines. He regretted only that the workings of evolution had failed to produce something equivalent to a hen to keep him company and listen to his bragging. There was a scientific explanation for this evolutionary flaw. Like every animal bred through eugenics (like the mule) and every revered dictator (like the uni-testicled Hitler),[6] God could not reproduce and thus had no need for a partner. Nevertheless, smug, roosterlike crowing was inevitable. Without meaning to, God laughed out loud. His laughter echoed through the wild, empty valleys, impressing him with how his voice could multiply so many times, resound so loudly, and carry so far.

This God was evolved, all right. He could not have been further from a Neanderthal, lacking any trace of the superstition or awe of a savage discovering the universe for the first time. His was the haughtiness and self-confidence of civilized man. Savage man, believing in the omnipresent existence of divinities, submits to and grovels before them.[7] God, discovering only his own greatness, believed that since he could control all things he need not rely on anyone else. The world would extend to meet his gaze and the ground would come up to meet his feet. In fear, the horizon retreated before him. Everything fed his arrogance and nurtured his vanity. Then, suddenly, he felt the need for a companion. What a dreadful bore it would be to continue living in this vast world alone. A companion would enliven things.[8] Coming to this realization, God pondered what his criteria for this companion would be. His conclusion may not have been as clear as what follows, but the gist was more or less the same.

First, this companion should understand him. This understanding, however, should be akin to that of a critic vis-à-vis a creative genius: appreciation without ability. The companion's knowledge should not enable him to copy or compete with him. At most, it should lead him to offer due praise and tickle him with sweet talk, because—

Second, this companion's purpose was to flatter his vanity. He should praise him tirelessly and indiscriminately, like a member of a rich man's entourage, a bought politician, or a newspaper editor on the take. But he wouldn't bribe this companion, whose praises would emerge willingly from the gratitude and happiness at the bottom of his heart; thus—

Third, this companion should be as loyal and honest to him as ... as *what* exactly? This naive and tentative God had no clue. Even we who are familiar with the ways of the world and have seen all sorts of relationships—between fathers and sons, elder and younger brothers, men and women, masters and servants, superiors and subordinates, leaders and their idolizers—can't suggest an apt comparison.

Some people are unable to sleep if a thought crosses their mind right before bed. Others drift off into slumber as a result of indulging in wild thoughts during their waking hours. God might well have evolved from this latter category of person, because these thoughts slipped him into a dream. The obedient world followed him into dreamland. In his dream he still saw barren mountains and wild rivers, and in the water he saw his own reflection. Inspired, he dug a ball of mud out of one of the more fertile sides of the jagged mountains. Following the image in the water, he shaped it into a figure and blew on it. The clay figure began to move and prostrated itself at his feet, crying: "Oh, true, omniscient, and omnipotent Lord! I will forever sing your praises." The surprise and joy that God felt at this moment is indescribable. If you or I were a young girl and heard the doll in our hands suddenly call out "Mommy!" or a female college student who saw the Hollywood star in our wall poster suddenly make eyes at us and intone in a baritone voice, "Little sister, I love you!" we might be able to surmise or imagine a minuscule fraction of what he felt. Unfortunately, we're not.

At this moment, all sacred religious texts' records of man being molded from mud were finally validated as fact rather than mere prophecy. God didn't realize that he was dreaming or that the dream was toying with him. He didn't know that this ball of mud, if you analyzed it, would prove to be but the stuff of dreams.[9] He thought that he had truly found someone to keep him entertained. From now on, he imagined, flattery would reach his heart without having to come from his own mouth. The best praise he could receive was that which he wanted to speak but instead heard, since it would be as thoughtful and apropos as self-flattery but come from someone else's mouth. Each one of us has an ideal, and we may all have dreamed someone up to make it come true. To fabricate such a person when awake, however, is not quite so simple. All we can do is take as raw materials the people already available to us and rework and adapt them, but the finished product will never be quite what we had hoped.

Without knowing it, God got a few lucky breaks by coming into being after mankind had gone extinct. In the past, when two nations went to war, for instance, Nation A would beseech him to punish Nation B, and Nation B would directly appeal to him to annihilate Nation A, leaving the brilliant and righteous God at a loss for what to do. Now he would never be faced with such a conundrum. If writers still existed, for example, his creation of man would surely have provoked a literary debate.[10] Judged solely by his molding man out of mud, God was undoubtedly a naturalist working in the mode of realism, since he saw human nature as despicable and drew his material from below. At the same time, he was clearly playing the classicist, since "all creation is based on imitation." Omnipotent though he might be, he still had to look at a reflection in the water in order to create man. Whether because classicist theory is inaccurate, because God's handiwork is below par, or because he had an ugly visage, the man God made in his image was not much to look at. Perhaps, he thought, this was because the mud was too coarse or because it was his first try and his technique was not yet refined enough. Accordingly, he selected the finest mud—from the very same mound under which Lin Daiyu had buried flowers countless years ago[11]—carefully picked out the gravel, and mixed it with morning dew that had not yet dried in the shady recesses of the valley. Having scrutinized the strengths and weaknesses of his first human creation, his experienced fingers fashioned a new figure from the mud. He chose curves from the ripples of the river to invent a new figure. He selected a gorgeous redness from the delicate rosy light reflected in the morning clouds for its face. He plucked the color azure from the blue sky and concentrated it in its eyes. Finally, he harnessed the gentlest rippling breeze and funneled it into the mud figure in place of his own breath. The essence of wind is inflation and fluidity, and as this figure came alive the first thing it did was to stretch its lithe and supple waist and give a long yawn, setting an example for all the world's lovelorn young ladies. This second figure was none other than woman—God's improvement on the original. Man was merely God's first try, while woman was his crowning achievement. This explains why appearance-conscious men always mimic women, and why women who push the envelope too far transform into vixens.[12]

From then on, God had work to do. He did everything he could think of for this male-female pair. He created all sorts of tamed animals and birds, as well as fruits and vegetables for their use and enjoyment. Whenever he made something new, brimming with self-satisfaction he would announce to them, "I invented another new thing. Am I skillful or what?" prompting the duo to exclaim in unison, "God, the merciful redeemer!" Before long, the couple grew accustomed to seeing his miracles and tired of thanking him. Soon, they began to resent his intrusion into their intimacy. God came to realize that, little by little, the pair's attitude toward him had cooled. Not only did their eulogies ring less loudly than before but their knees and backs no longer seemed to bend quite as briskly in supplication. This led to an unhappy realization. God had *invented* many things since creating humans, but this was the first time he had *discovered* something.

His discovery was that when it comes to male-female relationships, "three" is an integral yet intolerable number. As the newcomer, you will of course regard yourself as an integral member of the trio, as will one of the other two people. The other, however, will find your presence intolerable, though less so than you find his or hers. Should you be the original member of the trio who has subsequently been relegated to third-wheel status, you will continue to regard yourself as an integral party even though the other two resent your presence. In that case, you may consider one member of the pair integral, while of course finding the other intolerable. Mathematicians teach us that a triangle cannot have two obtuse angles, but there is always one obtuse angle in any love triangle. God's discovery was that this obtuse angle was not the thick-as-mud man but himself for having been such an indiscreet guardian. What an inhuman—no, ungodly—indignity![13] He hadn't created woman to be man's companion. He had simply created a plaything out of sheer boredom. The first mold was unsatisfactory, so he had created a second. Who could have thought that the two would have hit it off and cast him aside? He was flabbergasted that woman's attitude toward the Lord Creator on High would be to "respect him, but keep him at a distance,"[14] and that she would instead take up with a man who stank of mud. Consequently, God had another unhappy discovery, this time not mathematical but biological.

This discovery was that the universe had something called gravity. As a result of gravitational pull, all objects have a downward trajectory, including Newton's apple. This is why lower-class people are so numerous and upper-class people are so rare. The same principle also explains why upper-class people are inclined to oppress the lower classes; why youth go bad at the drop of a hat; and why public morality continues to deteriorate. When God created woman, he plucked dew and copied the ripples of the river, inadvertently validating the old saying that "women have a watery nature." Even less did he have in mind that other old phrase: "Water flows downward."[15] If the apple had fractured Newton's skull or broken his nose, he would have discovered gravity just the same, but he undoubtedly would have considered either demonstration to be excessive. Similarly, even though God thoroughly understood the human heart and the natural world, he always felt uneasy because the female mind was unfathomable to him. He even felt that his own greatness was an obstacle and regretted that it prevented them from getting closer. Contrary to his hopes, creating this pair of man and woman had only exacerbated his loneliness because their intimacy magnified the solitude of rejection. Even more infuriating was how they would come and kiss up to him when they had some unfulfilled need. When the fruit had rotted and they wanted the trees to grow new ones, for instance, or when they were tired of eating domesticated animals and wanted wild game from the mountains, they would pester him with endearments until they duped him into acquiescing. No sooner would their wishes be fulfilled than they would for a long time relegate him to the back of their minds. God had turned into their mere servant, and this infuriated him.[16] In the beginning, to make them love him, he had made them enjoy fresh fruit and wild game. In doing so, had he not lowered his own status to that of fruit and game? Given their ulterior motives, if he acceded to their every request, that would make him a stupid melon among fruits or a stool pigeon among wild game! Consequently, God decided that he would no longer grant their requests. But this pair had dubbed God "the Upright and Merciful," and he was embarrassed to cause trouble for them over such a trifle. He would have to bide his time until they made their next unreasonable request, at which time he could refuse them flat out. The beauty of it was that God was immortal and could outlast them no matter how long they waited.

One day, woman came alone to pay her respects to God. She sat by his feet, gazing up at him with eyes as limpid as two drops of water from the Mediterranean Sea, and exclaimed in a tender voice, "Oh, true Lord! No one is as thoughtful and capable as you. I really have no idea how to thank you!"

God mustered all his power to withstand her eyes' blitzkrieg and asked suspiciously, "What's your request?"

Woman laughed a cautious, ingratiating laugh that spread from the back of her shoulders down to her waist, accentuating the curves of her buxom figure. Her voice seemed to float up from the depths of her heart, each word rising and falling with her laughter: "You truly are the Omniscient Lord Creator! I can't fool you about anything. I'm so afraid of you. Actually I don't have any request. You're too good to us. Everything's perfect. It—it really isn't much of a request at all."

"What do you mean by 'it'? Spit it out," God demanded impatiently, excited by the thought that his chance to vent had arrived.

Deploying her entire reserve of charm, woman exclaimed with a twist of her figure: "Great Heavenly Father! You really are omnipotent. Merely an effortless lift of your hand fills us with wondrous admiration. I don't actually want anything new, I just want to request . . ."—as she spoke she pressed her face against God's unfeeling leg, pointing languidly toward man over in the valley—"I just want to request that you create another man like him. No, not exactly like him—with a slightly finer figure, and more handsome. Merciful Lord! You are most sympathetic and considerate!"[17]

God jumped up, kicked woman off his foot, and demanded, "You want me to create another man? Why?"

Woman rubbed the pit of her stomach with one hand and her cheek with the other. "You scared the heck out of me! Oh, mysterious God! Your power is so great! Your movements are so quick! Look, you hurt my face—but that doesn't matter. You were asking my reason, right? My man needs a friend; he's grown bored being with me all the time. If you make another man he won't be stuck with me all day. Am I right or what?"

"And you won't be stuck with him all night either, am I right?" God's angry voice resounded with a thunderclap in the blue sky. "Woman! How could you make such a brazen request? You covet and waste everything, even man. You have your fixed allotment, but you still demand luxury goods. Outrageous! Get out of here. I'll let you off this time, but if you come asking for more than your fair share again I'll punish you by taking away the man you already have. I'll annihilate him."

That last sentence worked. Her face flushing red, woman pursed her lips, got up, and departed. All the way back she mumbled to herself, "I make one joke and you get all high and mighty. To tell the truth, I could tell a long time ago you didn't have it in you to create a better man than him!" Fortunately, these words escaped God's ears. Having vented his frustrations, he was beside himself with joy. Afraid that woman would see his smile if she turned around, he hid his face behind a bank of storm clouds. He grinned broadly, and his magnetic white teeth flashed out from within the storm clouds. Just at that moment, woman turned around, but because she had never seen the drawing of the black man in the toothpaste logo,[18] she mistakenly took it to be lightning. "Ha, ha!" From a distance, the pitch of God's stifled, intermittent laughter sounded to her like thunder. She was both angered and frightened by God's deployment of scare tactics and hurried back to where man was. Since God had just threatened her that he would deprive her of her only man, she reverted to her former affection toward him. She sat beside his head, woke him with kisses, and hugged him, imprinting a kiss mark on every word, leaving it stained with the moistness of her lips: "I have only you! I love only you! I could never live without you. I won't let anyone take you away from me . . .

if anyone tries, I'll fight them tooth and nail!" Groggy from slumber, man awoke bewildered. Woman's reaffirmations of resolve made him uneasy because he was suffering a guilty conscience about a dream he had just had. Woman, exhausted from running and worn out by nerves, sunk into a deep slumber. Stealthily, man got up and selected a couple leftover pieces of fatty meat as an offering to God.

"Oh, most generous Master! Please condescend to accept this offering as a trifling token of my devotion. Everything we have was bestowed by you. Even this is yours—the only offering we can lay at your feet is our sincerity." So spoke man.

The happiness God had been feeling a moment ago intensified. "This is the first time the humans have made an offering," he thought. "No doubt woman had man bring it on her behalf to ask forgiveness. If they see delight on my face they're sure to think less of me." As such, he responded with silence, his facial expression projecting a meaning that French and Spanish novelists convey with the following punctuation mark: "?"

Man saw that God's expression was not unfavorable and mustered his courage: "I have a small favor to ask you, Lord . . ."

With a start, God suddenly realized that those two pieces of fatty meat were no different from woman's beguiling laugh and coquettish eyes: a bribe to accompany a request. Had man, too, been created beautiful and charming, he could have saved himself two pieces of meat.[19]

". . . Please create another woman for me . . ."

"Woman just asked me the same thing." God cut him off.

Once again, God was disappointed and angry, but muddleheaded man was surprised and delighted at God's words. "What a clever devil woman is!" he thought. "How would she know what I was dreaming about? No wonder she hugged me and said all that stuff just now. She was willing to make sacrifices and petitioned God on my behalf, but at the same time she also couldn't bear to have me snatched away by the newly created woman. Golly! She is so generous and thoughtful—how could I ever bear to abandon her?" As this was going through his mind, he lied to God, "That's right. She's been finding life a bit monotonous and hopes to have another female to keep her company."

"Wrong! She didn't ask me to create another person of the same sex; she made a request of the same nature. Did you know that she asked me to create another man, one better looking than a blockhead like you?"

Man's disappointment was no less than God's, and he hurriedly asked, "Lord! Did you say yes?"

Warming to the delights of venting his temper, God boomed, "I regret that I didn't. I really made no mistake in matching you two. A fine pair! Off with you!

If you don't watch your step, be careful that I don't annihilate woman." This threat didn't seem sufficiently forceful, so God added, ". . . and I won't give you any more meat to eat either!" Faced with this dual intimidation, man tremblingly begged for mercy and retreated, rebuffed. God sighed. How could his human creations have turned out to be such good-for-nothings? These two were so equally and symmetrically bad that they were like two lines of parallel prose or a couplet of regulated verse.[20] God reflected on what a well-balanced pair they were and admired the exquisiteness of his own art.[21]

Man and woman had each divulged a personal secret to God, and each had come away empty-handed. Man worried that God would reveal his request to woman, and woman was unaware that God had already revealed her request to man. Thus, without having planned it, both resented God and wanted to prevent him from spilling the beans to the other. Man declared, "We've already gotten enough stuff for our daily needs, so we don't have to go asking God for anything." Woman added, "He's exhausted his capabilities, so we wouldn't be able to get anything new out of him anyway. Just looking at his face makes me sick." They agreed in unison, "Let's keep our distance from him. Ignore him. Pretend he doesn't exist." And so, the divine and the human grew evermore estranged. Still unable to achieve his goal of bringing them closer to him, God thought of an ingenious oblique line of attack. Their life was too easy. If they were made to experience a little pain and suffering, they would learn that he was not to be trifled with and would "beseech Heaven when in dire straits."[22]

That night, man and woman were startled awake by the terrific sound of a faraway roar. Until now, humans had been the only meat eaters. Other beasts, such as cows, goats, and pigs were strict vegetarians. Put on the correct path by God, they maintained the lofty spirit of "I'd rather be eaten, but stick to eating grass."[23] Now, besides humans, there existed other meat eaters, who not only ate human flesh but also had a particular taste for it. Little did these creatures know that the meat of humans is as unpalatable as that of cats, dogs, and other meat-eating land animals. The reason the Tang monk Tripitaka's flesh made wild monsters drool with greed was undoubtedly because he had not broken his vegetarian fast for ten incarnations.[24] The sound that man and woman had heard was the roar of an impatient lion in search of food. They shivered instinctively, detecting the menace in that roar. The domesticated animals cowering around them suddenly straightened up, perked up their ears, and held their breath, as if on alert. This only increased the pair's uneasiness. The roaring soon stopped, and the night it had torn asunder gathered together again. After a certain interval of time, the domesticated animals seemed to realize that the danger had passed for the time being and relaxed with a sigh of relief. Man reached out and stroked the goat lying on its back beside him and discovered that its wool was wet and hot, as if it had just been sweating. Woman shuddered and said in a low voice, "God must be creating trouble for us. We'd better find a cave to sleep in. I'm afraid to sleep outside." They got up and herded the animals into a mountain valley, and then hid in a nearby cave, where they bedded down. Their bodies and minds gradually thawed, opened up, and sunk down. Just as the animals were about to disappear into slumber, they suddenly snapped to attention, and the humans were immediately wide awake. Cold waves of terror spread from their hearts to their limbs, freezing their bodies and throats. The cause of this terror seemed to be lying in wait for them in the dark, sizing them up. They dared not move or breathe, as cold waves of sweat coursed down their bodies. Time stopped, as if frozen in terror. Suddenly, the terror vanished, and a burden seemed to lift from the atmosphere. Dawn's rays crept into the mouth of the cave. Just then, a pig somewhere near the cave entrance gave a wild squeal, which stopped midway and was replaced with complete silence, as if it had been cleanly hacked off with a cleaver. The pig's squeal completely deflated the tension within the cave. Man put his arm around woman so that she could sleep in his embrace. Never since they had been together had they needed each other so much without sexual desire. When the sun had risen, each went out separately. Man counted the animals and discovered that they were short one pig. The cows, goats, and other animals also seem to have suffered a shock and were listless. As he was pondering the reason, woman rushed back from fetching water, panting for breath and crying. When she passed through the forest she had seen a large, coiled python taking a digestive siesta after having swallowed a pig. On the beach by the river lay a crocodile, its large mouth gaping at the sky. Luckily, she had run back quickly and it hadn't seen her. Danger seemed to lurk in every corner. No longer could they live as free from cares as in the past. "How could so many fearsome creatures have appeared in a single night?" they conferred. "The guy we've been revering as God must have created them to harm us. He's not God. He's the Devil—the despicable Devil. We've been blind to have let him dupe us for so long. Well and good! We've seen through him now!" Invisibly, these words resolved an age-old dilemma: "If this world was made by an omnipotent and supremely benevolent God, how could there be evil people running amok?" As it turns out, God is none other than the Devil when he is in a benevolent mood and willing to feed us, while the Devil is simply God when he is in a bad mood and trying to feed us to something else. Rather than being polar opposites, they are in fact two sides of the same coin or two names for the same thing—just as a "madman" is also called a "genius," a "thief" a "gallant," and a "lover" an "irreconcilable foe."

Man and woman's whispered deliberations went unheard by God. He still imagined himself to be their one and only, not knowing that, to man and woman, he had long since been "one" [written "一"] only in the spirit of the dividing "one" that Chinese physicians of antiquity marked below the name of the medicine on a prescription to indicate "two equal parts." Omniscient and omnipotent though he was, God was, after all, an upper-class personage who disdained to bother with what went on under the covers or listen to what was being said behind closed doors. At the moment, he was rubbing his hands in anticipation of a good show. Sure enough, though the two of them were dispirited and unable to come up with a plan, they did not come to God for instruction either. After a while, the python had digested the pig, and the lion and the tiger began roaring nearby. Man grabbed woman and sprinted in alarm back to the cave, where they stacked stones by the entrance. The unfortunate domesticated animals that remained outside ran about in a panic and hid themselves in crevices in the mountainside. "Superb!" God thought. "Once you see your animals eaten by wild beasts, you'll come begging to me, and when that happens . . . ha!" Who could have known that just as not all affairs under Heaven go as man intends, the affairs of mankind do not always proceed as Heaven wills. This strategy of depreciation failed to make humans accept defeat. Wild beasts, being wild beasts, meanwhile, lacked the moral cultivation that civilization instills. The python, for one, lacked an education and was unfamiliar with the ancient and enduring saying that one may "fail to taste lamb and end up reeking of mutton in the process,"[25] so having eaten the pig it wanted to try a new flavor and swallowed an entire goat.[26] The goat's two pointy horns pierced its throat, so that even though it did succeed in tasting goat, it paid for it with its life. Lion and tiger were also the picture of low-class coarseness: lacking table manners, they brawled over the cow they were having for dinner. The tiger died as a result and the wounded lion went to the river for a drink. The river crocodile was an illiterate who had never read Han Changli's famous piece "Offering to a Crocodile," so instead of eating seafood it instead wanted to try lion meat.[27] To the lion, it was bad enough that he had been denied eating someone else's meat—how could he bear to part with his own?—so he engaged the crocodile in a vicious struggle. Victor and vanquished were difficult to distinguish, and their fight to the death saw the death of both. The horrific sounds coming from outside the cave scared man and woman half to death. When things quieted down outside they peeked out from the crack between the rocks at the cave's entrance and saw that the domesticated animals had already been grazing for some time in groups of two or three. Relieved, they went outside and discovered that the horrid predators had all perished and that few of their own animals had been lost. Elated, they skinned the lion. Thenceforth, their cave had a rug, woman a leather overcoat, and man a few days of fresh meat. Woman had yet to be dazzled by American-made fake shark skin and was thus content with the leather from the skinned crocodile. The sole pity was that the giant snake hadn't slithered its way out of ancient Chinese books, so there were no pearls between its joints for the taking.[28] Fortunately, however, the vicious land animals weren't from ancient Chinese books either, otherwise the lion's heart and tiger testes that woman ate would have made her look fierce as well as bewitching,[29] and man's days would have been a trial!

As it was, they didn't end up enjoying many happy days. God saw that they had turned misfortune into good fortune and was as angry as he was disappointed. He realized that in order to make them suffer, he would need to create something that had no skin to flay and no meat to eat. Thus, the fur on the rug, the leather overcoat, and the domesticated animals suddenly had lice. At night, the entire sky was filled with disease-carrying mosquitoes. When the two of them ate, flies descended like large drops of black rain. Besides these, the humans were infiltrated with defense-resistant no-see-ums. As God anticipated, both of them fell sick, and a short while later, both breathed their last, realizing the vow that all lovers share to "die on the same day of the same month of the same year."[30] The flies continued to go busily about their work, and after a little while, the pair's corpses swarmed with fat, white maggots. Humans, who had consumed the flesh of cow, goat, pig, and even lion were reduced to bare skeletons by these tiny things. God, who when creating the insect world had gone out of his way to make them meticulous and efficient workers, was delighted. As he watched, he got carried away and forgot that he hadn't wanted man and woman to die—he had just wanted to make them suffer until they conceded defeat to him. He still wanted to keep them. Once the maggots and bugs had eaten through skin and flesh and had begun to drill through bone for the marrow, he finally came around, but by then it was too late. Whether because no-see-ums work too fast or because man and woman were too slow to catch on to the situation, God never saw them express defeat or contrition. He had created things—including humans, vicious beasts, and no-see-ums—to realize his own plan. Why did nothing go as he wished? God was filled with regret. . . .

His eyes opened and saw only the afternoon sun drooping lazily toward the mountaintops. It had all been a dream. As Lord of all, his will was law, but dreams enjoy extraterritoriality and were not subject to his governance. How infuriating! Then again, how could he know that this dream was not an omen? Creating a human for company would indeed be worthy of careful consideration. He was immortal. How lonely it would be to pass the endless years by himself! God stretched and let out a long, weary yawn at the sun, which was setting with a death-ly pall, and at the world, which was gasping for life. His gaping mouth seemed ready to swallow whole that stretch of time, which was inexhaustible and would be hard to while away.

CAT

∞

"'Don't beat a dog without considering his master's face,' they say," Yigu muttered. "In that case, I shouldn't beat the cat until I see her mistress's face."

Trying to suppress his rising anger was like combing a tangle of matted hair. The mistress, indeed, had yet to show her face, and that damned cat was off hiding who knows where, so he couldn't beat it anyway. It was his usual rotten luck—two and a half days of work wasted! Mr. Li was napping and, to judge by his routine, wouldn't come to the study until nearly three o'clock. But all this simmering resentment would have cooled off by then, and Yigu felt he had to let it out while it was still hot. Fortunately, at that moment Old Whitey brought in the tea. Pointing at the tattered manuscript on the table, its words and lines scattered like city dwellers after a heavy bombing, Yigu exclaimed, "Just look! I went home for lunch and came back to find this mess! Before I left, I gave the final draft to Mr. Li to read. Who'd have thought that after he finished with it he'd leave it on my table instead of putting it in the drawer? Now it'll have to be copied again!"

Having nodded along as he listened to Yigu, Old Whitey now shook his head and heaved a sigh. "What a disaster! This must be Taoqi's doing. Taoqi's so *taoqi*— so naughty! The mistress spoils her so nobody dares touch a single hair of hers. Mr. Qi, please ask the master not to let Taoqi into the study anymore." With that, he shuffled out slowly with his back hunched.

The Taoqi in question was the black cat who had made this mess. Back when she lived in a poor home east of the Forbidden City,[1] she was called "Blackie," but Mrs. Li found this name too vulgar. She laughed. "Wouldn't that make for a perfect match with our doorkeeper, Old Whitey? He'd have a fit if he heard that."

The day the cat was sent to the Lis' house, on Nanchang Street, Mrs. Li was having friends over for tea, and all the guests wanted to come up with a good name for it. A poet who admired Mrs. Li said, "During the Western Renaissance, a dark complexion was the ideal of beauty. When we read sonnets by Shakespeare or the

French Pleiades poets,[2] we see that the women they fell for were all dark beauties. I personally find black more mysterious than white, too—more suggestive and enticing. The Chinese have always favored women with white skin, but that's an immature aesthetic view, like children who only like to drink milk because they're not old enough to drink coffee. This cat is beautiful and dark, so why don't we borrow a ready-made name from Shakespeare's poetry and call her 'Dark Lady'?[3] Nothing could be more refined."

Hearing this, two guests grimaced at each other, because the poet was obviously alluding to the lady of the house. Mrs. Li, naturally, was delighted, but she found the name "Dark Lady" too long. Having received an American-style education, she was in the habit of calling everyone by his nickname to show her familiarity. Had she run into Shakespeare himself, she would have called him "Bill," so nicknaming the cat was just the thing to do. She took the poet's suggestion but settled for a shorter version: "Darkie."

Everyone applauded, "*Miao!*—Wonderful!"

The sound baffled the cat, who thought that people were imitating her own mewing and chimed in, "Meow! Meow!"

Nobody realized that the new nickname meant not "Dark Beauty" but "Blackie"—precisely the name that Mrs. Li found so vulgar. One eminent elderly man didn't say a word at the time, but after returning home stayed up half the night digging through books. First thing the next morning he called upon Mrs. Li and bad-mouthed the poet: "What does he know? I didn't want to argue with him at the time, so I kept my peace, but the Chinese, too, have always liked dark, beautiful women. For instance, in classical Chinese, Daji's[4] name was written with characters that meant that she was dark and beautiful. Daji is a perfect transliteration of 'Darkie,' and it's faithful to the meaning besides. Ha-ha! What a coincidence! What a coincidence!"

Secure in her mistress's affection, the cat seemed to take great delight in causing trouble. Within a week, people were slurring her foreign name, transforming it into a homophone of "Darkie"—Taoqi. And so, like a fashionable student from a missionary school, this rascal had both a Chinese name and a Western name. In addition, it had acquired a posthumous, hybrid name while still alive.[5]

The cat had been living at the Li home for less than two years. During those two years, the Japanese occupied three eastern provinces; Beiping's government was reshuffled once; Africa lost a nation and gained an imperialist state; and the League of Nations revealed itself to be a League of Dreams or a League of the Blind.[6] Yet Mrs. Li did not change her husband, and Taoqi still enjoyed her mistress's affections and her own naughtiness. In this world of never-ending calamities, how many people are as steadfast in their "isms" and beliefs?

This was the third day in Qi Yigu's probationary period as Li Jianhou's private secretary, but he had yet to have the good fortune to glimpse the famous Mrs. Li. When speaking of this Mrs. Li, we can use only what Chinese grammarians term "superlatives." Of all famous wives, her appearance was the most beautiful, her manners the most admirable and forthright. Her living room was the most tastefully decorated, she entertained the most frequently, the dishes and hors d'oeuvres served at her parties were the most exquisite and sumptuous, and she had the largest circle of friends. What's more, her husband was the tamest and never got in her way. If, in addition to according her all these virtues, we were to announce that she lived in prewar Beiping, you would immediately arrive at your conclusion: she was the most refined and elegant wife in the country with the world's most ancient civilization. This is because Beiping—the same northern capital that had been reviled by such Ming and Qing dynasty celebrities as Tang Ruoshi and Xie Zaihang[7] as the most vulgar and filthiest of cities—had, in the recent prewar years, suddenly come to be renowned as the most refined and beautiful city in the land. Even Beiping's dust, which lies three feet thick on any windless day, now seemed to have the very hue and aroma of antiquity. History museums from newly founded small European and American countries sent scholars to bottle it up for display, as though it contained the plundered remnants of the three imperial dynasties of the Yuan, Ming, and Qing.[8]

Ever since the capital had moved to the south, Beiping had lost its usual political function.[9] At the same time, like every useless and obsolete thing, it became a display item of historical value. Like a shoddy secondhand goods stall rebranded as an illustrious antiques shop, the reality remained unchanged but the psychological impact on the customer was enormous. Think how embarrassing it is to buy cheap things at a secondhand goods stall! To patronize an antiques shop, however, you must have money, an addiction to ancient things, and discriminating tastes. As such, those with no intention of accumulating secondhand junk begin buying antiques, and those who can afford to shop only at secondhand stalls have their status elevated to refined antique collectors. Should you happen to have lived in Beiping at that time, you could pass yourself off as worldly and brag to your friends in Nanjing or Shanghai, as if to live in Beiping conferred title and status. To claim that Shanghai or Nanjing could produce art and culture would be as ridiculous as to assert that the hand, foot, waist, or stomach could think as well as the head.

The discovery of the remains of "Beijing man" at Zhoukoudian further demonstrated the superiority of the Beiping resident. Beijing man was the most developed of the apes, just as the Beiping resident was the most civilized of the Chinese.[10] Therefore, at that time, when intellectuals were advancing the idea of a "Beijing [or Capital] school" in the newspapers, they traced their origins back to Beijing man. As such, even though Beijing had changed its name to Beiping, they did not call themselves the "Beiping school."[11] The "Beijing school" was composed almost entirely of southerners, who were as proud of residing in Beiping as the Jews were of their adopted countries, and Beiping never left their lips. Since moving to Beiping, Mrs. Li's foot fungus infection had not recurred—an unexpected bonus of living in the cultural center.

Mr. and Mrs. Li's fathers were both relics of the Qing dynasty.[12] Whereas Mrs. Li's father was famous, Mr. Li's father was rich. A few months before the Revolution of 1911,[13] Mrs. Li's father had accepted an appointment as a provincial governor, hoping that he could rustle up some money to compensate for his financial losses from prior years.[14] Yet the Wuchang Uprising seemed to have occurred specifically to foil his plans, and he cursed the Republic through clenched teeth.[15] Luckily, one of his former students had forfeited his integrity to become an important official of the Republic and honored him with a monthly stipend. Mr. Li's father lived in the foreign concessions in Shanghai, cherishing ideas of the past, enjoying the modern life of the present, and spending money of the future by borrowing on the security of his monthly stipend. Eventually, he hit upon the retired gentleman's road to riches. Today, some nouveau riche would be seeking an officiant for his son's wedding; tomorrow, a comprador banker would be looking for someone to preside over his mother's funeral. Each had a need for these Qing relics, and the honorarium would usually be equal to his monthly stipend. The beauty of it was that compradors' mothers would never all die out, and that sons of the nouveaux riches would all live to a marriageable age. His writing was unremarkable and his calligraphy undistinguished, but he discovered that so long as he affixed the seals from his several official titles, "Presented Scholar of Such and Such a Year" or "Governor of Such and Such a Province," there would be people willing to pay big money for both. He realized then that the fall of the Qing offered certain compensations, and that being a relic was worthwhile after all. He became so even-tempered and amiable that he even allowed his daughter to attend a foreign school.

Mr. Li's father, who was from the same hometown as Mrs. Li's father, was an extremely early promoter of Westernization.[16] As an expectant provincial inspector, he had written a report to the throne on how to "enrich the nation and the people" and been sent to Shanghai to procure machinery from foreigners. Yet the Qing dynasty fell too soon to reap the benefits of his report, so he ended up enriching only himself.

He once toured abroad as an attaché and upon his return to China summed up his gleanings in a four-line family motto: "Eat Chinese food, live in a Western house, marry a Japanese wife, and you'll have no regrets!" His in-laws' thorough knowledge of past, present, and future perfectly complemented his own thorough knowledge of China, Japan, and the West. Little could he have imagined that his muddleheaded son, Jianhou, would misremember his old man's motto in reverse order. First, he took a Westernized wife who was even harder to deal with than a Western wife. Aimo—now Mrs. Li—had graduated from a fashionable girls' school run by Americans. An irritable and irritating little girl to begin with, having been trained by Chinese Christian converts she not only was unsubmissive to her husband but even felt that he by himself did not suffice to wait on her. Second, as both husband and wife alike considered themselves to be civilized people, they were obliged to move to Beiping to live in an old-style Chinese house. Naturally, the facilities were far less Westernized than those in Shanghai. Third, eating Japanese food gave him stomach trouble—but that's a long story.

Since childhood, Mrs. Li had been dissatisfied with her looks on two counts: her skin was not supremely white, and her eyelids were not double-fold. The first point mattered little to her. Who cared for that kind of pale, pinkish foreign doll face?[17] Her natural looks were lovely enough. Her single-fold eyelids, however, were a serious defect indeed. The richness of her heart lacked a means by which to fully express itself, just as a landlocked country with no seaports has difficulty exporting its products. Not until she was in school did she learn that the single-fold eyelid was the national emblem of Japanese women, for which very reason that resourceful people, who had already stolen the sky and put up a sham sun,[18] had established beauty clinics. Unable to alter their height, they had to endure the national nickname "dwarf slaves," but there was no facial feature they could not improve. The ugly became beautiful and the grotesque were transformed into demonic seductresses.[19]

When Mr. Li proposed to her, she had set many conditions, item no. 18 being that they should spend their honeymoon in Japan. Immediately upon arrival, Mrs. Li went to a beauty clinic to have her eyelids altered and the dimple in her left cheek deepened. She knew that after the operation she would be unable to show her face for two weeks, and she was worried that Mr. Li, unable to endure the solitude of the honeymoon, would be unfaithful to her in such a romantic country. Thus, before checking herself into the clinic she had told him, "You know, I've undertaken this arduous, interminable eastern journey across the oceans to suffer here only for your sake. My only desire is to please you—my face is your pride. When my eyes are bandaged and I'm in pain and darkness, will your conscience permit you to live it up outside? If you love me, you'll do as I say. Don't go out running around with anybody. Also, you're such a greedy eater. After I've entered the beauty clinic, I don't want you going to Chinese restaurants or eating big meals. Every meal, it's only Japanese food for you. Promise? If you love me, you should share my suffering. It'll be a comfort to me while I'm in pain. Besides, if you don't eat so well it'll dampen your desire and you won't fool around and ruin your health. What's more, since you're on the short side, you'd be unsightly if you stuffed yourself and put on more weight. If you betray me or lie to me I'll find out and that'll be the end of our relationship."

Two weeks later, Jianhou went to the clinic to pay the bill and pick up his wife. He hadn't lost weight, but his face had grown sallow and saggy, and he looked listless. In contrast, Mrs. Li's eyes, newly bought for five hundred Japanese yen, further enhanced her original beauty, like the lights used in art photography. Her eyes and eyelashes worked in concert for every sort of expressive display—opening, closing, brightening, darkening, sharpening, and misting up—holding Jianhou spellbound. He wondered if two technicians were hiding in her eyes managing it all scientifically. How else could they move so confidently, convey feelings so exactly, or attain such precisely calculated effects? Jianhou had been his father's son; henceforth, he threw himself wholeheartedly into being his wife's husband.

Their friends discussed this privately. How could a woman as beautiful as Mrs. Li have married Jianhou? Surely there were more capable men out there with wealth and family backgrounds similar to Jianhou's. In fact, Heaven had not mismatched this pair. To be the husband of a woman like Mrs. Li was a lifetime occupation, a Trade No. 361 added to China's so-called three hundred and sixty trades.[20] This full-time job was busier than being a doctor and more exhausting than being a porter,[21] not allowing for other interests or goals in life. Although people mocked Jianhou behind his back for being "a husband whose prestige comes from his wife," or a minor celebrity who basked in her aura, Mrs. Li had never thought of it that way. Jianhou's vanity about his wife was not that of the ordinary man who possesses a beautiful wife—that is, it was not the satisfaction of the master. Rather, it was the satisfaction of the possessed, of being a servant. It was like the posturing of servants of rich families, entourages of famous people, or native employees in colonial administrations. This sort of vanity at being possessed was a rare virtue among husbands, one that enabled Jianhou to be tolerant and open-minded. Mrs. Li knew that such a husband was as indispensable as the zero in Arabic numerals.

Though zero itself has no value, without it one could not make ten, one hundred, one thousand, or even ten thousand. Any figure multiplies tenfold when a zero is added, so the zero, accordingly, gains significance by following it.

Ten years into their marriage, Mr. Li was happy and plump. His wife said he was a good husband, and his wife's friends considered him a decent pal. Yet last month, quite by accident, he had been badly upset. At a large banquet, a brash, young playwright had shared a table with the couple. This upstart playwright, having learned of Mrs. Li's presence, could not contain his enthusiasm. So busy had he been with praising Mrs. Li and showing off that his mouth had hardly had time to eat. By the time the third course had been served, he had persuaded Mrs. Li to grant him a visit and, having achieved his objective, could finally turn part of his attention to the food. It's difficult to keep one's mind on two things at once, and he was busy enough as it was. Paying Jianhou any attention was really beyond his capacity, so he never addressed even a casual remark to him. Jianhou was thoroughly displeased, and once they returned home he complained about the young man's ignorance of the ways of the world.

The young brat was as good as his word and arrived on their doorstep the next day with a batch of his writings in hand, asking specifically to see Mrs. Li. In a fit of childishness, Jianhou immediately hid himself just outside the living room to eavesdrop. After greeting Mrs. Li, the fellow spotted Taoqi sleeping on the sofa and exclaimed, "How cute! How content!" After asking for "advice" on his manuscript, he then inquired about a few of the guests who frequented the Lis' house, saying that he would like to meet them all if possible. Mrs. Li replied noncommittally that she would invite him to tea sometime and they could get acquainted. He still didn't leave and turned the conversation to Taoqi, saying that he loved cats too. Cats were creatures that possessed all of the three virtues: reason, emotion, and courage. When hunting for mice, they were like knights vanquishing bandits and making the world safe for good people. When sitting quietly and praying to Buddha, they were like philosophers contemplating the meaning of life. When mewing for mates, they were like poets singing to express their emotions. He added that although Thai cats and Persian cats were the best cat breeds, neither were the peers of Taoqi. In short, he flattered Mrs. Li and praised Taoqi without once inquiring after Mr. Li.

This incident caused Jianhou to self-reflect. He was silent and sullen for two days and then resolved to make a change in his personal life. From now on, he no longer wanted simply to bask in the reflected glory of his wife. He wanted his own career. He would either get a government position or become a writer. After some thought, he decided to try writing first. On the one hand, it would demonstrate that he was not just pretending to be educated, and on the other, writing itself might lead to a government position. Having settled on this plan, he kept it from his wife at first, fearing that she would rain on his parade. Then one day, when he could not hold back any longer, he told her his decision.

To his surprise, Mrs. Li agreed. "It's time you asserted yourself. I've been too selfish, not realizing that I've been hindering your career! From now on, you can focus on your writing; there's no need for you to accompany me at social events."

What to write about? Jianhou was not very bright. As a student, he had always borrowed notes from classmates, and while studying abroad, he had even paid a Jew to write his thesis. After their marriage, his circle of acquaintance broadened and he learned a slew of trendy terms and stock phrases that he could pass off as his own views at appropriate points in conversation. In fact, the contents of most famous works were nothing special. Having never written any books or articles in his youth, Jianhou took his book too seriously, becoming as apprehensive as a middle-aged woman about to give birth for the first time.

He carefully pondered which genre might suit him best. True, he had few brains, no ideas, and no ideals. But sometimes great works do not require good brains, just a good butt. According to Zheng Xuxi, Germans believed that having "sitting flesh" (*Sitzfleisch*) was a prerequisite for an intellectual.[22] If he could but sit down well, he would have no trouble, say, assembling a proper name index to *The Water Margin* or *Dream of the Red Chamber*. Such work represented Western scientific methodology as well as an academic tool for the twentieth century. But, regrettably, indexing was a job for college students or minor editors and was thus beneath him.

Alternatively, there was cookbook writing. When it came to cuisine, he was an indisputable authority. His wife could not give a party without his supervision, and his culinary prowess, needless to say, earned the praise of his friends. Suffering from stomach trouble and abstaining from drinking and smoking had made his sense of taste sharper and his palate more discriminating. Every fine meal he ate at least thrice. He first imagined its taste and ate it once in his imagination. Next, when actually eating he heeded the doctor's warning not to indulge himself and would linger at the table, reluctant to leave. Then he would recollect its taste afterward, savoring it in his mind all over again. Having chewed it over repeatedly, each meal's hidden defects and virtues were all exposed. It was true: if he deigned to write a cookbook, he could outdo Brillat-Savarin.[23] Yet the thought of Savarin was accompanied by unhappy thoughts. The name of Savarin had been mentioned by Chen Xiajun, the disgusting chap who had frequented their home the year before last. Knowing that Jianhou was fond of fine food, he one day brought over the first edition of Savarin's famous *Physiologie du goût*. Having forgotten all his French,

Jianhou spoke up rashly, "You are mistaken: I suffer from stomach trouble, not gout. There is no point in giving me a book about the physiology of gout."

To this day he could not forget the laugh of that bastard, who then remarked maliciously to Aimo, "It's a great pity that your husband isn't a translator. Someday you should ask Fu Juqing to appoint Jianhou to be the special editor of an *Anthology of World Famous Literary Works* and then throw a party with the money he earns." Worse still, Aimo had laughed along with him. His interest in writing a cookbook had thus been swept cleanly away. Besides, preaching the art of eating was hardly a serious career for a modern man.[24]

Xiajun had once teased him, "Foreign tea and coffee companies pay handsomely for *dégustateurs*. They are asked to taste all kinds of teas and coffees, after which the goods are graded and priced. These people usually drink about a hundred cups of tea or coffee a day. Fortunately, they only taste it quickly with their tongues and then spit it out without swallowing; otherwise, they'd get diarrhea or insomnia. What with your stomach trouble, this would allow you to taste the food without having to eat it. It's a pity that big restaurants don't have *dégustateurs* and that nobody is appointing you to be the examiner of the kitchen. That tongue of yours is going to waste!"

Jianhou was afraid that Xiajun would ridicule him if he got wind of his plan to write a cookbook. Having turned this over and over in his mind, he settled on a travelogue about Europe or America—something interesting as well as meaningful and neither too easy nor too hard. He could hire somebody to help without actually having to call it a collaboration. So long as one has indeed toured Europe and America oneself, there's nothing wrong with getting a scribe to set down the impressions. The assistant would be no different from a stenographer who records a speaker's words for a collection of lectures and has no claim whatsoever to its authorship. This approach perfectly suited Jianhou, who by nature couldn't motivate himself to pick up a pen. The first step was to hire a private secretary, preferably a college student looking to make some money.

At that time, patriots in Qi Yigu's school were causing an uproar. A large group of them had been arrested, charged, and thrown in jail. Yigu was timid by nature and his widowed mother, afraid that he might be implicated by his schoolmates, asked him to stay home for a while. Having been introduced in a roundabout way, he had called on Jianhou for the first time four days earlier. This big kid of nineteen wore a blue Chinese jacket, baggy Western trousers, and black, square-toed leather shoes, and had the habit of putting his left hand in his trouser pocket. His hair was pressed yet still unkempt, and his attractive face flushed as soon as he entered the house. His eyes were deceptively black and bright; neither his heart nor his intellect matched the profundity, intensity, and liveliness of his eyes. Jianhou was very pleased with this lad. After a few questions, he asked him to start work the following day, with a month's probationary period. Once Yigu had left, Jianhou went in and excitedly told Aimo that he had settled on a satisfactory secretary. Aimo was amused and compared him to a child who had just gotten a new toy. She also remarked, "I have Taoqi. Who cares about your secretary!"

Rubbing her face against Taoqi's body, she addressed the cat, "We don't care about his secretary, do we?—oh, no! How terrible!" Taoqi had licked some powder off Mrs. Li's face. Throwing the cat off her, she got up from the sofa and went to look in the mirror.

In the two and half days since he had arrived at the Lis', Yigu had gotten along swimmingly with Jianhou. Though shy, he was not intimidated by his employer. Jianhou, on the other hand, since the day he had first learned to speak, had never met anybody who would let him rattle on and on and still lend him an ear as earnestly, patiently, and enthusiastically as did Yigu. Never before had he realized he possessed such eloquence. In these two days, his self-esteem—like the mercury in a thermometer in the mouth of a typhoid patient—shot straight up.

Now he realized the function of a private secretary. Those who had them felt themselves magnified many times and elevated many levels. Jianhou first discussed with Yigu the title of the travelogue and how it would be written, and spoke in passing of many foreign customs. Thus it was that by lunchtime on the first day, Yigu already knew how popular Jianhou had been while studying in America; how much his annual expenses had been; how tough his college courses had been and how difficult it had been to graduate; how astonishing technological civilization was and how the cars in New York City alone, put end to end, would make a line long enough to circle the globe. He heard, too, how Jianhou had introduced China to the Americans; what the colors and designs were of the Chinese robes he had worn to fancy dress parties; how his landlady had cooked chicken for him every day when he was sick; and how an American girl had sent him flowers every day with a get-well note marked with an "X."

"Do you know what that means?" Jianhou smiled and asked mockingly, "Go ask your girlfriend, and she'll tell you that it stands for a kiss. This is a common convention overseas, where people socialize freely."

They settled on two possible titles: *Journey to the West* and *Roaming in Europe and America*.[25] The former was simple and straightforward, whereas the latter was modern.

Coming back to work after lunch, Yigu learned that in order to write the travelogue, in addition to taking down Jianhou's impressions, he would have to consult

America's *National Geographic* and *Travel*, as well as Baedeker and Murray's[26] city guides, for supplemental material. The next morning, Jianhou decided that the travelogue should be written in reverse chronological order, beginning with his return from America via Europe and Italy by ship. His reasoning was that travelogues typically begin with departure—one boards a ship and peers around commenting excitedly on commonplace things like your run-of-the-mill lower-class provincial. Having spent three years in America, he qualified as an expert on Western civilization, so he traveled to other countries for fun. Even new sights and spectacles would not cause him to make astonished exclamations and lose his dignity, like a country bumpkin visiting the big city. He said, "This return tour was at least akin to Lin Daiyu entering Rongguo Mansion, whereas going abroad at first was more or less like Granny Liu stepping into Grandview Garden."[27]

Yigu had been dragged along by some friends to listen to a magnificent rendition of "Daiyu Burying Flowers," sung by a famous Beijing opera female impersonator, so this wasn't the first time he had seen a plump and sturdy Lin Daiyu (as if, in *Sequel to Dream of the Red Chamber*, Daiyu had taken the invigorating pill given to her by the fairy Disenchantment before she went to bury the flowers),[28] but Yigu couldn't help laughing when Jianhou gesticulated and compared himself to Daiyu. This made Jianhou even more pleased.

Yigu hurriedly said, "If that's the case, Mr. Li, we'll need to change the title again."

Thinking for a moment, Jianhou remarked, "I happened to read in the newspaper the day before yesterday that someone is translating Hardy's *The Return of the Native*. The name's already there for the taking, so I'll title my book *The Return of the Sea Voyager*.[29] Good, don't you think?"

After lunch, Jianhou suddenly decided to write the preface first. As a rule, although the preface appears at the front of a book, it is written after the book is finished.[30] Yigu thought to himself that writing the preface first was, like the main text, a case of writing in reverse order. As Jianhou recounted, Yigu transcribed, rearranged, developed, and revised. Up till lunchtime of the day Taoqi made the mess, Yigu had been working on a draft for Jianhou's perusal. Two and a half days of labor had extinguished his reverence for Jianhou. Youthful extremism caused him to despise his master, seeing only Jianhou's dullness, vanity, and lack of intellect and overlooking his amiable nature. He should have been grateful that Jianhou was willing to pay him so handsomely for such a nonpressing job, but all he felt was resentment that Jianhou's wealth enabled him to waste a young man's time and energy by having him write meaningless stuff on his behalf. Seeing the draft torn to shreds by the cat, he had no choice but to suppress his temper and recopy it. Maybe the damn cat was a bold and sensible critic. Who's to say that its decimation of this cultural relic did not in fact constitute the most straightforward and effective criticism of this draft? Yigu smiled wryly at this thought.

When Jianhou learned of the matter, he not only expressed his sympathy but also apologized to Yigu for his own negligence, such that Yigu had no reason to be cross anymore. The next morning, as soon as Jianhou saw Yigu, he said, "My wife has invited you to tea at four thirty this afternoon."

Yigu, overwhelmed by this unexpected favor, managed a polite, sheepish smile.

Jianhou continued, "She has been looking forward to meeting you. Last night, I told her that Taoqi had made trouble for you. She was very apologetic and gave Taoqi a scolding. Since there happens to be a tea party today, she wants to invite you in for a chat."

This made Yigu feel unworthy of Mrs. Li's company. He was too ignorant of etiquette and lacked the proper attire to meet a fashionable lady, so he was bound to make a fool of himself. He declined, saying, "I'd feel embarrassed meeting all those strangers."

"There's nothing to be embarrassed about," Jianhou responded kindly. "You've heard of all the people who'll be coming today, and only in my home can you see them all together. Don't miss your chance. I have to go out to run some errands. In the meantime, would you please collect materials about New York for chapter one? At four-thirty I'll come to bring you in to tea. If I don't show up, please ask Old Whitey to take you in."

Yigu didn't feel like doing anything all morning. Fortunately, Jianhou was not there, so he could take breaks as he pleased. He wanted very much to meet all those people whose names exerted such a magnetic force, but at the same time he was afraid that they would make fun of him and look down on him.

"I wouldn't feel so shy if Jianhou escorted me in, but if Old Whitey did I'd be embarrassed to walk all the way into the living room without any protection. What if Jianhou does fail to return and I have to ask Old Whitey to lead the way? That'd be a problem! If I go in on time, none of the other guests will have arrived and the mistress will surely tease me for coming early and staying late for the food, like a brave soldier in battle who is the first to charge and the last to retreat. I can't risk it. But if I go in after the guests have arrived, all eyes will be on me, which would be even more unbearable."

After thinking it through, he saw that there was only one way out. "I must listen carefully for the doorbell around four thirty. Old Whitey will pass the study when he escorts guests to the living room. As soon as the first guest goes in, I'll follow right after. The hostess and the guests will be busy greeting one another, so no one will notice me and I won't get nervous."

In the end, Jianhou accompanied him in. They had no sooner entered the living room than Yigu's face flushed and his eyes clouded over. He was vaguely aware that a fashionable woman was greeting him with a smile. After sitting down, Yigu fixed his eyes on the carpet. He didn't have the strength to raise his head to have a look at Mrs. Li. He could only uneasily sense her presence before him.

Suddenly he found that his feet were stretched too far out, and he hurriedly retracted them, his blush deepening a shade. He had also failed to catch what Mrs. Li was saying about Taoqi.

Seeing how shy Yigu was, Mrs. Li took a liking to him out of pity. Thinking that the child must have never come into contact with women, she asked, "Mr. Qi, is your school coed?"

Mrs. Li knew very well that by that day and age a school that did not take in girls was as disreputable as a monastery that did.

"No."

"Really?" Mrs. Li was very much surprised.

"Yes, yes!" Yigu desperately corrected himself. Mrs. Li gave Jianhou a meaningful look and said nothing, only smiling at Yigu. This smile of Aimo's was exclusively for Yigu. Like the dog-skin plasters sold by boxers at Tianqiao[31] or the misty poetry of the European and American Pleiades,[32] the smile contained so much richness that one would never believe it if he heard that it encompassed such elements as consolation, protection, fondness, and encouragement.[33] Yigu still dared not look straight at Aimo, so Aimo's smile, like a prayer for victory, a charitable donation, or other well-meant offerings, did not confer any benefits upon its intended recipient. Just then, Old Whitey showed in more guests. Aimo went to receive them, but her mind was still on that intelligent-looking lad. She thought it was high time he received a lesson in the emotions.

Jianhou patted Yigu on the shoulder. "Relax!"

The Lis understood that Yigu was shy, so they introduced him to the guests only in passing as they arrived, pointing at him and nodding to him from afar. They let him sit on an inconspicuous sofa by the wall. Gradually, Yigu became more relaxed as he gazed upon these famous guests.

The tall man speaking in a loud voice was Ma Yongzhong, a noted political analyst who published editorials daily in the newspaper *Correct Argument*. No matter what political change may have occurred, abroad or at home, he always managed to demonstrate post-factum that it was precisely as he had expected or hinted. Now that his reputation was big, he began to talk big. Especially in private conversation, you would feel that he was a politician rather than a political analyst. He not only was able to hold forth about the domestic and international political situations, but did so as though he were a crucial mediator. He sounded like a meteorologist in his observation tower—come wind or rain, it was all under his control. Once, in one of his essays, he publicly told his readers about one of his personal habits: before turning in every night, he always tore off the calendar page of that day, unlike most people who would wake up to find it was still "yesterday's day." From this minor detail, one can infer the type of man he thought himself to be. Since Sino-Japanese relations were very tense lately, he felt no "dismay" for lack of topics for his editorials.[34]

The man leaning back on the sofa with his legs crossed, smoking, was Yuan Youchun. As a child he had been taken abroad by foreign missionaries, and following those pedantic Westerners had infected him with the most vulgar airs of Westernization: that of churches and the YMCA. After returning to China he condescended to take an interest in the culture of his homeland and began making efforts in that direction. He believed that China's old civilization was best represented by playthings, petty cleverness, and hack entertainment writers. In this sense, his enterprise was much like the Boxers' cause of "Supporting the Qing and Eliminating the Western":[35] he shelved high-minded Western religious theory and began to promote the style of intellectual hangers-on such as Chen Meigong and Wang Baigu. Reading his writing always felt like eating a substitute—margarine on bread or MSG in soup. It was even closer to the "chop suey" served in overseas Chinese restaurants: only those who had never sampled authentic Chinese cuisine could be tricked into thinking it was a real taste of China. He hoodwinked Chinese knownothings and hoodwinked foreigners—those who were merely know-nothings in Western suits. He had recently published several articles discussing the Chinese national psyche, in which he proposed that traits common to mankind were unique to the Chinese people.[36] His pipe was famous. He mentioned it frequently in his articles, saying that his inspiration derived entirely from smoking, the same way Li Bai's poems were all the product of his drinking. Some suggested that he must be smoking not pipe tobacco but opium, since reading his articles made one yawn, as with the onset of a habitual craving, or want to sleep, as if one had taken an anesthetic. It was suggested that his works be sold not in bookstores but in drugstores as sleeping pills, since they were more effective than Luminal and Ortal but had no side effects. All this, of course, was said by people who envied him, so naturally none of it could be taken seriously.

Among those who spoke unkindly about him behind his back was his friend

Lu Bolin, who sported a small Japanese mustache and whom he flattered and was flattered by in return. He never claimed to smoke pipe tobacco, but that was the only possible explanation for the color of his face. Not only did the black circles under his eyes seem to be the effect of smoke, but even their shape was like smoke, curling about and calling for deep thought. As for the dark redness of the tip of his nose, it could only be likened to that of steamed shrimps or crabs.[37]

Sunflowers excepted, nothing and nobody was more partial to the rising sun than was Lu Bolin.[38] The Chinese attitude toward Japanese culture had been that Japan had consistently been forced to content itself with being second-best. Since the West was too far away, the Chinese had to make do with Japan's jerry-built culture. Knowing very well that this kind of mind-set was detrimental to his aspirations, Lu Bolin conceived a brilliant idea. The Chinese, in their hearts, disdained the Japanese goods they bought in lieu of Western goods, while Westerners often bought old Japanese things, having mistaken them for rare Chinese treasures. The secondhand stores of London or Paris even displayed Japanese silk nightgowns embroidered with curved dragons, their tags all marked "for the use of the Royal Empress Cixi."[39] He believed that in order to convince Western students in China to treat him with greater respect, he had to propagate this kind of Western viewpoint. The Chinese were biased and looked down on modern Japan, which imitated the West, while he advocated ancient Japan, which imitated China. Because Japan was so adept at imitating the West, it was accused by people of being devoid of creativity. But though Japan did a poor job at imitating China, Lu nevertheless praised it as having its own distinctive style that deserved emulation by the Chinese. It was akin to saying that sour wine has the fine quality of thick vinegar, but he took this one step further and regarded vinegar as standard wine. Any Chinese cultural relic that was devoid of the spirit of bonsai, haiku, or the tea ceremony, he derided as mere trash.[40] He held that one's character, conduct, and writings should display a subtle and distinctive style. Unfortunately, however, his own writings seemed like "Greater East Asian Writing"[41]—half Chinese and half Japanese—conveying no "subtle style" at all. His writing was consequently famous for "giving food for thought." Yuan Youchun had this to say behind his back: to read his stuff, one could only feel that he was trying very hard to be subtle but somehow failed. He was like a dog whose tail has been cut: no matter how crazily it wags its tail bone, it fails to ingratiate itself. It was none other than he who had given Taoqi the name "Daji."

Zheng Xuxi, the scientist, though skinny and short, had a big heart and was not boring in the least. He had once studied astronomy in Germany. Perhaps influenced by German culture, he had decided to become a "whole man" (*Gesamtmensch*)[42] and an intellectual imperialist, embracing every field of knowledge as his own territory. He considered himself extremely poetic, full of romantic imagination and sentiments, and also possessing the skill to fuse the richness of life with scientific precision. As a consequence, he talked about the stars in Heaven as if he were talking about stars in Hollywood.[43] One middle-aged woman scientist who had vowed to remain single went to his lecture on electromagnetism. Amid the cheers and laughter of the audience packing the hall, she alone turned red with embarrassment when he explained the attraction between positive and negative electrons as being like love between the sexes. He often aired his views on political and social problems and was doted on by young people. Lately, however, he hadn't been feeling well. In an article in support of a strike by the students' patriotic movement, he wrote that his purpose in going to Germany to study astronomy had been to wipe away national shame. After the Boxer Rebellion, the Germans had taken away Chinese astronomical equipment; therefore, he wanted to introduce German astronomical theory into China, as he considered it to be a fine example of the "victory of the spiritual over the material." In other circumstances, his story might have been on everyone's lips and increased his fame accordingly. Unfortunately, since the League of Nations had decided to offer China only "moral support," young people had become disgusted with terms like "spiritual victory,"[44] and Zheng Xuxi was severely attacked.

The man dressed in a Western suit and with his head shaved, Zhao Yushan, was the director of a certain academic organization. This organization employed many college graduates to edit esoteric and profound research reports, the most famous of which was Zhao Yushan's "A Statistical Study of Misprints in Chinese Publications Since the Invention of Printing." It was said that this subject could not be exhausted in a single lifetime and thus could best foster the spirit of endurance required for academic research. He often claimed, "The import of finding one misprint is no less than that of Columbus's discovery of the New World." Since listeners had no way to interview Columbus himself about this theory, they could only nod their heads in agreement with Zhao Yushan. He was dry and uninteresting, a man of few words. But since he had sacrificed all his hair for Mrs. Li, he was entitled to frequent invitations to the Lis'. He and his young wife did not get along well. The lady loved excitement and was in such good health that she seemed totally impervious to noise. Whatever she did, she had to have noise in the background. All day long, if the phonograph wasn't on, the radio was. This, in itself, was enough to give Yushan headaches, but she was an avid moviegoer as well. On the silver screen, whenever the hero and heroine begin to kiss during a climactic love scene—be it on land, sea, or in the air—music always floats in from afar to enhance the mood. Therefore, at certain times in the bedroom she insisted on playing music, from hymns on Christmas Eve to the Qingyun Song on the night of National Day, driving her husband to the brink of neurasthenia.[45]

When they had first come to Beiping, the Lis once invited the Zhaos over for lunch. As soon as Mrs. Zhao saw Mrs. Li, she despised her eagerness for the limelight and her ability to have all the men at her beck and call. After the meal, everyone praised the meal, complimenting the cook's skill and Jianhou's supervision. Jianhou said, "Hold your praise! We have Mrs. Zhao with us today. She has a university degree in home economics and is an authority on culinary matters. We should ask for her opinion."

Mrs. Zhao didn't let this opportunity to belittle Mrs. Li slip by. Recalling a rule from her home economics lecture notes and feeling secure in the knowledge that she had strong backing, she said, "The dishes were delicious, but the colors were a bit monotonous. Too many of the dishes were steamed in clear soup and not enough were braised or stewed, so the colors were not well distributed and made no symphonic effect on the senses."[46]

It was mid-May, but each person at the table privately gasped at her words, as if hit by a gust of cold air. Zhao Yushan knew that every word his wife had spoken was a mistake, so there was no way of correcting it.

Mrs. Li joked with a smile, "Next time, we'll have to send the courses to the beauty parlor first to put on makeup and have them powdered and painted before we invite Mrs. Zhao to appraise them."

Chen Xiajun laughed heartily, "You can just borrow my painting palette and put it on the dining table."

Mrs. Zhao, having said something wrong, was chagrined and angry. On their way home from the party, Mrs. Zhao suddenly remembered that Mrs. Li herself was the product of a beauty clinic. She should have silenced Aimo at the time by saying, "A beauty parlor won't be enough. You should send them to a beauty clinic." She only regretted that she had seen the light too late and gotten the worst of it.

From then on, she became bitter enemies with Mrs. Li and forbade her husband to go to her house. Her husband, however, wouldn't listen. She then accused him of taking a fancy to Aimo. One day, the couple were quarreling about this yet again. Yushan had just gotten a haircut, and Mrs. Zhao obstinately asserted that he wanted-ed to please Mrs. Li with his sleek hair and shining face. In her anger, she chewed up a piece of gum and spat it onto Yushan's head. As a result, Yushan had to shave his head. Since it was late autumn and he could not use the weather as a pretext, he had to say that long hair would waste more of the blood in the scalp and decrease the efficiency of his mind. It didn't occur to him that this pretext would prevent him from growing his hair out later.

Knowing that Yushan had fallen out with his wife on her account, Mrs. Li began to invite him over for dinner and tea more often. Rumors flourished. One claimed that he had shaved his head because of a fight with his wife, while another said he did so because his love for Mrs. Li could never be requited. In short, he intended to become a monk. Lu Bolin once told him he should count the hairs he had shaved off; perhaps their number would match the number of misprints in Chinese books and he could be spared much future computation. His eyes wide open, Yushan replied, "Revered Bo, stop joking! Discovering a misprint is as momentous as discovering a new continent. . . ."

The genteel Cao Shichang was charming and soft-spoken. Listening to him from the next room, one became fascinated for the wrong reasons. But hearing a man speaking so softly to their face, many people became impatient and itched to turn up his volume as one might turn up a radio. Yet this cultured scholar, of all people, loved to give his readers an impression of rude barbarity, as if he combined the naivete of the savage and the ferocity of a superman. His past was shrouded in mystery. If he was to be believed, there was nothing he hadn't done. He had been a bandit in his native region; later he became a soldier for the government; and after that he had gone to Shanghai and become a gangster. He had also been a Chinese opera singer and a waiter at a grand hotel. Whenever he spoke of these and his many other romantic picaresque experiences, young men who had never lived outside of family and school would shake their heads and give the thumbs-up: "Amazing!" "Fantastic!"[47] Writing about what he had done turned out to be more profitable than actually doing it, so he decided not to change his trade again. In theory, since he had so many wonderful and interesting recollections, he really should have written an autobiography and packed them all into it. Instead, he wrote only bits and pieces of some autobiographical novels. Perhaps if he really had written an autobiography, there would have been a discrepancy between all his experiences and his age, since he was still in his thirties. And perhaps, once he had finished the autobiography, it would have been inconvenient for him to make new amendments to old experiences. As the Chinese saying goes, "End one thing and put a stop to a hundred others."

Famous as he was in literary circles, he could never forget how little schooling he had received as a child, and he felt that those who did have "proper academic credentials" didn't quite respect him. He was always on the lookout for some offense or insult from others. The honey-sweet voice hid that he was ready for battle, with sword drawn and bow bent.[48] Because of his position he had no choice but to socialize with the Lis' famous guests, but he really took pleasure in the company of young students—his "little friends."[49] Since he could not take part in the current conversation, he swallowed feelings of envy, anger, and scorn and carefully observed the buffoonery of the assembled "gentlemen" so that he could describe them thoroughly to his little friends when the occasion arose. Suddenly, he spotted the neglected Yigu, who looked like a little friend.

That day's tea party could not have excluded Fu Juqing. While *Hempen Robe Physiognomy*[50] is not entirely reliable, sometimes one's appearance can indeed influence one's life. A woman with deep dimples and good teeth, for example, will naturally love to smile at people, and as she becomes known as a "happy angel," her temperament should imperceptibly become less violent. Similarly, Fu Juqing had since childhood been somewhat slant-eyed; it was not known whether the cause was congenital or postnatal. In elementary school his teacher had always suspected that the child was looking askance at him to express his contempt. At the same time, his cold sidelong glances also seemed to find fault with the teacher's instruction. But since Fu Juqing's father was a member of the local gentry, teachers dared not offend him. By the time he had reached fifteen or sixteen, the intensity of his gaze had so increased that one glance from him would make you immediately feel uneasy and out of sorts, leaving you wondering if you had done something wrong, if someone had hung a strip of paper on the knot of your "melon skin" cap, or if you had forgotten to button your fly.[51]

One day one of his father's celebrity friends told him, "Every time I run into your son, he reminds me of He Yimen's book reviews.[52] Though He gave the impression of being superior, he actually only attended to details and nit-picking. Your son's gaze has that quality."

Fu Juqing didn't know exactly who He Yimen was. He had only heard that he was a critic from Suzhou and assumed that he must be someone like Jin Shengtan.[53] From then on, he believed that his appearance suited him to be a critic. When he was a junior in college majoring in liberal arts, among the assigned reference readings was a poem by Pope, in which he read the famous line about Addison, the editor of *The Spectator*, which said in effect that Addison was good at leering and sneering.[54] When he also read a chapter on "the critic eye,"[55] like an ant on a hot pan, he got all worked up in the reading room of the library. Thereafter, he saw to it that everything he did and said was consistent with the appearance of his eyes. Even the tone of his articles seemed to sneer between the lines. He knew that the British, of all people, had eyes higher than the tops of their heads and that the eyes of students at Oxford, Addison's alma mater, were higher than the tops of their top hats so that they could look down even upon the king. A few years in Britain had made him all the more contemptuous of mankind and his opinions all the more lofty sounding. One felt that, instead of being put on the table and read with bowed

head, they should rather be pasted onto the ceiling and read as one might appreciate Michelangelo's frescoes in Rome's Sistine Chapel. His lofty views could be appreciated only by those who didn't mind getting a stiff neck from looking up.[56] In
Britain, he had learned how to keep a straight face and look indifferent. Therefore,
at public gatherings, if a man were beside him, strangers would assume that he
was his brother and if it were a woman, that she must be his wife; otherwise, he
wouldn't be so indifferent. He, too, smoked a pipe, which, according to him, was a
mark of an Oxbridge education.

Yuan Youchun had once sneered, "Don't listen to him toot his own horn. So
what if he went to England! Anyone who wants to can smoke a pipe!"

Yet at heart, Yuan Youchun really did hate Fu Juqing's guts, for it seemed as if
Yuan Youchun were just "smoking a foreign pipe in secret," whereas Juqing could
borrow the words from the sign on a Vietnamese opium den: "Licensed Smoking."

Some guests looked at their watches. Others asked the host, "Should we still expect Xiajun today?"

Mrs. Li said to Jianhou, "We will wait another ten minutes for him. He's always
like this."

If Yigu had been more observant, he would have noticed that the present guests,
plus the host and hostess, made up ten. If Chen Xiajun were included, the number
would reach eleven. Such an odd number indicated that one guest who had not
originally been included had been added at the last minute. Yigu's mind had been
elsewhere, so this never occurred to him. He still entertained the old notion that
people should be judged solely by their appearance and thought that these celebrity seekers of truth, virtue, and beauty should have some corresponding mark, just
as butchers should all be fat and jewelers must all wear two or three gigantic rings.
Little did he expect their plain-looking appearances to be such a disappointing
contrast to their reputations. It was fine by him that there were no women guests.
Yigu had learned from school that female students who were passionate about literature and knowledge were seldom models of beauty.[57] Yet even if there had been
female guests at such a gathering of intellectuals, they would surely have been un-
pleasing to the eye and would only have magnified the beauty of the hostess.

Examining Mrs. Li closely, Yigu found that she was indeed a beauty. Her long,
Greta Garbo hairdo was in perfect harmony with the contours of her shoulders,
back, and waist, unlike many a woman whose hairstyle is an independent entity
that clashes with her figure. Now around thirty, Mrs. Li's prettiness had gradually
ripened toward full-blown gorgeousness. Her complexion was dark, making her
face suited to heavy makeup. She had fine eyes and teeth, with high cheekbones,
making her face amenable to smiling, talking, and changing expressions.[58] She of-

ten opened her mouth, but she didn't say much—just a nod, a smile, and an occasional word or two before she turned to converse with someone else. She wasn't the kind of woman who flaunted her talents and played the coquette. She simply enjoyed manipulating these people, like a juggler who could use both hands to toss and catch, keeping seven or eight plates aloft simultaneously.

Yigu found it odd that the guests were all longtime celebrities in their late thirties.[59] What he did not understand was that for these well-established middle-aged men, coming to Mrs. Li's home was their only chance for an economical and safe romantic relationship that involved neither trouble, scandal, nor expense. It was a place where they could seek spiritual rest, a club they could go to escape their families. Jianhou didn't mind their presence, but they were extremely jealous of one another. There was only one thing in which they could all cooperate: when Mrs. Li became interested in a new acquaintance they would, with one voice, disparage the person with clever, pleasant-sounding remarks. They paraded their friendship with the Lis, yet they did not lightly allow outsiders to step into the circle of friendship. Mrs. Li consequently became all the more inaccessible. In truth, they were not Mrs. Li's friends, merely her habits. Since they had all been together for five or six years, she knew them and they knew her. They were always at her beck and call, and within her grasp, so she didn't bother to foster new habits. Only Chen Xiajun, who came in at that moment, could be considered a relatively trustworthy devotee.

The reason for this was that Chen Xiajun had the least to do and could come to the Lis' more often. He had previously studied painting in France, but he didn't have to paint for a living. He once remarked that in addition to the capitalists and the proletariat there was another class that opposed both: the idle class—spoiled young men with inheritances and no proper careers—though he himself barely managed to belong to this class. When he first returned from abroad to Shanghai, he had wanted to make an effort to earn his living by painting. Yet in Shanghai, everything Western was deemed good except Western painting. The paintings displayed in houses furnished in Western-style were Chinese center-hall scrolls,[60] vertical scrolls, and horizontal scrolls. His eldest uncle was a famous painter of the traditional Chinese style, ignorant of perspective and realism. "Foreign cemetery mounds" and tap water excepting, he had never been exposed to famous mountains or beautiful rivers. Relying on collections handed down from his ancestors and Japanese collotype editions of *Southern Painting*,[61] he would paint rivers entitled "In Imitation of Dachi"[62] one day and trees and stones under the title "The Clouds and Forest Were Once Like This" the next. His paintings were in high demand, which made Chen Xiajun, who had an artistic conscience, furious. His uncle one day told him, "My dear nephew, you've taken the wrong path! I don't know Western painting, but it has neither the grace nor the subtlety of purpose of our classical painting . Three days ago, for instance, the manager of a bank asked me to paint a center-hall scroll for the meeting room of his bank. It should suit and flatter the bank but it mustn't be vulgar and obvious. How would you people who study Western painting say it should be done?" Xiajun couldn't think of anything, so he shook his head. His uncle guffawed. Unfolding a scroll, he said, "Look what I painted!" In the painting, there was a lychee tree overladen with fruits, big and small. Inscribed on the painting was: "An Investment Brings a Manifold Profit: In Imitation of Luo Lianfeng."[63]

Seeing this, Xiajun was simultaneously indignant and amused. His uncle then asked him how to paint "happiness." Thinking that he was really consulting him, Xiajun told him the whole story of how in Western mythology Fortuna was a blind-folded woman on a flywheel. Stroking his beard and smiling, his uncle unfolded another scroll depicting an apricot tree and five bats. The words on the painting read: "'Apricot' Plus 'Bat' Is a Homophone of 'Happiness.' Five Bats Allude to the Five Happinesses. My Own Creation." Xiajun had to admire his uncle in spite of himself. His uncle also had numerous women students, most of whom were mistresses of wealthy businessmen. These rich men were busy making money all day and worried that their mistresses would feel bored and nurture wicked ideas, so they often encouraged them to pick up some hobby to pass the time. Chinese painting was the best choice, since it could be shown off but wasn't difficult to learn. A painting tutor differed from other kinds of tutors in that he had to be famous, so as to increase one's own respectability. Furthermore, famous Chinese painters were mostly elderly men who would not seduce women, so they were more trustworthy. Xiajun was still young and had studied painting in the decadent land of France, so people took precautions against him. They had also heard that Western painters painted from models. It would be hard to say that they weren't painting what Silly Sister in *Dream of the Red Chamber* called "the fight of the demons."[64] That would be an offense against decency.

Cold-shouldered in Shanghai, Xiajun moved to Beiping, where his self-esteem was gradually restored by some friends who shared his interests. Yet he was never fully able to recapture the drive he had had when he first returned from abroad. He was so lazy that he was loath to do anything. Consequently, people thought that he was capable of anything, if only he were in the mood, and he became famous. Talking was the only thing he was not lazy about; he talked even in his sleep at night. He was especially good at talking to women. He knew that women didn't like men who respected them too much. He praised them in mocking tones and flattered them in offensive terms.[65] The previous month, for instance, Mrs. Li had given a birthday party. She had reached a point at which she wanted others to remember the day of her birth but not the year. When she predictably told the guests that she was getting old, they protested, "Not at all! Not at all!" Only Chen Xiajun commented, "You'd better hurry up and get old! Otherwise, you'll outshine all the young girls and they'll never be able to hold up their heads!"

Now that the guests were all present, the servants brought in the refreshments. Mrs. Li asked Yigu to sit beside her. After pouring a cup of tea for herself, she poured one for him and asked him how many lumps of sugar he wanted. Yigu hesitated out of politeness, "No, thank you!"

Gazing at him and smiling, Mrs. Li whispered, "Don't act like you did just now, denying that there are girls in your school. There's no need to be polite. The tea won't taste good without sugar. I went ahead and put in some cream for you."

Yigu was grateful that everyone else was too busy talking to notice his embarrassment. Mrs. Li's smile and the expression in her eyes made him so happy that his heart seemed to have been burned by something hot. He mechanically stirred the tea with a spoon, not hearing what other people were talking about for quite some time.

Jianhou said, "Xiajun, didn't you feel your ears burning as you came in? We were speaking ill of you."

"Who of us doesn't do that behind the backs of others?" replied Xiajun.

"I've never spoken ill of anyone," Aimo put in.

With his left hand on his chest, Xiajun bowed deeply to Aimo from his seated position, "And I've never said bad things about you." Turning to Jianhou, he asked, "Why were you bad-mouthing me? Let's hear it. As the saying goes, 'Correct mistakes if you have any and guard against them if you don't.'"

Ma Yongzhong, who had to go to the newspaper office to write articles after tea, hurriedly put in, "We were complaining that you put on airs, always intentionally coming late and wasting other people's time by making them wait for you."

Yuan Youchun remarked, "People have been saying that you must have picked up this artist's habit of yours in the coffee shops of the Latin Quarter in Paris. The French have no concept of time, so they had to borrow the expression 'Time is money' from the English. I hold a different view. I believe you were born with this habit—no, you had the habit even before you were born. You must have refused to come out of your mother's womb after ten months."[66]

Everyone laughed. Before Chen Xiajun could reply, Fu Juqing said coldly, "This humor is too dull and heavy. Put it on the butcher's scale and you'll find it to be a few catties on the heavy side."

His face slightly reddening, Yuan Youchun shot Fu Juqing an angry look, and replied, "The British measure by the pound, not the catty. You're not such an Englishman after all."

Taking a sip of his tea, Chen Xiajun said, "What a shame! What a shame! Such good tea is used to wet your throats for quarreling! I didn't mean to have you wait for me. I just went to the station to see off a friend and his family who were leaving for the south. That's why I was late. An inauspicious wind is blowing across the land these days. Many people want to leave here. Old Ma, do you think war will break out or not? You ought to be better informed than we are."

Cao Shichang said meaningfully, "You should read his editorials. No private interviews about state affairs now."

Several voices chimed in at the same time, "We need to ask him because we can't make heads or tails of his editorials." Yigu too felt that this was of immediate concern to him and waited for Ma Yongzhong to speak after finishing his sandwich.

Mrs. Li said, "Right! I need to be prepared. If Beiping is really all that dangerous, I'll have to reclaim the rented house in Shanghai, and Jianhou will need to go to the south to see to it. Yet that summer three years ago was even worse than now. Japanese aircraft were circling overhead and everyone was fighting for transportation to return south. The second-class corridors were full of passengers. In third-class, one couldn't even roll over at night. All kinds of funny things happened. The big problem later turned out to be no problem at all, and those who had left came back. Much ado about nothing. We're used to false alarms these past few years. It may be that nothing happens. Yongzhong, what do you think?"

Ma Yongzhong carefully chewed his bread, as if bearing in mind, as he had learned in his physiology class, that starch should be digested in the mouth. When he finished, he used the napkin beside the dish to wipe away the crumbs on his chest and frowned. "Hard to say . . ."

Mrs. Li coquettishly feigned anger, "That won't do! You have to tell us."

Fu Juging said, "Why are you so hesitant? Let's hear what you have to say. To tell you the truth, Mr. Ma, I've never taken what you say seriously. Unlike with your editorials, you don't have to be responsible for your talk here. For good or bad fortune, we can pray and draw divination sticks at temples, or prognosticate with the eight trigrams,[67] or consult those people who run the glyphomancy stalls.[68] We won't act based on what you big political analysts say."

Pretending not to have heard that, Ma Yongzhong said to Mrs. Li, "I don't think that war will begin immediately. First of all, we are not fully prepared. Second, I was informed that if Japan makes war on us, Russia might seize the opportunity to attack her. I can't tell you the source of this information, but it's quite reliable.

Third, Britain and the U.S., because of their interests in the Far East, will not sit around and do nothing while watching Japan invade China. I know they have a tacit understanding with our authorities concerning actual support. The Japanese are afraid of Russia and can't ignore Britain and the U.S., so they won't dare to start areal war. Fourth, our government is on excellent terms with Hitler and Mussolini. Germany and Italy sympathize with us. They won't help Japan in order to pin down Britain and the U.S. So, as I see it, there won't be a war for the next two or three years. But, there are always unforeseen circumstances."

Mrs. Li said angrily, "What an annoying person you are! Just as I was feeling a little bit relieved by all you had said, you came out with that one depressing line."

Ma Yongzhong smirked apologetically, as if an unexpected war were going to be the fault of his inaccurate prediction. Cao Shichang asked, "If that's the case, then how to end the present tense situation?"

Yuan Youchun said disdainfully, "Huh! What else can we do but give way?"

Ma Yongzhong replied gravely, "We can only endure and make temporary concessions."

"That's terrible!" Jianhou said. Yigu echoed him in his heart.

"It will get worse if we don't concede," Fu Juqing and Lu Bolin said simultaneously.

Chen Xiajun said, "Concede! Concede! How long can we continue to concede? At most, the nation will be subjugated. It would be better if we fought to the bitter end with Japan. Actually, we shouldn't be so reluctant about losing Beiping. In this atmosphere of compromise and momentary ease, we are quickening the pace of subjugation. I can't bear it! Fighting is the only way out." With this he struck the table to show that he was as good as his word, as if to say that this was how the Japanese should be fought.

Zhao Yushan, who was sitting on his right, was so startled that he jumped up, spilling tea all over his clothes.

"Look what you did!" Mrs. Li said with a laugh. "Be careful not to break my cups. 'Fight!' Will you go to the front to fight?"

Xiajun apologized to Yushan, "It's all my fault. Your wife will quarrel with you again about the tea stain . . ."

Hearing what Mrs. Li said, he turned back, "I will not. I cannot. What's more, I dare not. I am a coward. I am afraid of gunfire."

Jianhou shrugged his shoulders and winked at the other guests.

Fu Juqing said, "The fact that you can admit your cowardice shows the greatest courage. Nowadays, nobody dares to say that he's afraid of fighting a war. You are the only one who dares to speak so frankly. Some people conceal their cowardice under the guise of policy, saying that we should maintain peace, that we should compromise temporarily, and that we shouldn't act rashly and be swayed by personal feelings. Others shout loudly that we should fight. Actually, they only wish to make an empty show of strength and frighten Japan with shouting. They don't want the war, nor do they believe there will be one. In short, everyone is a coward, yet they pretend to be brave. No one dares to be an honest coward. You, on the other hand, support the fighting of the war. That's a little bit contradictory."

Xiajun poured milk onto his plate and summoned Taoqi to lick it. Stroking Taoqi's fur, he replied, "It's not contradictory in the least. It's a mentality shared by traditional Chinese and cats alike. We always say that 'Those who are good at fighting wars deserve the severest punishment' and that 'A good army is an inauspicious thing.' But we also say, 'Don't use an army unless you have to.'[69] We are afraid of fighting and fight only when it becomes impossible to avoid. Before we fight we are afraid of death, but when we fight we are so afraid that we forget death. I'm no Sinologist, but I vaguely remember a certain famous general once saying that soldiers' courage comes from fear. They are afraid of the enemy, but they are even more afraid of their own general, so they have to go all out against the enemy. To take another example, cats are the most cowardly domestic animals; yet we see children scratched by cats but never bitten by dogs. If you compare infants under one year old with puppies and kittens of the same age, you will see how kittens differ from those two other types of four-legged domestic animals. A child will cry if you pretend to strike him, while a puppy will lie down with its four limbs in the air and wave its two forepaws, as if to ask you not to hit it, rocking its body from left to right. A kitten, on the other hand, will become fiercer the more afraid it is. Its whiskers will stand on end and the muscles in its paws will tighten like the string of a drawn bow as it prepares to risk its life. Yet we all know that cats are far less brave than dogs. Therefore, to be afraid of war yet able to fight a war is not as contradictory as Juqing thinks."

Yuan Youchun realized that he could insert this discussion into his article about the traits of the Chinese and didn't say anything, as if he had not heard it.

Lu Bolin said, "I never knew that Xiajun was a speechmaker. What has happened today might well be made into the title of a chapter in a novel, 'Banging the Table, Chen Xiajun Makes a Vehement Declaration; Teacup Overturned, Zhao Yushan Becomes Soaking Wet and Angry,' or 'Chen Xiajun Compares Himself to a Kitten; Zhao Yushan's Wife Resembles a Tiger.'"[70]

Everyone laughed at Lu Bolin's wickedness. Shaking his head, Zhao Yushan said, "Rubbish! Poorly done."

Cao Shichang remarked, "I don't have Mr. Chen's courage. But we intellectuals have responsibilities toward our country and should hasten to do what we can. I think we should call for international sympathy. To begin with, we should get the media's support and sanction Japan for its perfidious actions. Those of you who know foreign languages should carry out this kind of unofficial propaganda. Mr. Yuan has made a lot of progress in this respect. Mr. Fu, perhaps you should try this too. Last spring, a Chinese art exhibition held in London drew the attention of cultured people throughout the world toward China. That's the best kind of opportunity. We shouldn't miss it! We must strike while the iron is still hot, and if it isn't hot, we'll strike it until it is!"

Yigu was fully convinced by this, thinking that Cao Shichang was quite reasonable.

Fu Juqing said, "You overestimate me. Only Youchun can do this. But you also overestimate foreign sympathy. Sympathy is merely an emotional luxury. There's nothing practical about it. We all sympathize with Yushan, for instance, yet who will help him tame his wife? We've seen with our own eyes that Chen Xiajun made him spill tea on himself, and our revered Lu Bo made caustic remarks to him. Have we defended him against the injustice? If foreigners know it's in their best interest, they will naturally come to our rescue. Modern media is unlike traditional Chinese pure talk.[71] In autocratic countries, the government controls the media, not the other way around. In democracies like Britain, all the nation's presses are in the hands of one or two publishing magnates. These people are not intellectuals with brains and hearts, just ambitious capitalists who want to expand their wealth and influence through the newspapers. How can they uphold justice? As for the London art exhibition, let me give you some food for thought. A British friend of mine wrote to me to say that Europeans took an interest in Japanese art because Japan had won the Russo-Japanese War. Now they are positive that if a Sino-Japanese war begins, China is going to lose. That's why they've suddenly become interested in Chinese art. When a big house is about to change hands, neighbors will go pay a visit."

"Talking about all these things is useless," Lu Bolin said with a yawn. "In any event, China can't bring credit to itself and has to rely on others. Whether we concede to Japan or seek protection from Britain or the U.S., it's either Tweedledum or Tweedledee. I see no difference between them. Both are a disgrace to the nation. The Japanese harbor ill intentions, to be sure, but how much better are the British and the Americans? I'd prefer Japan, which at least is of the same race and shares a great deal with us in culture. I know I'll be vilified for saying this."

Chen Xiajun said, "What else can we expect from an out-and-out 'Japanese expert'? Many peacetime 'Japanese experts' will collude with the Japanese when war breaks out. Revered Bo, I'm awfully sorry if I've offended you. We Hunanese speak crudely and know no taboos."

Lu Bolin went livid at this last utterance. His face turned white and his hand trembled over his beard. In China, only people from four provinces—Guangdong, Guangxi, Hunan, and Shandong (which barely makes the list)—could say such cocky things to others as "We people of such and such a place are born this way." It was as if their native places were themselves a principled debating standpoint or a battle slogan. Lu Bolin was a native of the area bordering the Shanghai-Hangzhou-Nanjing railroad. The name of his hometown didn't sound especially good. Others used his birthplace to mock him, or explain away his disposition, so it wouldn't enhance the force of his argument. Therefore, he couldn't think of anything at the moment to counter Chen Xiajun's "We Hunanese." Besides, he had just predicted that he would be vilified. Now that his prediction had come true, why complain?

Zheng Xuxi hastened to ward off an argument, "I can't decide whether or not it makes political sense for us to declare war, and I've already been disparaged by young people for saying too much. But from a suprapolitical point of view, war might be necessary for our national spirit. An epic war would stimulate our people's latent virtues and help us restore spiritual health and national self-esteem. Of course, we would be unable to avoid pain, casualty, horror, homelessness, famine, and all the disasters wrought by Ibáñez's 'Four Horsemen of the Apocalypse.'[72] But these are all necessary in the course of war. Amid the overarching atmosphere of glory and heroism, we would have compensation for local pain. Such is life. Beauty and virtue are distilled from ugliness and evil. The same is true of the fresh milk, snow-white sugar, fragrant tea, and delicious snacks on the table. Once inside us, these good things change property and shape through the biological and chemical processes of our intestines and stomachs, turning into a mushy and messy state too horrible to imagine. We should protest the injustice done to these fragrant and sweet good things. Yet, without this filthy process, how can the body become beautiful and healthy? I—"

Mrs. Li cut him short, "You're about to make people start vomiting. We women don't enjoy listening to such roundabout arguments. Life is full of disgusting and loathsome but unavoidable things. If this war can't be avoided, you don't have to find profound reasons to demonstrate that it's reasonable and good. Your attempt to justify war doesn't glorify war; on the contrary, it profanes the truth. Listening to you, we become suspicious of all truths and imagine that they, too, are merely compelling cover-ups for wrongs. Our task is not necessarily a good one. Your opinion sounds like self-delusion. I don't buy it."

Yigu was spellbound by Aimo. He turned and listened to her attentively, his eyes like two fires burning bright with surprise and admiration. Seeing this, the sharp-eyed Chen Xiajun winked at Aimo, smiling. Aimo turned to look at Yigu. Yigu was so embarrassed that he bowed his head. He twisted off pieces of bread and rolled them into little balls.

Chen Xiajun immediately asked, "May I know this gentleman's name? I came in late and didn't have the pleasure of making your acquaintance."

Yigu felt ten pairs of eyes setting his two cheeks on fire. He wished he could kill Chen Xiajun with one stab of the knife. Meanwhile, he heard his voice answering, "My name is Qi."

Jianhou said, "I forgot to introduce him to you! Mr. Qi helps me arrange material. He's very bright."

"I see, I see!" was Chen Xiajun's answer. If Heaven indeed obeyed human wishes, Chen Xiajun would have felt his cheeks burn as though slapped by Yigu.

"You haven't hired a woman . . . woman secretary?" Yuan Youchun asked Jianhou.

He had meant to say "woman clerk" but suddenly remembered that this title was too straightforward, and feared it might be unpleasant to Yigu's—the clerk's—ear. He congratulated himself for shrewdly switching to the more polite "secretary."

Cao Shichang said, "That's out of the question! Would his wife allow that? Besides, a woman secretary wouldn't be much help."

Mrs. Li said, "That's not true. He can use as many women secretaries as he wants. It's none of my business. Don't put it all on me. Right, Jianhou?"

Jianhou giggled foolishly.

Yuan Youchun said, "Only Jianhou can use a woman secretary without causing a scandal about seducing girls of good families. With a wife as beautiful as Aimo at home, he has high standards. It's hard for him to appreciate anyone else."

Glancing at Jianhou, Chen Xiajun said, "I doubt he'd have the nerve to seduce."

Suppressing his anger, Jianhou forced a smile, "How do you know I don't have the nerve?"

"Treason!" Xiajun shouted. "Aimo, did you hear that? You'd better keep an eye on your husband immediately."

Aimo replied with a laugh, "If someone falls in love with Jianhou, so much the better. It shows my good taste in my choice of a husband. I should be delighted if other people share my taste. I don't mind in the least."

Aimo's response was pleasant enough but actually beside the point, since Chen Xiajun was talking about Jianhou's falling in love with another woman, and not another woman's falling in love with him. But nobody corrected her.

Chen Xiajun continued, "Jianhou might have the nerve but not the appetite. For us who have reached middle age, so long as one of the two basic desires, for food and sex, is still strong, that means we aren't old yet. These two desires have something in common. From a man's diet, we usually can infer his libido . . ."

With his eyes on the teacup in front of him, Lu Bolin said, as if talking to his own beard, "Aimo said just now that she's not jealous! But she loves to eat fish sautéed with vinegar. Voilà!"[73]

Jianhou said, "That's right! Xiajun only spouts nonsense, as if he knew everything."

Paying no attention to Lu Bolin, Xiajun rolled his head as he told Jianhou, "I assume she's jealous since she loves to eat fish sautéed with vinegar. Be careful not to enjoy yourself too much."

Mrs. Li said, laughing, "That's irresponsible talk. Okay, okay, so I'm a vinegar bottle, a vinegar jar, a vinegar barrel. Go on."

Like a rubber ball that had been pricked and deflated, Xiajun said lazily, "There's nothing to talk about. Jianhou has a small appetite, so he probably isn't greedy for love affairs."

"He must also be constantly improving his skill as he does with cuisine. There aren't many women who can satisfy his aesthetic standards," said Fu Juqing.

Hearing this, Jianhou was very pleased.

"That's a completely erroneous statement," Xiajun burst out. "The women most likely to win men's love are not beauties. On the contrary, we should guard against plain and commonplace women. When we see a famous beauty, we can only look up to her. We dare not love her. Those of us who have grown ugly before we're old feel inferior and hopeless, so we don't lust after swan's flesh like a toad. Her beauty increases the psychological distance between her and us. It's like a danger sign that makes us timid and cowardly, and we dare not approach her. If we pursued her, we'd be like soldiers on a suicide mission, forging ahead with foreknowledge of failure. On the other hand, when we run into an ordinary woman whose looks are at best not repulsive, we go out with her with our guard down. Pow! One day, we suddenly discover that she's been stealthily making a nest in our hearts. We fall in love without knowing why and without justification. Beauties are like the enemy's regular army: you know how to guard against them, and even if you lose the war, you can account for it. But ordinary women are like Franco's Fifth Column in the Spanish Civil War, spying on you and subverting you while you're still daydreaming. Take our wives or other women we've loved, for example: none of them can be considered beautiful. Yet when we were wooing them, we still sometimes found it difficult to sleep and eat. Young as this Mr. Qi is, I assume you've had your fill of experience, eh? Ha, ha!"

Xiajun's earlier comments had made Yigu involuntarily admire him for his keen observations of human emotions. Little expecting the question to be directed to him, he turned red and speechless, and his hatred for Xiajun was rekindled.

Mrs. Li quickly put in, "You're disgusting, Xiajun. Mr. Qi, don't pay any attention to him."

Yuan Youchun said, "Xiajun, just now you said that our wives are not beautiful. Is Jianhou included in this 'we'?"

Both Cao Shichang and Zhao Yushan chimed in with him.

Mrs. Li said with a laugh, "He's certainly included. I used to be ugly even when I was young. Now that I'm old, I'm even more so."

Realizing that he had stuck his foot in his mouth, Chen Xiajun shrugged, scratched the back of his head, and grimaced. Even Lu Bolin laughed.

Ma Yongzhong said, "You're all being silly! My newspaper office has two women clerks who're very conscientious workers. Yushan, aren't there women researchers in your institute?"

Zhao Yushan answered, "We have three, and they're all quite good. Most young women would never come to our institute because they'd consider it boring. In my experience, women university students who major in the natural sciences, Chinese literature, history, and geography are honest and sincere. Only those who major in Western literatures are worthless. Their heads are filled with romantic ideas, but they know nothing. Nor have they mastered foreign languages. But they invariably want to figure out the meaning of life or become a woman writer or become a diplomat's wife and entertain Westerners—they're extremely restless. Juqing once introduced one of these precious creatures to our institute, but I finally got rid of her. Juqing is still mad at me."

Fu Juqing said, "The reason I'm mad at you is because you're obstinate and narrow-minded and intolerant toward others."

Zheng Xuxi said, "That's right, Yushan should have retained her. Maybe the academic atmosphere could have exerted a subtle influence on her, making her fitter for the environment and transforming her into a capable person."

Lu Bolin chuckled. "That reminds me of a joke. More than ten years ago, my family still lived in the south. One spring, I accompanied my wife to Mount Potuo to burn incense and stayed overnight in the guest room of the monastery. I wasn't pleased with the look of the bed and asked the monk if there were any bedbugs. The monk assured me that there were no bedbugs: 'Even if there are one or two, they're under the influence of Buddha and don't drink blood. Should they happen to bite—Amitabha!—don't kill them, sir. To take a life in a pure Buddhist monastery is a sin.' Good heavens! I was bitten so badly that night that I didn't sleep a wink. Later, I found out that some people really did listen to the monk. One old lady who went to burn incense with her daughter-in-law caught one bedbug and put it in her daughter-in-law's bed to 'free captive animals and accumulate virtues,'[74] making her daughter-in-law yelp. That joke has made the rounds. When Xuxi said that environment might change one's character by persuasion, I was reminded of the vegetarian bedbug in the monastery."

Everyone had a good laugh. After laughing, Zheng Xuxi said, "Revered Bo, you shouldn't mock the monk. There's some truth in what he said. Bedbugs are just too far removed from Buddhism. It's what Xiajun calls 'the vastness of their psychological distance.' That's why the bedbug didn't change its nature. Those creatures, which have higher intelligence, can be infected by their masters' habits. Biologists and animal psychologists agree on this. For instance, if the master likes joking and his guests laugh loudly, his dog will also acquire a sense of humor from its surroundings and behave comically, sometimes even stretching its face to imitate a human smile. Darwin once observed that dogs could imitate humans' humor. Over ten years ago, I read the German psychologist Preyer's book on child psychology,[75] which also mentions this. So it's not empty talk when I say that an academic atmosphere might alter a woman's character."

Lu Bolin remarked, "I haven't seen a dog smile; I'll have to keep a dog to experiment with later. But I'm all for your scientific demonstration. I love books, and the mice in my home are influenced by the master. They've taken a special liking to books and are always chewing on them. Perhaps the monks secretly ate meat and that's why the bedbugs in the monastery didn't abstain from blood. You were absolutely right." He winked at Mrs. Li, as if to draw her attention to his clever irony.

Zheng Xuxi shook his head, "You, old man, are incredible."

Yuan Youchun said, "Why use a dog as an example when we have Taoqi at hand? If you watch her figure when she moves, so supple and strong, sometimes she really does resemble Aimo, especially when she stretches. Being kept in the Lis' house, she has gotten accustomed to the beautiful mistress's example and changed imperceptibly."

Mrs. Li said, "I don't know whether to curse you or to thank you."

Chen Xiajun said, "His remark is totally incorrect. Taoqi has indeed spent many years with the Lis. But she also has a master. Why doesn't she imitate Jianhou? Don't laugh or Jianhou will think I'm making fun of him! If Jianhou were living in sixteenth-century France, many a woman would fall for the contours of his body and offer to be his secretary for free. Back then, it was fashionable for men and women to stick out their paunches, called *panserons* in French,[76] and the higher the better—a practice diametrically opposed to the modern one of women's binding their abdomens and exaggerating their hips. If Jianhou can be considered handsome by classical French standards, then he could certainly be Taoqi's model. That's why I say that Mr. Yuan has mistaken effect for cause. It isn't that Taoqi imitates Aimo. Rather, Aimo has made a thorough study of Taoqi and developed her own distinctive style. Aimo won't get angry when she hears this. The consummate Western beauty who brought an empire to its knees was the Egyptian empress Cleopatra. According to ancient Egyptian custom, the more a woman resembled a cat, the more beautiful she was.[77] Among our wives, Aimo is certainly the most attractively dressed. Come winter, for instance, my wife looks like a sack of corn flour. Only you look perfect. Your clothes don't seem to be made for the body; rather, your body seems to adapt itself to the clothes. You've imitated Taoqi and dressed up in furs. You couldn't say that Taoqi grew fur to imitate you, could you?"

Aimo laughed. "Watch out or Jianhou might punch you! You're just talking nonsense."

Passing an éclair to Xiajun, Jianhou said, "Could you cut it out, please? Here, put this in your idle mouth so that it'll stop spouting nonsense." And indeed Xiajun took the dessert and bit into it, thus ending his long-winded speech spanning antiquity and modernity.

Fu Juqing said, "I've been thinking about what Xiajun said. There is indeed a 'psychological distance' in love. That's why in the West Cupid shoots arrows only in secret. To shoot an arrow certainly requires the proper distance. If it's too close to the heart, the arrow can't be shot, while if it's too far away it won't reach its target. People of drastically different social position find it difficult to fall in love with each other. Yet, it's just as difficult for those who are close blood relations—this distance is not purely psychological. Have any of you had this experience? From afar a woman looks gorgeous and lovable, but when we get closer we discover it's all a sham: she's not beautiful in the least; nor is her makeup or her technique of applying it up to par. I can't figure out what women like this are up to. They take great trouble and time dressing up but in the end must be viewed from a distance of ten yards away! Perhaps they want men to fall deeply in love with them from afar, so that when they get closer and discover the truth, it's too late to repent. All they can do is leave their mistake uncorrected, make the best of it, and love them to the end. After hearing Xiajun, I realized that they are like guns and cannons in that their effective range is preset. I can't think how many women of this sort I run into every day. I detest them! They seem to want to cheat my love away and I almost get taken in, but, lucky for me, I live in modern times. China has opened up, and I have the opportunity to observe them carefully and rectify the illusion at first glance. If I lived in ancient times, when things were closed up, I would only be able to gaze at a woman as she leans on the railing of a high building or catch a glimpse of her when she pulls back her curtain while being transported by donkey cart. She would be within sight but beyond reach. My only option would be to fall in love with her at first sight and then take the trouble to woo her. How unfair! I shudder to think of it!" Fu Juqing shivered as he spoke.

Jianhou laughed so heartily that his entire short, stout body rocked, joining his mouth in the laugh.

Chen Xiajun, who had long since finished his dessert, said with a sigh, "Juqing is too haughty. If we middle-aged men still have desire, we shouldn't be so exacting. Not only do we have to lower our standards in the matter of looks, we also have to be less demanding when it comes to feelings. Ten years ago, I looked down on those old men who turned a blind eye to their young mistresses' messing around behind their backs. They played the fool and let it be. Now, I'm beginning to understand and sympathize with them. Unless you tolerate a woman's love for others, you can't expect her to tolerate your love for her. When I was studying art in Paris, I went out with a Corsican girl. Then I found out that she was a pious Catholic and would marry me only if I joined the church. It was as if she were a receptionist who solicited customers for the church. I had to get rid of her. At the time, I wanted a woman to love me heart and soul, leaving no place for anyone else. Even God was my rival in love. I felt she should forsake him for me, that her love for me should surpass any religious considerations. But now I am more content and completely lack such high expectations. If a lovely woman were so merciful as to bestow some leftover affection upon me, I would shed grateful tears like a beggar who gets leftover soup or cold meat. One glance, one smile, or one blush from her, and I would remember and savor it for days. Fight a war? We're too old, yet not old enough, since we still worry we'll be drafted. Fall in love? We're too old, but not really. We're so worried because we're afraid we'll be left out."

Ma Yongzhong stood up to say, "What Xiajun just said was demoralizing and shameless. It's getting late. I have to go now. Mrs. Li, Jianhou, thank you. Good-bye, good-bye! Don't bother to see me out. Mr. Qi, see you."

Cao Shichang also echoed that what Xiajun had said was a threat to public morals.

After listening to Xiajun, Jianhou looked dumbfounded, as if Xiajun's words had started him thinking. He stood up hurriedly when he heard his name spoken and joined Aimo in saying, "Won't you stay a little bit longer? Good-bye, good-bye."

Yigu took out his watch. Seeing that it was getting late, he too wanted to leave. He wished that all the guests would take their leave at the same time so that he could just say a polite word or two while the group was milling about and then sneak out. But the other guests were all snugly seated and didn't look as though they were about to leave. Fearing that his mother might be worried, he couldn't sit still any longer and began to plot out how to get through the awkwardness of repetitively bidding farewell to each of the guests.

Seeing him look at his watch, Mrs. Li said, "It's still early, but I dare not keep you any longer. See you tomorrow." Yigu mumbled a few words of thanks to Mrs. Li. Since it was the first time he had come as a guest, Jianhou saw him out to the gate. After leaving the living room, Jianhou closed the door behind him, but Yigu heard chattering and laughter, which the door could not contain. He groundlessly assumed that they were going on about him and felt his face grow hotter.[78] He jumped onto the tram and suddenly remembered Mrs. Li's "See you tomorrow." He carefully recalled what Mrs. Li had said to him at parting and sorted out the three words "See you tomorrow." Those three words had not yet turned stiff and cold, and Mrs. Li's voice still lingered. "Tomorrow" was spoken smoothly and therefore set off the "see you," which was clear and emphatic. Yet the emphasis was so light that the words seemed to have been touched only slightly. His memory preserved the phrase to the word, and his heart palpitated with joy. To Yigu, the next day was worth waiting for and worth desiring. A smile spread over his face. He was so overjoyed that he wanted to share his happiness with the other passengers on the tram. A middle-aged woman sitting across from him, seeing Yigu smile at her, misinterpreted his intentions and shot him an angry glance before frowning and turning her head away. Encountering this puzzling rebuff, Yigu calmed down.

After he returned home, his mother naturally inquired whether Mrs. Li was beautiful. Yigu insisted that Mrs. Li wasn't very beautiful, saying that her skin wasn't white, that her cheekbones were too high, and that she had other defects besides. If Yigu had not been so infatuated with Aimo, he might have said that she was very attractive, but he now seemed to have a new secret. Still a new arrival, this secret hid itself in his heart, too shy to meet strangers, so, without realizing it, he conformed to the protective diplomatic and military strategy of feinting east and attacking west. Back when his mother had gotten married as a young woman, the Chinese had yet to invent courtship, and if a go-between came and a girl's parents happened to ask their daughter if she were pleased with the man, she would blush, bow her head, and not utter a word. At most she would say, "Let mom and dad decide," and then rush off to her room. This would be the most discrete statement a girl could make to express her feelings. Who would have expected that some twenty or thirty years later the world would have changed so greatly and that her son's heart, a big boy's heart, would be so complex? Therefore, she only teased her son for being such a keen observer, and said nothing else.

That night, Yigu had several bizarre dreams, including one in which he dreamed that he had carelessly spilled tea on Mrs. Li's clothes. This so mortified him that he felt like crawling under a rock and had to escape that dream. He then dreamed that Taoqi had scratched his nose and that Chen Xiajun had called him a cat louse. He was furious and was about to retort when the dream shifted. He was stroking Taoqi's fur, and all of a sudden, he found that it was Mrs. Li's hair. He woke up feeling thoroughly ashamed of himself, too ashamed to face the Lis the next day. On the other hand, he was secretly delighted and revisited the dream over and over, against his conscience.

Mrs. Li hadn't taken Yigu seriously. As Jianhou was seeing Yigu out, Chen Xiajun said, "That kid looks quite bright. Aimo, he should be your private secretary. He would be at your beck and call for sure. He is just at the age to be infatuated with you."

Aimo answered, "I'm not sure whether Jianhou would agree."

Cao Shichang said, "Xiajun, you are impossible. You've bullied that kid enough today. He hasn't seen enough of the world. Poor lad!"

Xiajun said, "Who's bullied him? I saw him with his eyes wide open in astonishment. He's naive to the point of being pitiable. That's why I teased him—to loosen him up."

Lu Bolin said, "You think you were just teasing. You have no clue what's appropriate. No wonder Jianhou was angry with you." Everyone agreed with him. At that point, Jianhou came back. The guests stayed for a while and then departed, one by one. In the latter half of the night, in the middle of a dream and without any reason, Aimo thought of how Yigu looked at her and what Chen Xiajun had said that day. She suddenly woke up, elated by the feeling that she was not yet a middle-aged woman, and then turned onto her side and fell back asleep.

The next day, Yigu was describing for Jianhou how he, Jianhou, had gazed down from the top of a big hotel in New York—how the electrical wires, pedestrians, and cars had made him so dizzy that he almost tumbled out of the window. Aimo knocked on the door and came in. She glanced at them and then turned as if to leave, saying, "You're busy. I'm not going to interrupt you. It's nothing."

Jianhou said, "We're not busy. Do you want to read the preface to my travelogue?"

Aimo said, "I remember you already told me the gist of the preface. Fine, I'll read it together with the first chapter after you finish it. It's not interesting to read the preface by itself. Jianhou, may I ask Yigu to write invitations, when he has time, for our party three days from now?"

Yigu hadn't expected Mrs. Li to take the cover off his name—no surname, no

"Mister"—leaving his name stark naked, like a man going into a massage parlor for the first time and not expecting the masseuse to take all his clothes off.

He said hurriedly before Jianhou could answer, "Certainly, certainly! But I'm afraid that my handwriting isn't good enough—"

With this modest remark, Yigu had meant to appear at ease, instead of clumsy to the point of incoherence. Jianhou, of course, agreed. Yigu took the guest list from Aimo's hand and willingly began to write invitations for Aimo, leaving the dizzy Jianhou by the window of the thirty-second floor of the New York hotel. Writing Jianhou's travelogue had made him feel as if he had been wronged, but in doing something as trivial as writing invitations he became, on the contrary, as pious as a monk using his own blood as ink to copy Buddhist sutras. After returning home, he still considered this trifle proof that Aimo thought highly of him. The next day, he answered several unimportant letters for Aimo. On the third day, he read a new novel that Aimo had been given by the author and gave her a synopsis of it, because the author would be meeting Aimo the following day. Far from being a chore for Yigu, these tasks made him return home in the afternoon with the feeling that his day had been extraordinarily fulfilling and nurtured in him hopes for the next day that he otherwise would never have dared contemplate.[79]

The day Yigu had been asked to write the invitations, Mr. Li had already been feeling somewhat unhappy. By the time Mrs. Li asked Yigu to read the novel for her, Mr. Li thought that this would not only stop the writing of the travelogue but, like a hot knife cutting lard, would waste the best part of the day—the time before and after noon. He couldn't expect Yigu to work for him any more that day. At the moment, he had been too embarrassed to blow up, but he harbored a vague fear that Aimo would snatch this secretary from him. In Aimo's presence, he said to Yigu sulkily, "You go read your novel. Give the draft to me. I'll write it myself."

With a faint smile on her face, Aimo asked, "What's the hurry? One day matters little to your writing. What if I offended the author tomorrow? If I weren't expected to keep house for you, I would have read the book ages ago."

At the time, Yigu knew only that Aimo wanted him to work for her and failed to grasp the implied meaning of Jianhou's words. He gave the draft to Jianhou, which Jianhou took. Though he didn't say anything, Jianhou's yellow face turned greenish.

Casting a glance at Jianhou, Aimo smilingly said to Yigu, "Thanks!" She then left the study.

Yigu sat down to read the novel. What bad luck for the author! Eager to show Aimo the severity of his discernment and the loftiness of his standards, Yigu felt compelled to be overcritical of the plot and the writing, as if he had been instructed by Fu Juqing. Jianhou sat absentmindedly in front of the spread-out draft, unable to write a single word. It had always been his job to watch the time and tell Yigu to go home and have lunch. Yet that day, not until the servant came in to ask him whether he would have lunch did he give Yigu a forced smile, implying that he could leave. Seeing Yigu take the novel home with him, Jianhou became even angrier. He went into the dining room and sat down to drink his soup. Neither he nor Aimo said a word. Women, after all, are creatures that have been oppressed since the dawn of creation and are thus more patient.

Jianhou broke the ice by saying, "Would you please not use my secretary later? I have important things for him to do. If you want him to do those trifles, you should do so in the afternoons, when he has finished with my serious business."

"Hm." Aimo said in English, "So you're blowing up at me, are you? The maid is standing close by and listening. Aren't you embarrassed? Is this the appropriate place to start a quarrel? Just now, you embarrassed me in the presence of your dear secretary. Now you're finding fault with me over lunch. I suggest that you not get angry at mealtimes, otherwise you'll have a relapse of your stomach trouble. One of these days, you're going to bully me so much that I'll have stomach trouble too. Would that make you happy? Besides, today we're having fried lobster, which is difficult to digest."

Although the maid didn't know English, she understood enough from Aimo's tone and countenance and sniggered to herself, "They must be boiling over with anger at each other! Your gobblygook can't fool me."

After lunch, the couple went into the bedroom. As soon as the maid had made up the bed for Jianhou's nap and had left the room, Jianhou burst out, "Did you hear what I said?"

Sitting on the sofa and smoking, Aimo said, "I heard! How could I not hear? Maids, old and young, heard it too. Your voice could be heard by people at Tiananmen and in the Haidian district. Everyone knows you're scolding your wife."

Jianhou didn't want to expand the war and give up his nap, so he said in conclusion, "Just so long as you heard it."

Without looking at her husband, Aimo said as if to herself,[80] "But you want me to obey you. Certainly not! It's up to me when I want to use him. Quite the big husband, scolding me in front of the secretary and the servants!"

Jianhou felt that his prone position was not advantageous for quarreling. The bed was a woman's territory. Only a woman could talk to a guest while lazing in bed. Women and beds were fit for each other, and each shone in the other's company. If a man lay in bed, he would be like an army that loses its esprit de corps without a secure defensive position. Jianhou sat up and said, "I'm the one who hired this secretary. He should listen to me. If you want him to do odds and ends, you should ask me first."

Aimo threw away her cigarette so that she could use her mouth exclusively for arguing. "As long as you're employing him," she said, "I'm going to call on him if I have things to do. To be honest, the work you give him is not necessarily more meaningful than what I ask him to do. If you had any talent, you'd write the book yourself instead of asking somebody else to write it for you![81] Cao Shichang, Lu Bo-lin, and Fu Juqing have all written many books. None of them used a secretary!"

Jianhou was so angry he struck the bed and barked, "All right, all right! Tomor-row I'll send that Qi kid packing and *nobody* will have a secretary."

Aimo replied, "If you fire him, I'll hire him. I have so many little things to do, whereas your travelogue . . ."

"If you're busy," Jianhou retorted, "why don't you hire another secretary instead of grabbing mine?"

"And why shouldn't we economize when we can, my dear sir?" Aimo asked. "I'm not a mindlessly extravagant woman. Besides, have I demanded a share of the fam-ily assets?"

"I wish that the boundary between us were clearer." Jianhou said.

Aimo stood up. "Jianhou, make sure you don't regret this later. If you want to divide up the family assets, then divide them we will!"

Jianhou realized that he had gone too far but insisted stubbornly, "Don't deliber-ately misinterpret me. You're making a mountain out of a molehill."

Aimo sneered, "I didn't misinterpret you. You always feel that others look up to me more than to you, so you're jealous. You believe the nonsense Xiajun was spouting two days ago and have made up your mind to find another woman. Don't worry, I won't get in your way."

Losing momentum, Jianhou gave an awkward laugh. "Ha-ha! Isn't that sheer exaggeration? Sorry, I'm going to sleep."

He lay down and pulled the covers over his head, not uttering a sound. Five minutes later, he poked his head out.

"Will you get the novel back from that kid?" Aimo asked. "I'm not going to ask him to read it for me."

Jianhou replied, "You needn't feign benevolence and righteousness. I have some errands to run in the afternoon, so I'm not going to the study. If you want to use Qi Yigu, go right ahead. I'm not going to write anything anymore. It's all the same. Whatever is mine you always take over in the end. All my friends are estranged from me and drawn to you. All the servants busy themselves for you first, while my affairs are always delayed. Your convenience trumps my command. It's a good thing that we don't have children. Otherwise, they would be like beasts and barbarians, acknowledging only their mother and not recognizing me as their father."

Mrs. Li's attitude on breeding children resembled the slogan of the Soviet Union's state abortion institution: "First-timers welcome, but please don't come again." Mrs. Li's gynecologist, however, had given her a severe warning that she was not fit for childbirth. Therefore, not even one soul had reincarnated in her womb. Behind her back, their friends called her a true "peerless and heirless beauty."[82]

"How pitifully you talk!" she retorted. "What a wretched husband! Servants listen to me because it's me who keeps house. Who wants to do that? All the worry has given me a headache. Starting tomorrow, you can take care of it, then all the servants will flatter you. As for friends, that's even more absurd. Why is it that all my friends from school days have abandoned me since I married you? You haggle over your friends with me, but who's to blame for the loss of my friends? Besides, aren't our present friends common to both of us? What's the point in distinguishing whether they're good to me or to you? You're so naive. As for the secretary, these are precarious times. Who knows how long we can employ him? If we move back south, we can't take him with us, can we? But, if you fire him now, you still have to give him a month's salary. I don't necessarily need him. But even if you're not going to write anything, there's no need to dismiss him right away. He might come in useful occasionally for errands. Let's see how the situation looks in a month and then decide. If you consider this merely a woman's pettiness, I'll be provoked into saying something you dislike again. Anyhow, you take care of everything. It's all up to you."

Hearing his wife speak plausibly and at length and call him "naive," Jianhou found it difficult to go on quarreling and waved his hand. "Don't say that! You're always right. Let's call a truce."

"See how easy it is for you to say 'truce'!" Aimo replied. "If I were to believe you, we'd have broken up long ago." She left the room as she said this, ignoring Jianhou's hand, which was stretched out for her to grasp and seal their truce. Jianhou lay there alone, wondering how it was that even though reason was on his side, he seemed at a loss for words and reason after a short quarrel and had to apologize to her, only to be given a cold shoulder. The more he thought about it, the more indignant he became.

For the next four or five days, Jianhou seldom came to the study. He was always out, and no one knew what he was doing. Once or twice, he failed to accompany Aimo to dinner parties, but Yigu's work was not reduced. Jianhou did not tell him that he had decided not to write the travelogue and kept him busy by telling him to translate material to arrange later. Aimo also frequently asked Yigu to write invitations and thank-you notes for her. Occasionally she would sit for a while and chat with him.

Yigu didn't have any sisters, and he had few contacts with his relatives. As his widowed mother's only son, he was kept under strict guard. Thus, despite having been in college for a year, he had never spoken to a girl. Even a tightly sealed bottle of soda pop will reveal floating air bubbles when the bottle is held up against the sunlight, and so it was with Yigu. Though he was outwardly uptight, deep in his heart a kind of foolish, unclaimed love had been stirring. The number of women in the heart of your average girlfriendless boy of eighteen or nineteen is equal to that in the thirty-six harems of an emperor, while the filth in his heart sometimes surpasses that of a public restroom. In the meantime, he entertains lofty ideas about love, hoping to find a woman whose sentiments match his for an intimate yet chaste relationship. He pushes aside physiological impulse or conceals its true nature beneath layer upon layer of gloss.[83]

After Yigu got to know Aimo, his general and aimless affections gradually focused. To a boy with no experience in love, the charms of this mature, middle-aged woman were like late spring weather or a down comforter—snug, soft, and hard to wake up from.[84] A love object is merely a means to fulfill one's life's needs. Therefore, in one's youth, one tends to fall in love first with someone older, because a young person needs to mature and will unconsciously choose a more experienced partner. In old age, however, one always falls madly in love with someone younger, because an old man dreams of rejuvenation, which we also see in his final endeavors.

After his second week at the Lis', Yigu had admitted to himself that he loved Mrs. Li.[85] What would come of this love? He had no time to think about that. He only wished he might often have the opportunity to continue being close to her. Whenever he heard her voice, his heart would thump and his face would flush red.[86] This could not escape Aimo's eyes. Yigu dared not fantasize that Aimo loved him. He was sure only that Aimo liked him. But sometimes he lacked even this much confidence, thinking that he was only dreaming and that Aimo would certainly despise him should she learn of it. He would then busily search her small gestures and expressions—ones that Aimo herself might not remember—for evidence that his hopes were not just wishful thinking. But this was not enough. What on earth did Aimo think? He had no way to determine this. What if she didn't like him? Fine! He didn't care. So be it! To hell with her! He would put her out of his heart. But after he had done this and awoken from his sleep, he found that she still occupied his heart, and that his first thoughts were about her. One moment he would feel as happy as if he had risen to Heaven; the next, as dejected as if he had fallen into Hell, swaying on the swing of lovesickness.

When Yigu arrived at the Lis' on Monday of the third week, Old Whitey informed Yigu as soon as he opened the door that Jianhou had gone back south the day before. Yigu immediately asked why and whether Mrs. Li had also gone. Only after ascertaining that Jianhou had gone to Shanghai to see to the house and that Aimo wouldn't be leaving right away did he calm down. Yet he still felt uneasy. The possibility of parting had cast a shadow on his heart. He moped about for quite some time before Aimo came to the study. She told him that Jianhou had returned home on Saturday saying that news from outside was not good, that war was inevitable, and that they should move as soon as possible. He had thus left for Shanghai the day before in a hurry.

Pretending to be calm, Yigu said, "Mrs. Li, you're not leaving Beiping right away, are you?"

He waited for an answer like a patient waiting for emergency treatment.

As Aimo was about to answer him, Old Whitey came in to report, "Madame, Mr. Chen is here."

Aimo said, "Please ask him to come to the study—I will pack up and leave too after Mr. Li comes back. Yigu, you should go to school in the south. It will be safer than here."

Though he had expected such an answer, Yigu still felt desperate and heartbroken when it actually reached his ears. It was all he could do to keep himself from crying.

Chen Xiajun shouted as he came in, "Aimo, I never expected that you would take my advice and that Jianhou would let you have his private secretary."

After saying hello to Yigu, he said to Aimo, "Jianhou took the train back south yesterday."

Aimo said, "You're well informed. Did Old Whitey tell you that?"

"I was the first to know. I saw him off yesterday."

"That's strange. Had he informed you ahead of time?"

"You know that the sight of me gives him a headache. Why on earth would he tell me? Since I haven't had much to do these days, I've been going to the station whenever a friend leaves. I manage to see all kinds of people this way. Yesterday, I was seeing a relative off, and quite by chance, I met your husband. He seemed to feel uncomfortable running into me and wanted to hide, but I called out to him. He told me that he was going to Shanghai to look for a house. Why didn't you go see him off yesterday?"

"We've been married many years, so we're not like lovers who can't bear to part. Anyway, he's only going to Shanghai. There's no point in my seeing him off, and besides, he didn't want anyone to see him off. He didn't have any large trunks, only a briefcase."

"He had one female second cousin returning with him to the south, didn't he?" Xiajun fixed his gaze at Aimo.

Aimo jumped up. "Ah? What?"

"It was just him and a girl of seventeen or eighteen in his sleeper. She looked quite humble and by no means attractive. She also wanted to hide when she saw me. Is that strange or what? Jianhou said she was his second cousin, so she must be your second cousin too. Isn't she?"

Aimo turned pale. "He doesn't have any female second cousin! Isn't this a bit odd?"

"Yes! At the time I also asked, 'Why haven't I ever heard you mention her?' Holding the girl's hand, Jianhou said to me, 'Go ask Aimo, she knows.' His tone was quite solemn, and I felt it a bit odd that he didn't say much at the moment. Jianhou looked very out of sorts! I parted with him then and there."

Aimo's eyes could not have opened wider. She said, "There's something shady going on here. What did that girl look like? Did Jianhou tell you her last name?"

Suddenly, Chen Xiajun slapped his side and rolled with laughter. Aimo was incensed. "What's so funny?"

Yigu hated Xiajun for coming and interrupting their talk. Now seeing Aimo angry, he was angry too. Still laughing, Xiajun said, "Sorry, I can't help laughing. That idiot Jianhou really was as good as his word. Now I understand. That girl is his new lover and they were stealing away south for their honeymoon. Little did he expect to run into a disgusting fellow like me. He knew that the matter couldn't be disguised, so he simply asked me to inform you. Ha-ha! I had no idea that Jianhou would pull such a trick. He was goaded into doing this at that tea party. I find it hilarious that he carried out my suggestion to the letter. Even the girl he chose was plain looking and behaved awkwardly. She looked like no more than an ignorant child who would exchange friendship for being treated to a meal and a couple of movies. Beiping is full of girls like that. In her eyes, Jianhou is wealthy and great; one might compare her to that divorced American woman who got to know Britain's Prince of Wales! Ha-ha! How will this end?"

Aimo was so angry that she could hardly hold back her tears. She said, "Jianhou is such a jerk! Treating me like this—"

At that moment, all Aimo's fashion and competence faded away, leaving behind only the weak and pitiful nature of a woman. Seeing Aimo cry, Yigu was at a loss.

He suddenly found that when Aimo cried, her age and all the defects in her looks were laid bare. Her tearstained face, like ink-written characters that have been splashed with water, had become obscured and swollen.[87] Her tears, meanwhile, reminded him that she was still Jianhou's woman. Those tears were for him.

Chen Xiajun knew in theory that a woman's anger could lessen once she had cried, just as a fierce wind can be stopped by the rain, but when he actually saw tears he became confused and kept repeating, "You're crying? Can I do something? I'll do anything to help."

"It's all your fault," Aimo said angrily. "What can you do? Go away. I'll call you if I need you. I'm fine. I'm only mad because Jianhou has left me in the dark. I've been so muddleheaded."

Knowing Aimo's temper, Xiajun said something inconsequential and left. Aimo didn't see him off but sat on the sofa, her teeth clenched. The tearstains on her face were like dried streaks of rain on a window.[88] Yigu saw that, in hatred her face had assumed a sharp, hardened, even murderous look. He sensed that this was a formidable woman and grew scared. It occurred to him that today it would be better if he went home. He got up. "Mrs. Li . . . ," he began.

As if awakening from a dream. Aimo said, "Tell me, Yigu, do you love me?"[89]

Yigu was taken aback by the sudden question and didn't know how to answer.

"Don't think I don't know," Aimo said playfully. "You're in love with me."

How to deny that, yet not annoy the other person? An impossible question. Yigu didn't know what Mrs. Li meant. Nor did he want to reveal his feelings to her. He only felt that the situation had turned grave and wanted to escape.

Seeing that he had not taken the bait the second time, Aimo demanded impatiently, "Say something!"

Looking frustrated, Yigu stuttered, "I, I dare not."

That wasn't the answer Aimo had expected. His awkwardness enraged her, yet when she thought of Jianhou her will hardened and she replied, "That's interesting. Why don't you dare? Are you afraid of Mr. Li? You've seen how absurd Mr. Li is. Are you afraid of me? What's so scary about me? Please sit down. Let's discuss this in detail."

Moving to one side, Aimo vacated half the sofa and patted it, inviting Yigu to sit down. The meaning in Aimo's question was unmistakable. Yigu felt like he had awakened from a dream. Day and night he had fantasized an exquisite scene of himself wooing Aimo. Never had he expected it to turn out like this. He suddenly remembered Chen Xiajun's laughter just now. To others, Jianhou's love affair with that girl was merely a joke. All flirtations and clandestine love affairs, to the persons concerned, were incomparably sentimental, romantic, and bold. But to outsiders they were dubious, ludicrous, and fodder for gossip; as a rule, they could only win a lascivious smile. Yigu, as yet untempered by the ways of the world, recoiled in fear at the thought.

Already incensed and seeing Yigu's hesitation, Aimo grew even angrier. "I asked you to sit down. Why don't you sit down?" she demanded.

Hearing the order, Yigu had to sit down. No sooner had he sat down than he jumped up and exclaimed, "Ouch!"

The sudden recoil of the sofa springs also jolted Aimo. Startled as well as enraged, Aimo asked, "What's wrong with you?"

"Taoqi was hiding under the sofa and scratched my heel," Yigu replied.

Aimo burst out laughing. Yigu pursed his mouth and protested, "It hurt! My sock might be torn."

Aimo caught Taoqi and put the cat on her lap. "Now you can sit down and be at ease," she told Yigu.

Yigu was frantic because he couldn't think of any pretext for refusing. Wearing a serious expression, he blurted out rubbish: "This cat may not be human, but I always feel she understands what we're saying. She's like a third party. There are so many things that are inconvenient to say in her presence." Only after he had said it did he find it ridiculous.

Aimo frowned. "You're such a difficult lad. Fine, you put her outside."

She passed Taoqi to Yigu. Taoqi struggled. Yigu grabbed her by the back of the neck, an act that was itself upsetting to Mrs. Li, held the study door ajar, threw Taoqi out, and immediately shut the door. Taoqi yowled nonstop, the sound so high-pitched it pierced the nerves of one's ears. It turned out that he had shut the door too fast and it had caught the tip of the cat's tail. Aimo could stand it no longer. She stood up and slapped Yigu in the face. As she opened the door to free Taoqi, she said, "Get lost, you big fool!"[90] Taoqi scurried in with a painful tail, and Yigu ran out to the street with his cheeks burning. He didn't even wait for Old Whitey to open the gate. "Big fool! Big fool!" The words resounded in his head like the sound of rice being husked with mortar and pestle.

Now that Yigu had gone, Mrs. Li regretted that she had been so rude. She realized that she had been acting strangely today and was amazed that she had gotten so worked up on Jianhou's account. All of a sudden she felt old, so old she seemed to be crumbling away. Fame, status, and appearance were like so many heavy burdens that she was too tired to shoulder any longer. She wished only that she had a place to escape to where she could forget her pride, avoid her current friends, not have to dress fashionably or put up a glamorous front, and not be obliged to look beautiful and young for anyone.

At that moment, the train, which had started out in Beiping the day before, had entered Shandong province. Jianhou looked out the window. His heart was as dry and withered as the yellow soil that flashed past. The previous day's excitement, like the exhilaration of drunkenness, had left behind only a hangover. Jianhou figured that Chen Xiajun was sure to report to Aimo, and that it would be impossible for him to back down with good grace if things got complicated. The girl sitting beside him was plain and naive and not worth breaking up his family for. He acutely regretted having set a trap for himself in a moment of muddleheadedness when he had been unable to swallow an insult. The girl who held Jianhou's arm and watched the scenery outside the window was ignorant of all his thoughts. She felt only that her future was like the never-ending tracks of the train, stretching out limitlessly ahead of her.

Translated by Yiran Mao

INSPIRATION

There was once a famous writer, but strangely enough, we do not even know his name. It was not that he had not taken a name, or that he had done away with it.[1] Nor was it that he had somehow remained anonymous, or that something about him was perhaps so peculiar that it defied naming. The reason was simple: the ring of his fame was too deafening for us to hear his name clearly. This was hardly a unique case. The postman, for instance, would unhesitatingly deliver an envelope addressed to "The Greatest French Poet" to Victor Hugo.[2] Likewise, the telegraph company was sure to route a telegram for "The Greatest Living Italian Writer" to Gabriele D'Annunzio,[3] making it absolutely unnecessary to specify name and address. This writer of ours was even more famous, for his was a name that needed no written or spoken forms. The name was completely obscured by the reputation, as it were. Mention "writer," and everyone knew you were referring to him.

Being a genius, the Writer was prolific, but, having an artistic conscience, he suffered labor pains with each act of creation. Then again, writing was not quite the same as childbirth, since a difficult delivery did not cost him his life, and his fecundity was a burden only to his readers. He penned numerous novels, prose pieces, plays, and poems, thereby moving, inspiring, influencing countless middle-school students. Overseas, sales of a literary work are dominated by the tastes of the middle class. But China, that ancient and cultured land of ours, is a country where material wealth matters not. Here, the value of a work rests, instead, on the standards and wisdom of the middle-school student. After all, the only ones willing to spend their money on books and on subscriptions to magazines are those who are still in middle school: unthinking adolescents, eager to hear speeches and lectures; ever ready to worship great men; and full of the unremarkable sorrows of young Werther. As for university students, they themselves had authored books and hoped to sell their own products. Professors, of course, would not even bother with books, writing only forewords for others and expecting complimentary copies in return. Those more senior in position disdained even forewords, limiting themselves to gracing the cover designs of friends' works with their calligraphy; books, meanwhile, would of course be respectfully dedicated to them.

This Writer of ours knew only too well where the key to his success lay, having seen that middle-school students made great customers. It comes as no surprise that his works would be collectively titled *For Those Who Are No Longer Children but Have Yet to Grow Up*, or, alternatively, *Several Anonymous, Postage-Due Letters to All Young People*. "Anonymous" because, as previously mentioned, nobody knew his name, and "postage due" because the books had to be paid for out of the young readers' pockets. The Writer was able to disguise his ignorance as profundity, pass off shallowness as clarity, and speak with the voice of a radical who proceeded with caution and good sense. The volume of his production was such that he became the unavoidable author whose works one would run into wherever one went. Customers of food stalls, of peanut hawkers, and street-corner stands selling panfried cakes regularly received his novels or plays in loose, torn-out pages, thereby unexpectedly acquiring spiritual nourishment. Thus, his contribution to the literary world, a matter of popular recognition at first, eventually won official endorsement. He had become a nationally certified talent. The government commissioned a panel of experts to have his masterworks translated into Esperanto, so that he could compete for the Nobel Prize in literature. As soon as this was announced, one fan wrote the "Readers' Forum" of a newspaper:

It's about time the government took this action. One need only consider how many characters figure in his works. Put together, they would be numerous enough to colonize a totally uninhabited island. Now that the nation's population has been depleted by the war, there is no better time than the present to encourage accelerated growth. By the sheer quantity of production, therefore, the Writer deserves official honors, and should be recognized as a model for public emulation.

It was most unfortunate, however, that Esperanto did not always mean *espérance*, the hope that very name stood for. Although the Nobel judges had no trouble with English, French, German, Italian, Russian, Greek, and Latin, not one of those moldy relics from a bygone age could handle Esperanto. No matter how they wiped and cleaned their pince-nez, they just could not decipher the masterpieces that our Writer had submitted for consideration. After a great long while, one of them, a Sinologist senior both in years and standing, finally saw the light.

"That's it, that's it!" he proclaimed. "This is Chinese, what they call Latinized

Chinese. We've mistaken it for some European language—no wonder we didn't know what it is!"

This eased the committee's anxieties, and they heaved a collective sigh of relief. The one who was seated next to the Sinologist asked him, "You should know a bit of Chinese. So what does it say?"

"My dear venerable sir," came the solemn reply, "it is through specialization that learning ascends to the pinnacle of excellence. My late father devoted his entire life to researching Chinese punctuation, and I have spent forty years studying Chinese phonology. But your inquiry just now lies in the area of Chinese semantics, which is quite outside my field of specialization. Whether the Chinese language contains meaning is a topic I should not blindly pass judgment on before I have obtained unimpeachable evidence. This stance of mine, my dear sir, you would not want to question, I am sure."

The chairman, observing that the Sinologist was not at all agreeable, quickly put in, "I don't think we even have to bother with these works, since they don't conform to our regulations to begin with. According to our eligibility requirements, only works written in a European language qualify for consideration. Since this is written in Chinese, we need not waste any more of our time on it."

The other old fogies indicated their unanimous agreement, noting at the same time their admiration for the Sinologist's scholarly circumspection. He himself, however, was quite humble about it, insisting that he was nowhere close to the American ophthalmologist who had won that year's Nobel Prize in Medicine. The doctor, he explained, specialized only in the left eye, and did not treat any malfunction of the right. Now, there was the true specialist. In such an atmosphere of graciousness and mutual respect, these senior citizens pleasantly parted company. That was just too bad for our Writer and his single day of hoping. The announcement of the winners plunged the entire Chinese population into a righteous wrath, to say nothing of our Writer himself, who was driven to despair. Earlier, quite a few of his fellow writers, their green pupils seeing red, had armed themselves with mental notes, waiting for the moment he was declared Nobel laureate to attack his works in public. With one voice they were to assert that such recognition was unwarranted. These same people now all turned sympathetic, and were loud in their lamentations. Perhaps because of the cleansing effects of the tears of commiseration they shed, their sight and their pupils returned to normal; indeed, their eyes were now awash with the kind of luster that infuses the sky after a rainstorm has subsided.

One newspaper ran an editorial admonishing the Swedish Academy for having "forgotten its origins." Was it not true that Nobel made his fortune from explosives, and China was the country that had invented gunpowder in the first place. The prize thus should have been intended for the Chinese to begin with, a point the administrators would do well to keep in mind in the future. What a pity that the "Sinologist" on the selection committee had not yet begun his research on the semantics of Chinese, thus allowing this forceful essay to escape his attention.[4] Another paper was quite imaginative, attempting to comfort our Writer by actually congratulating him. He had been a successful author all along, the paper argued, and he now qualified as a wronged genius and an overlooked and unsung but truly great artist. The paper went on to say, "There is no more unlikely pairing than success and injustice; yet he has now attained it. What a rare and enviable turn of events!" Still another paper made a concrete suggestion:

While there is much to be gained through the policy of securing foreign loans, to accept a foreign prize would be shameful. In order to recapture the respectability our country has lost, we should establish China's own literary award as a protest against the Nobel Prize, and to save the right to criticize from falling into foreign hands. The most important eligibility requirement for our prize would be to restrict the medium to Chinese dialects, with the stipulation that admissible also as Chinese dialects would be English as spoken by residents of Hong Kong and Shanghai, Japanese as spoken in Qingdao, and Russian in Harbin. Once this prize is established, the Nobel would cease to be a unique attraction, and Western writers would strive to learn and write Chinese, in the hopes of winning our prize money. China's five-thousand-year-old culture would therefore penetrate the West. Since the Nobel Prize is supported by private funds, our prize should follow the same format. It would only be appropriate, if we may suggest it, that our great Writer implement the above proposal by way of retaliation, and start an endowment fund with his royalties and fees.

In addition to practical-mindedness, the editor of a fourth paper demonstrated much psychological insight. He agreed that the literary arts ought to be encouraged, adding only that those who were willing to contribute funds to that cause should themselves be honored too. Therefore, as incentive for the rich to make grants, some honor had to first be bestowed upon selected men of wealth. Since this was to be no more than a gesture, the amount of their cash prizes did not have to be substantial. The wealthy writer surely would not mind. "Would our great Writer," he concluded by asking, "be willing to set an example for others to follow by making the first contribution?" Who could have guessed that all this goodwill and these kind suggestions would only drive the Writer to his deathbed?

He took the confirmed announcement of winners so hard that he fell sick, his misery and bitterness mitigated only slightly by the outrage and support of the population. While awaiting articles rallying to his defense to appear in the paper, he made plans to dictate an interview the next day, to be transcribed for publication. By long-standing practice, news stories about him were, without exception, his own submissions. In them, he would often insert some minor factual errors, in order to create the false impression that the piece had been written by someone else. This also gave him the bonus of having a correction appear in the next issue, thus ensuring that his name would see print twice for one iota of trivia. It so happened that while he was making these plans, those editorials came to his attention one after another. The first one alone was enough to make him fly into a rage. "Missing out on the Nobel Prize means a loss of personal income," he reasoned. "The minute lofty things like the nation, the people, and so on got dragged into the show, I myself would be crowded out of it!" He then noted the congratulatory heading of the second editorial and became so furious that he tore the sheet in two. Suppressing his anger as best he could, he went on to the third editorial; by the time he had finished reading it, he felt nothing but ice-cold water being poured on his head. The moment he finished reading the fourth, he passed out.

That night, quite a few visitors gathered at his bedside, including journalists, fans, and representatives of various organizations. Besides the reporters, who were busy scribbling in their notebooks items that would make for a good article entitled something like "A Profile of the Writer Indisposed," everybody was nervously gripping his handkerchief to wipe away tears. All knew that this was the last they would ever see of the Writer. Several young, sentimental females were in fact worrying that one hankie might not be enough. The flowing sleeves of the men's mandarin gowns might come in useful in such an emergency. But the girls' sleeves, so short that they barely covered their armpits, would be of no help. Looking up to find all those people standing at his side, this Writer of ours found the scene matched quite well the scenario for his dying moments that he had fantasized about. The only thing that irked him was that he was no longer master of his own mental powers and organs. He could not recall completely or properly deliver the farewell speech to the world he had prepared long ago. At long last, a few words managed to dribble from his lips: "Don't collect my writings into a series of complete works, because—" Perhaps this line was too long, or what was left of his life was too short, but he was unable to make it to the end of the sentence. Many in the audience pricked up their ears like terriers, only to let them droop like a hog's in disappointment. Once outside his room they enthusiastically debated the meaning behind the Writer's last words. Some said he had written so much that it was simply impossible ever to make any collection a complete one. Others conjectured that since additional hundreds and thousands of novels, plays, and songs had been planned, what little there was in print would hardly be representative. This controversy between the two schools soon grew into the most intriguing chapter in the history of Chinese literature.

During the memorial service for the Writer, one literary critic passionately intoned, "His spirit shall endure. His masterly creations shall never perish, for, indeed, they are his most valuable legacy!"

Privately, though, one young reader remarked, somewhat in relief, "At least he must be physically too dead to keep putting out new books! I would've gone broke before long." The fact was, this young reader had to pay for all the books out of his own pocket, whereas the critic's entire collection was of course autographed, complimentary copies.

Meanwhile, in that other world of the deceased, the spirit of our Writer soon found that the afterlife was not quite as bad as one might have expected. For one thing, the release of mental tension was like shedding a heavy overcoat at the moment one is about to be smothered. Together with those fleas that had established themselves in the seams, whatever ailments had previously plagued him were gotten rid of too. He was dead, no question, but he had been wondering what it would be like after death. "For someone who has made the contributions to culture and society I have," he pondered, "Heaven should have sent a welcoming party to receive me long ago. Could it be true that Heaven is nothing more than a product of superstition? Maybe it doesn't exist after all? Even if that's so, they should hurry to build one just to accommodate me!" But then it also occurred to him that staying in Heaven all the time was bound to be mighty boring too. Unless it was the Heaven of Muhammad's design, a place where one had possession of seventy-two beauties, all with large black eyes, who could be restored to the virginal state at will. There, one also found swans and plump ducks, their meat roasted to perfection, and the skin still crisp, flying through the air, all rushing toward one's mouth to be eaten. "Now, that would be quite something, wouldn't it?" The Writer was lost in thought. "What a shame that overwork has given me heartburn and ulcers! Too much of that roasted stuff might do more harm than good. There won't be bottles of Heartburn Relief, Ulsooth, or Clear-It hanging from the swans' necks.[5] That supply of seventy-two women is somewhat overabundant too; it would take a while to sample all their charms.[6] If their looks are all different, it could very well happen that some of these lovers will be favored over others, because of the peculiarities of personal taste, leading to a jealous war. How could someone who cannot cope with two arguing females handle seventy-two of them? That's not even taking into account their having the traits of India's preserved vegetables, liable to turn from sour to hot enough to burn one's system. But legend has it that these seventy-two houris—'hot ones' would have been more appropriate—all come from the same mold, with the same black hair, dark eyes, serpentine waists. In short, all their features are identical. Sticking with one woman is boring enough, so just imagine this one woman magically multiplied into seventy-two copies . . ."

Our Writer was so scared that he had to change his line of thought. "When it comes to falling in love, most men of letters indulge in it out of vaingloriousness—the desire to impress people with the mesmerizing effects a genius has on the opposite sex. The lovers of the literati are just like the new cars and mansions of the rich: they serve to generate envy, not fill dire needs of their owners. If every man ascending to Heaven had six dozen women to his name, nobody could use it to show off his sexual prowess. This, however, would undoubtedly be a superb opportunity to collect materials for lyrical poems or confessions. The question is: do people read in Heaven? Well, perhaps a climate for reading could be fostered after my arrival. In that case I might as well bring along a few volumes as gifts." So thinking, our Writer sauntered into his study.

As soon as he stepped inside, he had the sensation that he was treading on something funny. The floor was like an empty stomach about to cave in under a load of rocks; and yet it was gasping for air, struggling to buttress itself. It turned out that there were such an incredible number of his works on the shelves that the ground could no longer carry their weight and started to come apart. Before the Writer could leap to save his books, the ground split open with a loud crack. There, off the shelves and down the gaping hole, his books, big and small, fell helter-skelter. The Writer lost his balance and, engulfed by that torrent of collapsing books, plummeted straight down. Curled up though he was, with neck tucked in, he could not avoid being the target of all those books, which hurt his head, bruised his shoulders, and lacerated his skin. Only then did he realize firsthand the impact of his works. It was too late to regret that he had lacked the self-discipline to write fewer books, and each one several tens of thousands of words shorter. After an interminable period all those books finally found their way past him. Bearing the marks and scars from this attack, he trailed the books, drifting down into the bottomless darkness. He was becoming more and more scared. If this continued, sooner or later he would surely pass through the center of the earth and bore straight through the globe! All of a sudden the geography he learned in primary school came rushing back. "The other side of this shell is nothing but the Western Hemisphere, and the Western Hemisphere is where the American continent lies. For all writers of the old continent, America is the Treasure Island where the unsuccessful become successful and the successful reap rewards. That's why every writer should visit, give a lecture tour, and create a market for his works there. In doing so, he would also be helping relieve Americans of the burden of their gold dollars and at the same time recovering some of our country's financial loss stemming from the importation of American goods. To fall all the way to America would be fantastic! A perfectly straightforward, effortless, yet refreshing experience, which avoids that motion sickness business on board a ship or airplane."

With such thoughts in his mind, the Writer found his spirits soaring higher with each inch his body dropped. He was so thankful that Providence was after all what it was, and his ceaseless toils of a lifetime were not about to go unrewarded. The reward of being a good writer, so it appeared, was not to ascend to Heaven, but to descend to America. The saying "Slipping to fall, one falls upon the best of fortunes" had all but come true.

As he was thus comforting himself, he suddenly hit bottom. Amazingly enough, it didn't hurt. He stood up and found himself inside a huge room, with maps hanging on the walls. He had fallen through the ceiling, but since he had landed on his books on the floor, the cushioning effect saved his bones. Just a moment ago he had been regretting the volume of his works, but now he was only too happy to discover the benefits of numerous and voluminous writings. "But what now? I've smashed someone's ceiling!" As if in answer, the books he was standing on suddenly started to push upward, tripping him. At the same time a great many uniformed people rushed in through the door and pulled him down from the mound of books. Shoveling, kicking the books aside, they managed to clear them out of the room. Then they helped a person sporting a huge beard, bruised black and blue by the books, up on his feet. Now that the room's decor and appointments came into full view, our Writer began to realize that he was in an elegant private office. Some of the uniformed men were now busy patting the dust off the bearded man, straightening his clothes by giving them a tug here and a pull there while the rest went about tidying up the place, righting overturned desks and chairs. Finding himself in such grand surroundings, the Writer was quite ill at ease. He knew this person he had just knocked down must be some dignitary or other.

The bearded man was surprisingly polite to him. He bade him sit down, and at the same time ordered his men to leave the room. Not until now did the man's mustache catch the Writer's attention. It circled his lips, continued all the way down to the chin as a massive beard.[7] The growth was so black and thick that the words that came out through this curly grove seemed somehow dyed with the color of that beard, every one of them dark.

"My goodness! Your works are really as weighty as gold, my dear sir!" The man sat down himself as he spoke, massaging the swollen parts of his head, a weak smile curtailed by that mouthful of whiskers that screened his lips. Our Writer, seeing that the man was not giving him a hard time, and thinking that he had praised his works for being "worth their weight in gold," felt instantly emboldened.

"They aren't really *so* expensive," he said, visibly arrogant. "Maybe I should first ask whether this is America—calculated in American dollars, my prices don't come out to be very high at all."

"No, this isn't America."[8]

"Where am I then?" the Writer asked.

"This is none other than the legendary Hades."[9]

"That's ridiculous!!" The Writer jumped up in shock and consternation. "I'm darn sure the way I led my life doesn't call for such a reward—being sent to suffer in Hell!"

The bearded man waved his hands, motioning for calm, and asked him to sit down. "That you don't have to worry about, sir, as Hell has already moved to the human world. You see, you've been so busy writing you don't appear to be too well informed about the current state of the world. Oh well, I don't blame you for that."

The Writer realized that it must be Yama, king of Hell, himself before him. "No wonder he has the liberty to sport such a flamboyant beard!" So he hurriedly stood up again. "Your Netherly Majesty, I beg your forgiveness—" he said, bowing so low as he spoke that he was about to split his ass (*saluer à cul ouvert*), as French slang has it.

"I'm afraid you're mistaken, sir," the man chortled. "And you must excuse me for not being able to return your greeting. My back is still aching a bit from the burden of your books, so I'll just have to take your bow remaining in my seat. This place was indeed formerly Hades, but I certainly am not any abdicated emperor of a fallen dynasty, nor am I a newly appointed director of some national palace museum. One would think that with the abolition of the monarchy, palaces should be converted into repositories for antiques. But then all antiques in the eighteen levels of Hell are torture devices. Humanity has progressed in many respects through the last thousand years or two, except for its cruelty toward its own kind. That hasn't become any more refined or exquisite. Take for instance the extracting of confessions by brute force inside intelligence agencies and the punishment of prisoners of war in concentration camps: they share the virtues of being simple, homespun, and effective—thoroughly in the time-honored tradition of savagery. If you look at China, it's only in the brutality of her various forms of torture that you can still see the essence of her culture. You know, pumping water down the nostrils, poking a red-hot branding iron in the armpits, tightening up the hand with wooden pins stuck between one finger and the next, and similar features of the indigenous culture. So those torture instruments in Hell, far from being antiques that had outlived their usefulness, have all been called to active service in the human world. At any rate, this place is the Public Administration for Chinese Territorial Production.[10] And yours truly happens to be its administrator."

The Writer was beginning to regret his unduly courteous bow, and was feeling embarrassed. But the man's last line made his interest surge again. "I'm a prodigy," he mused, "and this man here deals in products—the two words even alliterate. What perfect partners we'd make!" So he asked, "Products of the land are of course valuable commodities, but this is smack in the center of the earth—who's going to do business with you here? Oh, wait a minute, I get it. Everything's been scraped clean off the face of the earth by those corrupt officials. And in these times of war, people all over are digging tunnels as shelters from air attack. Since you businessmen will go to any length to make money, you figured that you might as well do what everybody else is doing, and so you bored your way underground here to open up shop. Right?"

The administrator replied in a matter-of-fact tone, "Are you implying that being in 'Chinese territorial production' our purpose is to sell out China? There would indeed be plenty of potential customers, but who could afford the price of that priceless land? If I were a typical businessman, I'd hold firmly to a policy of tangible profits. In other words, I'd never close a deal at below cost, nor would I accept bad checks. That's why the China deal will never be closed, and for the same reason I won't be offering China for either retail or wholesale, as those foolish politicians are doing. I'm afraid you've totally misunderstood our name. We are in fact the agency in charge of the production of newborns within Chinese territory. You see, although Hell has relocated to the human world, human beings are still destined to die, and someone still has to manage the reincarnation of souls, the business of karma, and the like. Our mandate here is to handle the assignments for any person or animal to be born inside China."

"Why 'Public Administration' then?"

"The 'Administration' part is simply handed down from tradition. Aren't there such agencies as the Rewards and Commendations Administration, and the Punishments Administration, in the world of Hades? My title is therefore naturally 'administrator,' and not 'president,' as you might expect of a business concern. As for 'Public,' all that does is to give the idea that the affairs of our organization are open to public view. Everything's fair and square. We don't take bribes or send good people to be reborn into the wrong family. This thick black beard of mine symbolizes the spirit of our administration."

"I see the double meaning," said the Writer, eager to show off his cleverness. "Since those who grow beards like yours must be old enough to be grandfathers, your beard, Mr. Administrator, must symbolize impartial justice."

"Come, come, sir, your sharp mind has flown off at a tangent again! Well, perhaps this weakness is just common to all you men of letters. It doesn't take a beard for a person to be called 'grandfather,' you know—look at those eunuchs of various dynasties in our history. You must also be aware that the insignia of high justices in the West is none other than a silvery *white* wig. I expect you're familiar with all those best sellers on Chinese civilization made for the export market that are so popular in the human world? Anyway, our country, people, customs, mentality, are, by their accounts, all exact opposites of Westerners', isn't that true? We're an Oriental race, and so they have to be Occidental. We're Chinese, so they'll always be foreigners. When we beckon, our fingers point down, but somehow when they do it their fingers have to point upward. We kneel to worship, but when they greet you in salute, quite conversely, they raise a hand. A foreign man kneels to propose to his lover before marriage, while his henpecked Chinese brother ends up kneeling in front of his wife after marriage. These and many other things are all quite bizarre. If you extrapolate from this, since we value face, Westerners must be shameless. In mourning we wear white, but they wear black. It's obvious, therefore, that if their impartial officials wear white wigs on their heads, their counterparts in our culture should endeavor to grow natural, black beards on their chins. This is the only way we can avoid violating the pet theories of those scholars who make comparisons of Eastern and Western civilizations.[11] And then, of course, it also makes a statement. That is, aside from this beard, which won't stay pitch-black forever, there's nothing in this wide world that's allowed to be a deal in the dark!" The administrator's beard flew about with every word he spoke, making his delivery forceful and impressive indeed.

At this moment, our Writer was busy taking stock of his own situation. "Fair people are also the most obnoxious and unsympathetic. If left to this fellow's disposition, I'll have no hope of getting to America. I'd best clear out while I still can." Thus, he put a smile on his face and stood up to take his leave.

"It was very inconsiderate of me today to have allowed my bookcases to fall down here and damage your office, and also to have taken all this precious time away from your working hours. I sincerely apologize for all this. But I have learned a great deal through our chance meeting, sir; it's been a true pleasure. Someday when I write my memoirs, I'll make a point of saying many good things about your administration. For the moment, however, I shouldn't tarry any longer. Would you be kind enough to have your men bring in the works of mine that landed here just now so that I can autograph a few to be presented to you? They should make fine souvenirs. Besides, books carrying my signature are sure to fetch a handsome price from collectors of later generations, so please take this as restitution for my having smashed your ceiling."

"Oh, that's quite all right, don't you worry about that. But now that you've come, I'm afraid you can't leave so easily." The administrator stroked his beard peacefully in his seat.

"Why not?" the Writer shot back, incensed. "Your subordinates wouldn't dare to try to restrain me! Don't you know I'm a genius? And I didn't make this mess on purpose either. My fall was completely accidental and unintentional."

"There's no such thing as an 'accident' in the world. It's just a planned occurrence in disguise. People of the human world all end up here upon their deaths, and each comes in his own way. Indeed, the routes they take are governed by a fair enough principle: 'To your own designs shall you fall victim, and victim you shall be.' In simpler terms, whatever it was that you did for a living would be the very cause of your own undoing, sending you to report to me here. See, you're a writer, so the books you've written bored their way through the ground, taking you along with them. Just this morning a sanitary engineer's soul arrived. Could you believe how he got to this place? One way or another he fell into the toilet, and some unthinking fool flushed him all the way down here! My ceiling does get broken once in a while, or at least damaged enough to leak, and I myself sometimes get hit on the head, or splashed all over with dirty water. But then when one is in public service, one simply can't afford to be concerned about such things."

"Well, what are you going to assign me to be then?"

"Oh, that I'm still trying to decide. In your lifetime you consumed an enormous quantity of ink, so I could very naturally reincarnate you as a squid, so that you'd keep spitting it back out. But then you also wasted a lot of paper, and for that you ought to be reincarnated as a sheep, whose skin could be used for paper manufacturing. And you've presumably also worn out countless brush tips, so I should turn you into a rabbit or a mouse—or maybe that same sheep would do. What a shame that you're a writer of these new times; you handle a brush about as well as a foreigner handles chopsticks. What you use most often are nibs inserted into holders and platinum-tipped fountain pens. I'm not too sure which animals produce metal, so I may just have to make you a ranking government official, from whose heart and countenance one could scrape off iron or steel. As for platinum, well, don't we have that handy stereotype, the platinum blonde? Finally, considering the way you make a game of hiding yourself behind all those pen names, you should in your next life be made a fugitive from justice constantly under the pressure to create aliases. The problem is, you have only one afterlife and simply couldn't be a woman, man, fish, rabbit, and so on all at the same time! So . . . so—hey, you can't just run away! There are a lot of people waiting for you outside; they have accounts to settle with you yet."

Our Writer, finding the administrator's talk getting more unsavory by the minute, had pulled open the door and was ready to make a run for it. Now stopped by his words, he turned around and sneered at him. "What? Settle accounts with me? Aha, Mr. Administrator, didn't you make a fool of me just now for not being aware of the current world situation? I'm throwing that right back at you. You think geniuses of today are the same old down-and-out Bohemians, or dreamers who know nothing about financial management. By thinking of them as long-haired artists with a string of creditors at their heels you're showing residual symptoms of an infection known as romanticism. I'm afraid you're totally out of touch with reality! We're not idiots, you know. We do realize the importance of personal finances in daily living. In fact, as if we weren't smart enough, we hire lawyers and managers to safeguard our interests. Royalties and fees that total substantial amounts we invest in business partnerships. Of course, there are those cultural personalities who are nothing more than cultured paupers, but I'm not one of them. To tell you the truth, at the time I died, I left royalties on several novels and income from performance rights to several plays unclaimed. There were some thousands of shares I haven't had the time to sell, and dividends from one corporation not yet cashed. I may have a lot of collecting to do, but certainly no creditors to settle accounts with me! Who're you trying to fool?"

"Sir, your grasp of reality—of the marketplace, that is—has never been doubted. The crowd outside hasn't come here to clear financial accounts, but to file charges against you."

"What 'charges'? It couldn't be anything more serious that calumny, plagiarism, or immoral influence. If a man of letters gets sued, it must be for one of these three reasons." As the Writer was well aware, a literary figure who has never been involved in a lawsuit, jailed, or put under house arrest—like a socialite who has never faced divorce proceedings—could never make a name for himself.

"They are suing you for murder and robbery"—the last three words from the administrator's lips came out crisp and cold, as if forged from steel.

The Writer was scared stiff. His past, decades of it, instantaneously flashed through his mind in minute detail. Yet there was nothing in his earthly existence that even came close to such heinous crimes, only that for a while his writings did promote revolution. "Well," the Writer pondered, "maybe a handful of foolhardy young men who could not resist any instigation really did pitch in everything they had—blood and neck included. So this would be a sinful debt, I suppose. But at the time my wife wanted children and I wanted to buy life insurance for myself—and all this takes money. If, in the interest of my and my family's well-being, I did write stuff that indirectly cost a life or two, that's no big deal. Besides, those fools with their blood boiling in their guts were too ready to die for a cause to regret it and demand settlement." The Writer regained his nerve. With a sneer he pushed open the door of the office. But before he had taken a full step outside, he found himself bombarded from all directions by shouting and yelling.

"Give me my life back!"

"My life! I want it back!"

The throng completely packed the courtyard, even overflowing out of the main gates. Only the uniformed men at the steps were keeping them from coming up to the corridor and rushing the office. The administrator, patting the Writer on the back, spoke from behind him: "Well, since things have already come to this pass, you'll just have to face their questions." He walked him out the door.

Catching sight of the Writer, the crowd stretched out their hands, jostling to come up close, shouting, "Give me my life back!" However, despite their numbers, their collective voice was weak and lifeless. Each was able to contribute only a wisp of sound, one not cohering with any other to form the stentorian roar it should have been. Taking a closer look, the Writer found that the people came in all shapes and ages and counted among them rich and poor, male and female. What they did have in common was a sickly look. They were in fact so emaciated that even the shadows they cast were blurred ones. From the exertion in their movements one could see their dire lack of strength. The arms they managed to stretch out were all trembling, not unlike a voice shaken by anger and sorrow, about to lose control any second. They also reminded one of the strands in a spider's web hung between two twigs. "With such a crowd, what do I have to be afraid of?" the Writer concluded. "And then there're even old grannies with bound feet, kids no older than five, effete women with whatever seductive vitality they once had almost totally drained from them. None of these could be among the martyrs who took to revolution under my influence. Unless . . . unless these are lives taken by those revolutionary heroes and are now tracing the responsibility to me. If you look at that old lady, you can tell at one glance that she must have been a stubborn mother, a prime target for family revolution. Well, people like that deserve what they get! They asked for it. Since I'm in the right, I have nothing to fear."

Clearing his throat, he took a dignified step forward, and announced, "Quiet down please, quiet down. I'm afraid you folks are mistaken. Frankly, I don't even know a single one of you."

"But *we* know *you*!"

"Oh, that's not surprising. For people whom a person doesn't know to know about him is just a measure of his fame. You might indeed know me, but that's not saying an awful lot. The problem is, you see, I don't know you."

"What? You don't know us? Don't play dumb! We're the characters in your novels and plays. *Now* you remember, don't you?" They were edging closer, craning their necks, turning their faces up to him so that he could take a better look. And they went ahead all at the same time to identify themselves.

"I'm the heroine in your masterpiece *Longing for Love*."

"I'm that country bumpkin in your *Chips Off the Emeralds*."

"I'm the genteel young lady in your famed *Dream of a Summer's Night*."

"I'm the grandmother in your fascinating *Fallen*."

"I'm the well-bred daughter of that distinguished family in *The Thug*."

"Remember your much-admired work *Embraceable Me*? Yes, I am that intellectual who lost his bearings at the crossroads of the '–isms.' "

"I'm the spoiled brat born into the country squire's family in your own favorite, the novel *The Nightmare of the Red Chamber*."

His memory now refreshed, the Writer responded, "Very well, we're all one family. What's going on here then, if you wouldn't mind telling me?" Actually, deep down he was beginning to have a vague inkling of their intentions, which, like something drifting in the depths of the sea, started to show up under the sunlight.

"We're here to demand our lives back. The way you portrayed us in your works was so dull and lifeless! Our every act and speech was like a puppet's; we were just too far from being vivid characters. You created us but didn't give us life, so now you need to reimburse us!"

From among them a woman with ill-defined features broke in, "You remember me? I suppose only the way I dress gives any inkling of what kind of a character I was supposed to have been in your book. You were going to depict me as a femme fatale, the ruin of countless youths who otherwise had the most promising of futures. But what really became of me under your pen? I was neither a woman who looked like a human being, nor a human being who was like a woman. I didn't have the personality to support any clear, sharp image at all. You said I had 'watery,' not 'limpid,' eyes, and that my gaze was so 'pointed' that it could pierce the soul. Good God! How could anyone even think of such lines? My eyes, sharp and dripping wet, had to be icicles on the eaves during a spring thawing. You wanted to make me a metropolitan temptress, draining the mental and physical energies of men. But on your pages I wasn't given one breath of life—I wasn't concrete enough to be a sponge! I was more like a piece of worn and tattered blotting paper. You described me as a person who spoke 'frankly and boldly.' Right—'frayed and broken' is how I'd describe the voice I have now. You've made a total waste of my life. Now what are you going to do about it?"

A well-dressed, elderly gentleman next to her spoke up too: "In your work I got old as soon as I was given life." He gasped between words. "That I don't mind, but an old man should act his age. Should I be fancying a concubine, what with my health and all those years behind me? Isn't that asking for trouble? You scoundrel, you not only denied me life but also made a mess of my second life—my reputation. And I couldn't even risk my life to get even with you, since I never had one. But now our paths have finally crossed. Let me first wrest out of you the life that's due me, and then risk it to—" Choking with excitement, the old man couldn't go on.

"Mister, you've said enough. It's my turn to ask him something," a swarthy man, patting him on the shoulder, interrupted. He turned to the Writer, "Hey, you recognize me? I'm one of the uneducated roughnecks you created. You think I look the part?—wearing a short vest, sleeves rolled up, pounding my chest all the time, with expressions like 'your daddy' and 'his mama' crowding my speech. Your book claimed that I used gutter language, but doesn't all the 'daddy' and 'mommy' talk add up to one big happy family? It's nowhere near the streets![12] Since I'm uncivilized, I was thinking of giving you a couple of slaps on the face before we even start to settle accounts. But then if you slapped me back, I wouldn't even have enough in me to fight you. What a shame!"

It was a good thing that the Writer had not portrayed this roughneck true to life, or he would have been in for a sound beating. At the moment, however, he was really too harried to indulge in this kind of self-comfort, for the characters were now all clambering forward to speak to him. Some of them appealed to the administrator directly, urging him to hand down a verdict with a proper sentence without further delay.

"Although this case we have at hand is not exactly a phonograph record," the administrator grinned, "we've still got to listen to both sides, right? Eh, Mr. Writer, what do you have to say in answer to their charges?"

The Writer rose to the occasion. He faced the crowd at the foot of the steps: "What you've just said is not entirely groundless, but how else would you have existed if it were not for me? Since I am your creator, I must be considered a forefather. 'Of everyone under Heaven, only parents make no mistakes': that's how the ancient saying goes. In other words, one should be ever mindful and respectful of one's origins. So stop giving me trouble." While the administrator was snorting at this, twisting his mustache, a male character yelled in outrage: "In the book you made me start a family revolution because of my ideological beliefs, driving my own father to his death. How come you're talking about filial piety all of a sudden?"

"If you're my father"—a female character picked up the questioning, a smile forming at the corners of her lips—"where's my mother, then?"

Another man, sobbing uncontrollably, put in, "All I know about is motherly love—exalted, unadulterated motherly love. While in your work I never felt the slightest need for any fathers."

Then it was a middle-aged man: "Even a father who is supporting his children doesn't necessarily win their sympathy. You're supported *by* us, so why should you be let off easy? You made us all lifeless in your works, but out of that you gained your livelihood. Isn't that both murder and grand larceny? At the very least it is criminal intent on an estate. And that makes *us* your ancestors."

The old man nodded in total agreement. "Well said, well said!"

"Yes, here I am, one of his ancestors!" chimed in the roughneck.

"Ancestors?" the metropolitan temptress protested. "I'd hate to be that. And there are cases in which the old live on the young. Don't you see all those young girls sacrificing their bodies for their fathers? There're lots of those around all right."

An unexpectedly loud voice boomed forth from the middle of the crowd: "I for one certainly am not a product of your making!" This one drowned out all the other voices, mere whispers in comparison.

The Writer looked up and could not have been more delighted. It was none other than his best friend from the human realm, a cultural entrepreneur who had died just a few days before the Writer did. Son of a nouveau riche family, he had since his younger days been a man of principle. The principle, as it turned out, was not to spurn the family's quick yet sizable fortune but rather a deep regret that they hadn't been enriching themselves long enough. Their wealth was, one might say, glittering so brightly that it hurt the eyes, stinking so much that it was an offense to the sense of smell. There was no touch of class to it. His father shared these misgivings and made every effort to give the family name the ring of long-established status, much like one who, wearing a gown made of a down-home fabric, crumples it on purpose to reduce somewhat its feel of the countryside and the rustling noise it makes. The father had always hoped to further his goal by having his children marry into families of corrupt bureaucrats or gentry who had fallen on hard times. The son, on the other hand, devoted all his time and energy to playing the Bohemian poet, singing in praise of alcohol, opium, loose women, intoxication, and sin in general.[13] Thus knocking around in life, he made it with a number of women, and the brands of tobacco and alcohol he consumed could well have formed a League of Nations. But he failed to commit any sins at all, other than producing some freely plagiarized free verse.

One day while eating out with his mistress, he suddenly noticed how lipstick always got swallowed with the food a woman ate. Naturally, then, after the meal her lips would be robbed of color, and she would have to put on lipstick again. This stirred his inherited business instincts, which emerged as if awakened from a dream, or like a snake coming out of hibernation. From the next day on, he exchanged Bohemian living for entrepreneurship, starting a factory with money his father had made. The first thing rolling off the lines was Vitastick, a new product so great that only his advertising chief's catchy sales slogans could do it justice: "For Both Beauty and Health—What Else?" "Never Before Have Kisses Been So Nutritious." That last line was actually the caption to a picture showing a young man dressed as a Daoist priest embracing a girl not unlike an unshaved nun. So this scene was supposed to be Jia Baoyu of *Dream of the Red Chamber* tasting rouge. Another line was: "What Fulfilling Love!"—this one being a caption to a picture of a fat man gleefully holding the hands of a woman with pouting lips. Her gesture was meant to focus attention on the thick layer of blood-building Vitastick on them. The chemical composition of this particular lipstick was no different from others for cosmetic use; all our entrepreneur did was concoct a name. The result turned out to be so appealing to the mentality of the masses that he multiplied the capital his father gave him several dozen times. He kept at it, coming up next with products such as Intellegrowth, an ointment that promised to stimulate the growth of both hair and intellect, canned Diet-Rich Chicken, which promised not to put weight on slim misses, and Cod Liver Gum.

At forty, having made enough money, he thought of old times, and his youthful hobby of patronizing the literary arts came back to him. Since drama was the genre that appealed best to both the learned and the popular taste, he, with a sustained effort, advocated a movement for "healthy drama," in much the same spirit he had earlier pushed his new products. He thereby succeeded in rallying quite a few writers to his camp. He figured that comedies made one laugh, and laughing was undoubtedly good for one's health. But then unrestrained laughing would add wrinkles to the face, and a mouth wide open invited germs. Besides, that would also lead to cramps of the stomach muscles, dislodged jaws, and a host of other unhealthy conditions. Thus the kind of comedies he promoted abided by the rule of causing audiences only to chuckle. As for tragedies, he thought them good for the health too. The daily functioning of any opening on the physical body meant one form of elimination or another. However, modern man, raised in a mechanized culture, lacked the normal range of human emotions. This resulted in insufficient elimination from the eyes. The moderate quantity of tears that tragedies produced would do the job of preventing diseases that were to the eyes as constipation or gas was to the digestive system.

By that time our Writer had already made a name for himself and was in the process of turning out scripts from all his novels. These plays of his all satisfied the conditions set for healthy theater, except that they were not totally in line with the entrepreneur's original intent. But the Writer's reputation was so imposing that it amounted to a threat, a terror. No reader of his dared not to rave about his works along with the others. To do otherwise would be to risk being criticized as deficient in the appreciative faculties and unworthy of works of literature. At performances of his tragedies, the audience had the urge to laugh, but, cowering under his fame, they dared not laugh out loud. Every one of them hid his reactions from the person in the next seat, smothering his chuckles with the handkerchief that was brought along for tears. Of course, nothing could have been more in keeping with the spirit of the healthy drama than this. When it came to his comedies, not a soul in the house was not bored. But who had the guts to stand up and leave? Who wanted to be branded an unknowing fool? So everybody just settled on making himself comfortable, and dozed off. Sleep was of course an important part of healthy daily living. Thus, between the entrepreneur and the Writer they had a great act going, and they forged a strong friendship out of it. On the former's fiftieth birthday, our Writer even took the trouble to solicit essays for an anthology in commemoration of the occasion.

Now, seeing that the person talking to him was the entrepreneur, our Writer became very much heartened and beckoned him. "You appeared at just the right moment! Come help me argue my case!"

"Argue your case!" the entrepreneur scoffed, "I'm here to settle accounts with you myself!"

The Writer was dumbfounded. "Good heavens! Since when did we become enemies? Don't you remember your fiftieth birthday? Didn't I guest-edit a special section in the papers in your honor? Remember the congratulatory essay I wrote in the vernacular language—practically singing in exultation? Who could have known that you could have too much to drink that night, and die of some acute illness! I wasn't at your deathbed, and that has been bothering me ever since. So we should only be overjoyed at this chance meeting today. Why have you turned so hostile and ungrateful?"

"Pah! It's precisely at your hands that I died. We have no more friendship to speak of! That special edition of yours was just special perdition. Your commemorative essay was closer to a funeral oration. You call that 'exultation'? Execution, that's what it was! You aren't even aware yourself how destructive you can be. Your pen is nothing but a razor, your ink poison, and your paper might as well be a death warrant issued by Yama, king of Hell, himself. It's not just the characters in your works that are like puppets, or clay dolls, not showing a glimmer of life; even the living human beings you describe or write about have their lives and blessings terminated. If you hadn't written that essay, I would have enjoyed several more years of life. Just think: your tone was so reverent in that article, so virtually trembling with respect and awe, that it read like a bereft son's memories of his father, or at least an epitaph commissioned for a princely sum. How could I take that kind of overdone adulation? You were using up all my good fortune. And I've been waiting here for no other reason than to get even with you."

As the Writer was listening to this dressing down, an unpleasant idea flashed across his mind and lodged there like a hard food particle in the stomach resisting digestion. "Didn't I, just before my death, complete an autobiography, with the intention of publishing it as soon as I got the Nobel Prize? According to the entrepreneur, whomever my pen lands on dies. If that's the case, I didn't die of frustration over not getting the prize but because of a fatal autobiography.[14] Why, oh why did I have to have such a murderous pen? Why, oh why did I have to have such a secretly murderous pen? Why, oh why did I have to write such a suicidal autobiography? I have nothing left but regret! But wait a second—how foolish of me! The mistake's been made, so the thing to do now is to turn it to my advantage. So first let me use it to get rid of this bunch of devilish creditors."

"If what he says is true," the Writer declared to the crowd, "my crimes have already caught up with me, and I'm suffering my just desserts. I have paid for my acts with my own life. Didn't I write an autobiography, and wasn't that suicide? Forget it! Forget it! Let's consider this matter settled; we don't owe one another a thing anymore."

But they protested in unison, "You aren't getting off that easy! Your death wasn't suicide. Suppose you loved to eat and feasted on globefish; if you got poisoned and died from it, that wouldn't mean you killed yourself because you had grown tired of living. You wrote that autobiography to toot your own horn. You just never knew you could be slain by your own pen—that knife of a pen! We're going to get our lives back from you no matter what. Give us our lives back!"

The Writer started to panic, wringing his hands and pacing back and forth, muttering, "The way this is going, you're going to end up getting *my* life!"

"I think I'm ready to hand down the verdict now," the administrator announced. "For your next life I assign you to be—"

"Mr. Administrator," the Writer interrupted, bowing, "could you let me say one word before you go on? I really suffered everything that could be suffered in the literary life in my last existence, so I had been fantasizing of a good life of glory and riches for my coming incarnation. Now of course I've given up all those wild thoughts. I fully realize how serious the sins I've committed are, but I'm appealing to you to consider my past good deeds as mitigation of my wrongs, and exercise leniency in your sentencing. Why don't you, as punishment, simply designate me to be a writer again in my next life?"

"A writer *again*?" The administrator was taken aback. "Aren't you afraid of another crowd demanding their lives of you in the future?" The reaction of those gathered below was similar: all stared at the Writer in disbelief.

"Oh, I'll just translate," he explained. "No more creative writing for me. That way my life won't be in much danger, I'm sure. Besides, I'll do literal translation—I definitely won't try anything even close to free translation—just to make sure that the liveliness of the original isn't lost, and also to prevent myself from being hauled into some foreign court. Take for example that fashionable American novel *Gone With the Wind*. I vow I'd faithfully render its title as *Swept Off by the Storm*—notice how 'Swept Off' [*kuang zou*] conveys both the sound and meaning of the word 'Gone'! Dante's masterpiece would be entitled *The Heavenly Father Joking*. In the same vein, I could give Milton's epic the interpretive title *A Blindman's Song on the Fall of Suzhou and Hangzhou*, but I promise I won't do that, even though the old saying does claim that Suzhou and Hangzhou are paradises on earth, and Milton had indeed lost his eyesight. And whenever I have a problem translating, I'll just follow those celebrated examples of transliteration: *youmo* for "humor," *luoman-tike* for "romantic," *aofuhebian* for *aufheben* [sublate][15] and so on. Since the whole thing would then be, one might say, spelled out in Chinese, how much closer could the reader get to reading the original? That's like taking out a life insurance policy for the characters in the work.

"Or, if you're not happy with that, I won't even do translations but just stick to playwriting and specialize in historical tragedy. There's plenty to work on. Well-known historical figures such as Lord Guan, General Yue Fei, Consort Yang, Lü Zhu, Zhao Jun, and so on. Historical figures are quite dead to start with, and on top of that, tragedies should of course entertain a lot of deaths. That would make deaths here doubly warranted, so I couldn't possibly be charged with murder. There's a third possibility too. I could retell Shakespeare. The venerable Bard came to me once in a dream, complaining that the characters in his plays lived way too long. After these endless centuries, they had become plain sick and tired of living and were more than happy to put an end to it all and simply drop dead. So he asked me to do an act of charity, to send them off to a painless, natural death. He added this was what that foreign culture of theirs called 'mercy killing.' Before he left, he complimented me, saying I was a young man to be reckoned with, even bowing to me, and repeating his words of appreciation."

"I have a good idea of my own," the administrator said. "All of you listen carefully. His intention in writing an autobiography was not suicide, it's true, but he didn't write the congratulatory essay with an intent to kill either. The effects of these two events could be considered to have cancelled each other out; hence there's no debt outstanding between him and the entrepreneur. But as for his depriving the characters in his works of lives, he should have to pay for that. It wouldn't be a bad idea at all to make him, as a penalty, a character in a novel or play of some other writer's and let him have his own taste of being suspended between life and death. The problem is, there're so many writers of this sort that I don't know whom to send him to. Oh, I've got it! Yes! In the human world there's a young man who is currently planning to write an epoch-making mixed-genre work. He'll be adopting the syntax of those causeries written in the style of collected sayings while employing the rhythm, meter, and form of modern poetry. The product will be a novel in five acts and ten scenes. He has the paper all ready now; the only thing he's waiting for is inspiration. When the propitious moment comes, we can smuggle a spirit into his mind." The administrator turned to our Writer: "Sir, no one could be a better choice than you for the hero in this work. You're a genius, and it just happens that your successor plans to write about the genius's sense of life."

"Mr. Administrator," the hoarse voice of one of the Writer's characters asked from down in the crowd, "did you say 'sense of life' or 'sex life'? If that fledgling author is to focus on the latter, wouldn't that be too easy"—he pointed at the Writer—"on this common enemy of ours?"

The administrator smiled. "Relax, relax, don't you worry about it. Our Writer's mantle must have fallen on this young man. As soon as a person ends up in his work, the character will have a hard time telling whether he's dead or alive, much less living life."

"In that case, we have no objections!" Rejoicing and jubilation. "Long live the fair administrator!"

Our Writer made his final despairing protest. "Mr. Administrator, I've already dropped all consideration of my own interests and am prepared to take the rough with the smooth. I do have that much grace. But at least you should have some respect for the literary arts. This youngster is waiting for a stroke of 'divine inspiration,' not 'ghostly intervention.' How could you send my ghost to cast an evil spell on him? I can take whatever hard times you give me, but if you're going to play a malicious joke on the arts, which should be held in the highest respect, I'll simply refuse to go along with you. Should the Writers' Association ever find out about this, they'll surely issue a public statement of protest."

"'A genius is but the most inspired of ghosts.' You more than rate it. Everything's going to be all right, just take it easy."

Taking the administrator's archaic phrasing as a sign of erudition, and thinking his claim must therefore have been based on the great books—little knowing that the line had just been invented on the spur of the moment—the Writer was reduced to silence.[16] Thereupon, amid the jeering and ridicule of the crowd, his spirit was escorted on its way by a uniformed elf.

By now, the fledgling author had been waiting for his inspiration for three solid years. The reams of paper he had stocked up had by now appreciated to more than ten times their original value. But his inspiration just would not come, no matter what. Perhaps it got lost somehow, or had altogether forgotten where he lived. Finally, the enlightening thought occurred to him one day that in order to write a maiden work, he should seek it through a maiden. It was therefore no coincidence that just as the elf was bringing the Writer's spirit over, the young man was in the process of exploring—with the principles of the experimental sciences as his guiding light and his landlord's daughter as his coinvestigator—the secrets of life. The elf happened to be quite the gentleman, and averted his eyes. At this crucial juncture our Writer made up his mind instantly. He decided that anything was better than getting dispatched to the young man's mind and ending up coming out of his pen. So, while the elf's back was turned, with a swish he scurried into the girl's ear. Indeed, since at that time the couple was one inseparable body all tangled up, only her ears allowed unimpeded entry. Thus it was that the Writer personally, but unknowingly, gave substance to the explanation medieval Christian theologians had offered for the conception of the Virgin Mary: the female aural passage is a passage to conception (*quae per aurem concepisti*).

From that moment on the young man lost a character for his book, while the girl gained a baby. He had no choice but to marry her, and the book was never to be. Whatever writing ability he once had was henceforth put to use in keeping daily accounts for his father-in-law's grocery store. One comfort he did find, however. In traditional Chinese bookkeeping, a new line was very often begun before the previous one was completely filled, and that approximated the visual appeal of modern poetry. The language of accounting, moreover, was neither the literary idiom strictly nor the vernacular, for which reason such writing rightfully belonged in the genre of collected sayings, wherein a cross between the literary and the vernacular was the norm.

The elf, upon his return, was severely reprimanded by the administrator. Only then did he realize that to be a subordinate meant that one could not afford to play the gentleman. To serve a superior well and conscientiously, one simply could not let a matter of honor bother the conscience.

Later, it was reported that the baby boy grinned right from the moment of his birth. And whenever he saw his father, his smile would wax triumphant. The relatives all agreed that the baby had to have been blessed with good fortune of the highest magnitude. But so far, nobody could tell whether or not he would grow up to be a writer.

Translated by Dennis T. Hu

SOUVENIR

Although this was a city surrounded by one range of mountains after another,[1] spring, like raiding enemy planes, entered it without the least difficulty. Sad to say, the arid mountain region was not suited to a luxurious growth of flowers and shrubs, so though spring had arrived, it had no place to take up lodging. Nevertheless, spring managed to create a vernal atmosphere in this mountain city with no other help than the fermenting effect of a damp and stuffy Lantern Festival[2] and of a few ensuing sunny days. The air of such bright, cloudless days was heavily laced with the busy dust of this mountainous region. Illuminated by the twilight of the setting sun, it imparted to the spring atmosphere a ripe yellow hue. They were the kind of days when one could dream while awake, become drunk without drinking. A wonderful season it was!

From a street where twilight still lingered, Manqian turned into an alley deserted by the sun. The early evening chill of spring alerted her to the fact that without realizing it she had reached her home. She had no idea how she had come home, but she knew her legs were very sore. The uneven gravel road hurt her feet and made her worry about her high heels, the last luxury she had bought two years ago when she passed through Hong Kong on the way to the interior. She was a little rueful that she had not allowed Tianjian to hire a rickshaw for her. But after what had happened today, could she continue to accept his gallantry? Wouldn't that indicate tacit approval of what he'd done? He was just the type to interpret it that way.

Engrossed in thought, after wearily passing a few homes near the entrance to the alley, Manqian saw the mud wall that circled her own courtyard. In this area, where there was a shortage of bricks and tiles, mud walls were common. But contrasted with the neighbors' brick and stone walls, this mud one was unsightly and had brought lots of embarrassment to its mistress. When Manqian first looked at the house, she was reluctant to rent it because of that ugly wall. Sensing her displeasure, the landlord offered to reduce the rent. It was precisely because of the wall that the deal was made. But only recently had she made her peace with the wall and become willing to accept the protection it offered.

Her husband, Caishu, not only accepted but also endorsed, bragged about, and praised the crude mud wall. That is, he was unwilling to accept it but used words to camouflage his true feelings. Whenever he had friends visiting him for the first time, Manqian heard Caishu say gleefully, "Its appearance is plain and simple, especially appealing for city dwellers long accustomed to Western-style homes. I took an immediate liking to it. There are so many kids who play in the alley, and my neighbors' whitewashed walls are filled with their pencil scrawls and pictures. But my mud wall is dark and coarse—the kids can't do a thing to it. After the last bombing raid, the police told everyone to paint their walls black. Our neighbors, terrified of bombs, scurried around getting their walls painted. But mine was naturally camouflaged already, which saved me a lot of trouble. Otherwise we would have had to hire people to paint it black. The landlord certainly wouldn't have refunded the money for the job, so that we would have had to pay for it ourselves. And shortly after the neighbors' walls were painted black, the kids went at it again and crisscrossed drawings in white chalk. It was just like setting up a big blackboard for the kids. It really wasn't worth all the trouble." At this point, Caishu's guests would politely join him in laughter. And if his wife were waiting on the guests, she, out of a sense of obligation, would smile too.

What Caishu neglected to mention was that the kids, unable to write on his wall, had scrawled all over his front door many *Xu Residence*'s of different sizes, more or less in the manner of the two ideograms Caishu had written on the red strip of paper pasted at the top of his door. This was a fact that his guests would politely refrain from mentioning.

Manqian pushed open the door. The maid, a native of the area, asked gruffly in a loud voice, "Who is it?"

Manqian entered and asked casually, "Has the master come home yet?" The reply was negative. Of course, she had expected that answer, but today she felt relieved. She was timorous, afraid that her husband had come home before her and would ask her where she had been, and as yet she had not found the most succinct and effective lie to tell him. Lying to his face seemed much more difficult than being unfaithful to him. She knew very well that because of the noon air raids, offices opened at three in the afternoon and her husband would not be home until well after dark. But one could never tell—what had happened to her a while ago was a complete accident. Yes, indeed, the meeting she had with Tianjian this afternoon had gone beyond the expected. She was totally unprepared for what had happened. Yes, she had encouraged Tianjian to admire her, but it had never occurred to her that he would take the initiative and force her. She had only hoped for a tender, subtle, delicate emotional relationship with him, one ornamented with complications, filled with doubts and uncertainties, without verbal commitments or traces. In short, she wanted this relationship merely to enable them to touch each other's souls with remote antennae. For a woman like Manqian, that was the most interesting form of recreation, and also the safest, with her husband a convenient buffer to prevent her and her lover from overstepping the bounds.

But who could have known that Tianjian would be so bold and direct? The substantial, physical love he had offered only frightened her, and somewhat disappointed her, since what she had obtained was more than she had hoped for—like someone with a weak stomach filled with greasy food. Had she known him to be that aggressive, she would not have gone to see him, or at least she wouldn't have gone out without first changing her undershirt. The thought of her old undershirt, which should have been washed, still made her blush, even at this moment; in fact, this thought embarrassed her more than what had taken place.

Home. After walking through a small courtyard and through the room that served as both living and dining room, she entered her tiled bedroom. The maid went back to the kitchen to prepare dinner; like all household help from the countryside, the maid had no idea that now that the mistress was back it was time to bring her tea. But Manqian was too exhausted to speak to anyone. Her heart confused, she was unclear about what to think. Here and there, certain parts of her skin, such as her face and lips, that had been kissed by Tianjian seemed to retain some lingering impressions. Each place seemed to have a mind of its own, briskly alive, standing out from a feeling of general fatigue.

The room, with its old-style framed windows, had been dark for some time. Manqian preferred the darkness, as if under the cover of night her conscience would not be laid bare like a snail without a hiding place after it leaves its shell. So she did not turn the light on. In truth, the lights in the interior of China were only a shade better than darkness; the gleam they provided was so insubstantial that it seemed as if the color of night had been diluted with water. After she settled down in a chair, the heat generated from walking surged out of her body. She felt she just couldn't believe what had happened; it could only be likened to a relief carved on the surface of a dream.

She wanted to lie down in bed, with her clothes on, for a little rest. But she was, after all, a woman. Tired as she was, she took off her street clothes and put on her housedress before she lay down. Her fur coat was shedding, and the color of her flannel-lined *qipao*[3] was no longer fashionable. Ever since last summer, this place had been busy. Along with government offices evacuated to this city were numerous stylish married and single women, who dazzled the natives. What Maqian had, from her innermost underwear to her overcoat, was what she had bought for her wedding, and she wouldn't have minded having some new clothes. But her dowry had been spent long since, when she and her husband fled their home; what Caishu earned was barely enough for monthly expenses, and there wasn't any money left over for her to indulge in clothes. She was sympathetic to her husband. She never asked him for money for clothes, and she kept her yearnings to herself. Yes, in more than two years of married life, she had not had it easy; Manqian had to grin and bear the hardships of life with her husband, using her pride to sustain love, and never complaining to anyone. A wife like that had certainly done right by her husband.

It should be said, however, that her husband had not done right by her. Before their engagement, Manqian's mother insisted that Caishu had cheated her of her daughter, and she blamed her own husband for having introduced Caishu to her. Some of Manqian's girlfriends had also commented that, despite Manqian's shrewdness, she had made a foolish mistake on such a vital matter as choosing a mate.

But what mother doesn't object to her daughter's choice of a mate? What woman doesn't disparage her friend's lover behind her back? At college, every young person, besides aspiring to a degree, must also aspire to a lover. In colleges that require students to live on campus, the distance between men and women is greatly reduced. Without the factor of their families, when men and women meet, they get to know one another. Thus this type of contact leads to what the families would call a mismatch. Moreover, love, as legend has it, is blind. It opens its eyes only after marriage. However, many students do not regard love as blind. They want to be loved, to offer their love, to beg to be given some residual love. But love seems to see them as totally unlovable and ignores them altogether. This proves that love is still blind, too blind to see their lovable traits. Thus coeducation not only increases the number of married couples through freedom of choice, but it also leaves behind many rejects from the love game, especially old maids. But the old maids, unlike Manqian, had at least not been willing to be mismatched!

Manqian was somewhat lethargic, and her image of herself was of a poised, refined young woman from a good family. Her long eyelashes, her egg-shaped face, her pale complexion, and her slim figure all contributed to an impression of gracious aloofness in her. She was especially known among her classmates for her love of art, and this caused her admirers to detect an indefinable elegance about her. Some men might consider her beauty too pure and lacking in sensuality, but her detractors, so vulgar in taste, would never have attracted the attention of her curved, slightly nearsighted eyes in the first place. By exploiting her inborn bashfulness, she developed self-appreciation. Some people called her arrogant, but arrogance in a woman is an enticement to a man's spirit, just as wantonness in a woman is a stimulant to a man's body. Thus, though Manqian was perhaps not as elegant as she perceived herself to be, she did have a few suitors. She was slow by nature, and her attraction for men was low-key and cumulative. Her admirers were schoolmates of many years. Precisely because they had been together for so long, she was used to their ways and bored with them. None of them could arouse a fresh reaction in her. Until the year of her college graduation she had had no lover. When she was bored and in low spirits, there was an emptiness in her heart that no one could fill. It must be said that she had failed to benefit from the opportunities of college coeducation. At this time, Caishu appeared, seemingly from nowhere.

Caishu was the son of an old friend of Manqian's father's. Because of the political situation, Caishu had transferred to Manqian's school from a college in the south. In view of Caishu's family's straitened circumstances, Manqian's father had invited Caishu to stay with them before school started; he even set up a couch for Caishu to use on weekends and holidays, the idea being to give Caishu a home away from home. Years of education in the city had not eradicated Caishu's rusticity or his childishness. His naive rudeness, his unsophisticated civilities, and his native smartness made him look ridiculous and yet charming. Ever since the day when Manqian's father told her to take Caishu to register at school, Manqian had vaguely felt that she was much more experienced than this big, newly arrived country boy, and she relished the joy of being the competent elder sister. On the other hand, Caishu felt strongly for her from the start and stayed at her home frequently. They became very good friends, almost as if they were of the same family. In his company, she forgot her usual reticence, partly overlooking the fact that he was, potentially, an attractive man. Her feeling toward him was like that of a comfortable foot that has forgotten that it still has a shoe on, a feeling she had never had with other men. What was at first companionship gradually turned to love, not passionate love, but a slowly and steadily growing intimacy. It was not until her girlfriends began to tease her that she realized how much she really liked Caishu.

When her parents found out about this, they quarreled with each other, and Caishu was too scared to come spend the night with them anymore. The mother blamed the father; the father scolded the daughter and blamed the mother; father and mother joined in scolding Caishu and in counseling their daughter, pointing out that Caishu's family was poor and his prospects dim. Manqian shed some tears, but her parents' chiding stiffened her resolve, like a piece of hemp rope that has become wet and so become stronger. At first her parents forbade her to see him; later they prohibited an engagement; they hoped time would erode her love for him.

But love, like a habit, takes a long time to grow, and, like a chronic illness, even more time is needed to be rid of it. So, after two years, Manqian remained steadfast in her love for Caishu, who, of course, took everything in stride. It was because of the opposition of friends and relatives that their relationship, not nurturing itself as much as it should, began to turn into a unified force against outsiders and an alliance against snobbery. They had waited a long time when the war suddenly broke out, and political uncertainties easily divide families.

War, which traditionally produces many widows and widowers, ironically became the catalyst for Manqian and Caishu's marriage. Her parents felt they had done their best by her and should stay out of her affairs. So Manqian and Caishu were married without too much ceremony, as they blandly listened to the usual wedding benedictions and to such clichés as "lovers eventually get married." Soon afterward Caishu and his fellow employees were evacuated to this city.

Purchasing items hard to come by in the interior, packing their luggage, looking for affordable transportation and lodging, buying or renting furniture, hiring a maid, and returning courtesy calls to the wives of Caishu's colleagues took up a lot of their time before they settled down. After the wedding they were so busy they had little time to savor any sweetness. Manqian, who had never paid any attention to domestic chores, now had to worry about daily necessities such as fuel, rice, oil, and salt. She was not extravagant, but she came from a respectable family. Caishu's income was limited, and they felt the pinch even though prices in the interior were low at first. People had not become accustomed to poverty since it was the first year of the war; Manqian and her husband were just poor enough to want to hide theirs, and could manage to get away with their pretenses. It was really hard on Manqian. For this Caishu was both sympathetic and apologetic. Husband and wife both wished the war would end soon so they could lead a better life.

It was not long before Manqian discovered that Caishu was not an aggressive or enterprising person. He would never do more than to go to work at his square desk in the office. Even if the war came to an end, his prospects would not improve. His ignorance of the ways of the world made her feel vaguely the absence of anyone to support her. It intensified her fear that she alone had to take care of them both; that she would always have to be a gentle, protective mother to him. All the luxuries associated with being a woman—playing coy, being naughty, and throwing temper tantrums—were denied her, just like material luxury goods. Caishu himself was a child; he could not accommodate wanton coyness.

Except for some activities in the morning, there really wasn't much for Manqian to do at home. After lunch Caishu would go to work; the maid would be washing clothes in the courtyard, and she would be sitting leisurely in the center of the room, gazing at the sun climbing the wall—a regular diet of ennui and silence that she could share with no one. She did not care to gossip with the wives of Caishu's colleagues. In the same city lived a number of friends whom she had known before she got married. Those who were men she felt it would be improper for her to associate with anymore. As for women, some were married, and those who were single had jobs or were preparing to get married—all of them were busy with what they were doing. And, because she was trying to save money, she had few activities, and so her friends dwindled in number. Only in the evenings or on weekends would a few of Caishu's friends occasionally stop by. She felt no desire to cultivate the friendship of those that didn't come to see her. She loved to read, and her only regret was that there were few new books she could buy in the interior. The few old and tattered foreign novels she borrowed were not enough to fill up the hours in the day, nor the gaps in her soul. Knowing she must be bored, Caishu had suggested she take walks by herself. Out of extreme boredom she went to a movie theater once. She did not go to see the move per se, but to see what constituted a movie in the interior. It was a bizarre old foreign film, and the long benches in the movie theater were crowded with local moviegoers. Whenever a kissing scene appeared on the screen, the audience would clap their hands and yell, "Good, how about another one?" After chatting with her husband a bit after coming home from the movie, she went to bed, but was deprived of sleep by the fleas she had picked up at the cinema. From then on, she was afraid to go to the movies.

In this manner two years went by. And there was no sign of a baby. Every time the wives of Caishu's colleagues saw her, they would say, "Mrs. Xu, you should have a baby by now!" Because Manqian was a woman with a modern education and a knowledge of science, the old-fashioned wives speculated wildly as to why she wasn't pregnant. They would remark with a meaningful smile, "Young people these days sure put comfort first!"[4]

The previous spring enemy planes had bombed the city for the first time. Some houses were destroyed, and, as usual, some common folk who were not worth bombing got killed. But this was enough to frighten the citizenry of all social classes in the city. Even the most naive aborigines knew that bombers were not hens laying eggs in the sky, and they no longer dared gaze at the sky from the streets, clap their hands, and make noises after the air raid sirens had sounded. Air raid precaution measures suddenly became a matter of supreme concern; in editorials and readers' correspondence columns local papers repeatedly stated the area's importance for the War of Resistance in the interior and called for air protection. Protection by the air force, detractors argued, would only make the city a military target and induce the enemy to bomb; but such views were not expressed by the papers. After the summer, the city had its air force academy and its airports expanded, and the people began to get used to seeing their country's planes flying in the sky.

One day late in September, Caishu came home to say that an acquaintance who was distantly related to him had moved to town. Earlier that day a cousin from the air force academy had visited Caishu in his office. This cousin had been a brat who refused to pay attention to schoolwork, Caishu told his wife. Not having seen his cousin for six or seven years, Caishu said he could barely recognize him. He was big and tall now, but just as naughty and flippant as ever. He added that the cousin, after learning Caishu was married, had joked that he would like to "get acquainted" with Manqian in a couple days.

"Should we invite him for a simple meal?" asked Caishu casually. Without much enthusiasm, Manqian replied, "We'll see. Those guys in the air force are accustomed to good food and fun. He may not think much of our inviting him to dinner. You'll spend lots of money, but he may not appreciate the dinner, or, worse yet, he may feel he's been imposed on. Why bother? If you invite him for only a mediocre dinner, you'd be better off not inviting him at all. Most likely he just said he'd like to visit you. So long as he has seen you, that will probably be the end of it. Someone like that probably won't spend the time to find your house."

In view of his wife's disdain for the whole matter, Caishu lost half his excitement and replied quickly, "We'd better wait. He said he would come. He asked for my address. He also said that he has heard you were beautiful and gifted, with both 'talent and looks,' and that he must see you. He had a good laugh with me about it."

"Humph. Please ask him not to come. I'm old and ugly, nothing more than your housekeeper. If he sees me, wouldn't we be embarrassed?"

"Come, come," Caishu comforted his wife, fondling her hair. "If you saw him, you'd certainly like him. He's talkative, funny, affable, and kind." Then he changed the subject, wondering why his wife should turn so caustic when she was told she was both pretty and talented. In truth, Caishu was born to be a subordinate or assistant who would be allowed only to take orders and would be good at only that. As he never heard any complaints from his wife, who appeared complacent, he had taken her for granted. Now he was astonished, but dared not ask any questions. Hurriedly, he finished his dinner and dropped the matter.

It would be Sunday in a few days; Saturday night Caishu remembered that Tianjian might show up the following day, and he told his wife. On Sunday she bought a little more food than usual, preparing for Tianjian to come to lunch. Since Tianjian had not committed himself to coming, they prepared just a bit more than usual, so that if Tianjian showed up, he would not get the impression that they had prepared a special meal for him. They also supervised the maid, who swept the living room and the courtyard more thoroughly than usual. As husband and wife made preparations, they laughed to each other, stating that they really shouldn't make too much of this, because the guest, if he showed up, was no one very important. Despite all that was said, Manqian put on a traditional Chinese dress, which she would hardly wear every day. She also put on a little more rouge, and even applied some lipstick, something she seldom did.

Shortly before noon, there was no sign of Tianjian. The maid, famished herself, urged them to eat. Since they had no choice, husband and wife sat across from each other and began to eat. An even-tempered man, Caishu said smilingly to his wife, "He was never that firm about coming. We were the only ones who were certain. Lucky we didn't spend too much. The courtyard hasn't been cleaned like that for some time. I wonder how the maid usually sweeps it?"

Manqian said, "It isn't a question of the money, but rather of all the planning that went into it. A fine Sunday has been spoiled by him. If he was coming, he should have said so; if no, he should have made himself clear. He was noncommittal, and we've been kept busy for him. Only someone as naive as you would take a casual remark as a solemn promise."

Her unpleasant expression made Caishu put in quickly, "Even if he comes, we won't entertain him. That boy's been inconsiderate since childhood. After lunch we can take a walk in the park. Since the weather is so nice, you won't have to change your clothes."

Manqian assented. In her heart she judged Tianjian to be genuinely disgusting.

Another week and more went by, during which time Tianjian did not come. After Caishu got home one day, he mentioned that he had seen Tianjian with a young woman. "He was very vague about the whole thing; he didn't introduce the girl. Must be some new girlfriend of his. That kid is too much. The girl looks all right, except for the way she was dressed. Too provocative—definitely not a native of this area. When he heard we'd been waiting for him to come to lunch, he apologized. He said he had intended to come but couldn't because something else had come up. He said he'll visit us in a few days, and he wanted me to send his regards and his sincere apologies to you beforehand."

"Come here in 'a few days'? How many days, then?" Manqian asked coldly.

"Let him come whenever he likes; we don't have to make any preparations anyway. He and I are relatives, and there's no need for formality. I think he's madly in love right now, and it's likely he won't have time to come in the immediate future. I'm afraid we're getting old. For example, when I saw the young couple together today, I wasn't jealous at all. For some reason I felt them naive enough to be pitied.

There are so many ups and downs awaiting them; they have yet to be fooled and manipulated by fate. For us married folks, life has settled down—like a boat that has entered its harbor and no longer fears the storm. Though we've been married for only two years, we can consider ourselves an old married couple."

Manqian smiled and said, "Don't say us, just *you!*"—a line she borrowed from *Heroic Sons and Daughters,*[5] spoken by Thirteenth Sister to a "faceless" woman. Manqian and her husband had borrowed and finished reading that novel, and they had appropriated expressions from it to tease each other. When Caishu saw his wife being naughty and teasing him, he begged for a kiss. Intoxicated with his own passion, he did not sense her indifference.

For better than half the night, Manqian could not fall asleep. The snores of a tired Caishu did not relieve the tense vibrations that permeated her whole body. Quietly she lay there wondering why at such a young age she should be so tired of love. No, not only of love, but of everything. She had been married for only a little over two years, but the marriage was as stale and boring as if she had been married a lifetime. "For us married folks, life has settled down," was what he had said. Yes, the truth was that since meeting Caishu she had never experienced any fluctuations in her feelings. The fear of outside forces interfering with their love affair did once exist, but there had always been sufficient mutual confidence and assurance. Groundless suspicions, deliberate misunderstandings, and other assorted delicate torments associated with romance were wholly outside her experience. There never was any bitterness, spiciness, sourness, or harshness, but always the taste of clear tea.

Her relationship with him now was like fresh boiling water poured over old tea leaves—the tea gets weaker after each infusion. Days went by as if she had not lived them, eventlessly, as if time bore no relationship to her. Soon she would be thirty—the way she aged, it really wasn't worth it. It would be better if she did have a baby, to reduce some of the emptiness of life; she might as well reconcile herself to being a mother. In the beginning she had a faint hope of getting a job so she could be part of society and not confined to her home. She was unwilling to lose her role outside the family after she got married. At first she feared a baby would be a hindrance to love and she'd rather not have one. Then she didn't know if Caishu would want a baby; she was afraid he couldn't afford it. When would this dreadful war come to an end?

Manqian rose late. By the time she had gotten up, Caishu had left for work. She had not slept for the better part of the night. Her head felt heavy and her eyelids too weighty to lift themselves, and she was afraid to take a good look at her long, sallow face in the mirror. After washing her face and rinsing her mouth, she had little energy for anything else. No one would come this morning, and she was too lazy to tidy herself up. After resting a bit she felt better. The maid had gone to the market and returned. Donning her plain green cloth apron, she helped the maid prepare lunch. While they were in the midst of this, they heard a knock on the front door. She wondered who could be visiting at this hour. The maid ran to open the door. Suddenly she remembered that she had not combed her hair, had not made up her face, and that she smelled of grease. She definitely could not receive a visitor, and she was sorry she had not told the maid so. She heard the maid running all the way to the kitchen yelling, "Madam, madam," and saying that the man was surnamed Zhou, who said he was a relative of the master's, had come to visit the master and mistress, and was standing in the courtyard. The maid wondered if she should invite the guest in.

Manqian knew the caller was Tianjian. Flustered and annoyed by the maid's garrulousness, she did not know what to do. Scolding the maid, her first impulse, would not help matters. Should she go out to greet the guest? She felt ashamed of her condition, and since this was their first meeting, she did not want to be too embarrassed. If she were to put on some makeup and receive him, she must go to the bedroom and to go to the bedroom she must pass the courtyard, which was right outside the kitchen. Not wanting to be seen in her condition, and there being no chance to make up, she was forced to tell the maid to inform the guest that the master wasn't home but would be informed of his visit and that the master would return his visit shortly. The maid answered in a loud voice, and left.

A wave of shame overtook Manqian, and she didn't trouble to find out if the maid had relayed the message correctly. She felt she had been less than civil to her guest, who certainly knew she had been hiding in the kitchen, unwilling to come out. Perhaps he would have forgiven her for her less-than-neat appearance and for not having had time to make up properly. Yet it was truly disgraceful that the cousin's so-called talented and beautiful wife had been unable to receive her guest because she smelled of kitchen smoke. Really it was Tianjian's fault. Of all the times he could have called, why did he choose that time to come, and so abruptly? While she fumed, the maid came back to tell her the guest had said he'd come again on Saturday afternoon. Manqian, full of frustrations, scolded the maid for having yelled at the top of her lungs when a visitor called. The maid, peeved, threatened to quit. This only exasperated Manqian more. When her husband came home for lunch, she told him what had happened in the morning and blamed him for having a mischievous troublemaker from God knows where for a cousin.

Even though husband and wife said they didn't want to go out of their way to entertain Tianjian, Caishu brought some pastries when he came home around noon on Saturday. And after lunch, Manqian herself spent some time making herself presentable. The last time she had made herself up, she had merely wanted to show her respect for her guest. Good manners dictated that she not be seen with her hair uncombed and her face unadorned. But this time, it was completely different, for she was still subconsciously very much affected by the shame and embarrassment she had felt two days ago when she couldn't see Tianjian. Though Tianjian had never seen her, she felt he must have an image of her as a smoked-up, greasy, untidy woman working by the stove. So today she must pay extra attention to her appearance to restore her tarnished reputation. Unconsciously, she put powder on her face in a more obvious way, to appeal to someone with Tianjian's crude sense of aesthetics.

A little after three, Tianjian came, with some gifts. On meeting him, Manqian was pleasantly surprised. Tianjian did not appear to be the slick, crude young man she had expected to dislike. Like all air force personnel, he was tall and strong, but his facial features were finely chiseled, and his manner of speaking seemed more refined than Caishu's. What was more, his suit was well tailored without giving the impression of being either unsophisticated or slick. Even during their first meeting, his words of courtesy toward her seemed affectionate, and one could tell he was experienced in social relations. Of course, Caishu had much to say to him, but she could tell he didn't want to spend all his time talking about his past with her husband and ignoring her. From time to time he broadened the conversation deliberately so as to involve her in it. Yes, the facts wouldn't allow her to dislike Tianjian, unless she was offended by his frequent, sly glances at her. One time, when he was gazing at her, she was looking at him at the same time. She blushed instantly and her eyes blurred like a mirror someone had fogged with hot breath. But then he gave her a candid smile and asked casually what she did for recreation.

What a smart man Tianjian was! Since Tianjian's gifts to them were quite expensive, husband and wife felt they had to invite him to eat with them the next evening. The long-scheduled dinner had to be given after all.

The next day Manqian was busy all afternoon until she felt she could entrust the remaining housework to the maid, and then went to her room to change. Tianjian came shortly, and since Caishu had not yet returned from visiting a friend, the job of entertaining the guest fell to Manqian alone. Trying to be calm, she searched the fringes of her brain for things to say. Fortunately, Tianjian was a good conversationalist. Whenever she, in embarrassment, ran out of things to say, he would subtly touch on something else as if erecting a floating bridge to connect the ever-widening cracks, so linking the threads of conversation. She realized that he knew her predicament and was sympathetic. As she pondered this she felt the situation was a bit amusing, and she also felt grateful toward him.

Tianjian said he wanted very much to try Manqian's cooking, but he feared that would give her extra work, and hence he felt a conflict in himself. He added that he enjoyed cooking too and would demonstrate his culinary skills sometime.

Manqian smiled. "It's lucky I didn't know you were so talented. I don't know much about cooking. Next time, if you come here to eat, I won't dare prepare dishes for you—I'll just have to serve you plain rice."

Tianjian had the ability to make new acquaintances feel like old friends, and his enthusiasm was so infectious that it made social intercourse easy. Without being aware of it, Manqian relaxed.

When Caishu came home, he saw his wife and cousin in a happy mood, and his wife with some animation in her gentleness. He knew that her prejudices against his cousin had all dissolved and was very pleased. When they sat down to eat, the three cast formalities aside—especially Manqian, who had never known that being a hostess could be so easy and entertaining a guest so relaxing.

Tianjian told them about many of the things he had done before coming to town. He also said that a man from the same province had recently prepared a room for him at his house, and that sometimes when it was too late to return to the academy he would stay there.

Caishu then thought of Tianjian's woman companion and asked, "I imagine you must have quite a few girlfriends. Who was the one I saw you with the other day?"

Taken aback for a moment, Tianjian asked, "Which day?"

Manqian interrupted wickedly: "What he meant was 'Which one?' I think he has girlfriends with him every day, and he doesn't remember them all."

Tianjian laughed, looking at her. "Now I can see for myself you've got a sharp tongue, Biaosao,[6] but frankly, I don't remember."

Making a funny face, Caishu said, "Don't play dumb. It was the day I met you around Sun Yat-sen Road. She was round faced and wore purple. With all the evidence, aren't you going to confess?"

"Oh, that one," Tianjian said. "That's my landlord's daughter."

Manqian and Caishu thought they would hear more about this, but their guest paused and had no more to offer, as if a torrent of words ready to flow had been dammed and reclaimed by silence.

Unable to bear the suspense any longer, husband and wife commented simultaneously, "No wonder you want to live with her family!"

To explain himself, Tianjian said, "It's like this. My landlord is an old lady, and her nephew and I were very good friends when I was in Sichuan. When I came here, her nephew wrote me a letter of introduction, and it happened that she had a lot of space, and she let me have one spare room.[7] She has a son and a daughter. The son still goes to school, and the daughter, who graduated from college this past summer, works as a clerk in some office. She's quite pretty and knows how to apply cosmetics and dress herself up. She loves fun so much that her mother can't do much about her." He stopped at this point; then he added, "Many colleagues from the air force academy go out with her. I'm not the only one."

A clerk himself, Caishu realized that she was a "flower vase."[8] Before he could say a word, Manqian's laughter exploded like bubbling water as she said, "You could call that girl an aircraft carrier." Caishu laughed involuntarily. Tianjian seemed momentarily stunned by the remark, but he quickly regained his composure and started to laugh too.

Having made the remark, Manqian was irritated with herself for not having weighed her words before uttering them. As she looked at Tianjian she saw that his smile was perfunctory at best and was doubly unhappy that she might have offended him. After all, that girl might be his girlfriend. She felt she had spoken more than usual, and her garrulousness had caused her gaffe. As she mulled this over, she lost her enthusiasm and began to watch her words. At the same time she noticed that Tianjian had become inhibited. Maybe she was just being too suspicious.

The only one who remained unruffled was Caishu. He kept talking about this and that and eased the discomfort between host and guest. The dinner seemed interminably long. When it was finally over, Tianjian said good-bye to Caishu and Manqian, thanking her again and again and praising her excellent cooking. She, of course, knew this was his social routine, but from his repeated thanks she could see his respect for her and felt somewhat pleased. As she and her husband saw Tianjian out of the courtyard, her husband said, "Tianjian, if you don't mind this place being shabby, just drop in and visit us when you have the time. In any case, Manqian is home most of the time, and she's bored. You two can talk."

"Of course, I'd love to come. But I'm afraid people like me are so crass that we aren't qualified to speak to Biaosao." Though a smile lessened the severity of his tone, his reply implied hostility and challenge. Fortunately, the dark night by the front door concealed their faces and allowed Manqian to blush in safety.

Assuming a normal tone of voice, Manqian said, "I'm only afraid you wouldn't be willing to come. If you came, I'd be more than pleased. I've been a housekeeper for so long that I can only talk about homemaking. What's more, I've never been a good conversationalist."

"Don't be polite, either of you," Caishu interrupted. Thus, amid abundant "Good-byes," and "Take cares," Tianjian left them.

Two days later, in the afternoon, Manqian was just planning to knit something new from the yarn she had unraveled from an old sweater, soaked, and hung out in the sun to straighten, when suddenly she heard Tianjian coming. She felt that he had come especially for her that day, because he knew it was too early for her husband to have returned from work. This knowledge made her very constrained and ill at ease. She said hello, she asked how he had found the time to come, and then she couldn't think of another word to say. The friendliness of two days past seemed to have disappeared.

Spying the yarn on the table, Tianjian smiled. "I came especially to give you a hand," he said. Hoping to ease her own unnatural reserve, Manqian suddenly became unusually bold and said, "You came at the right time. I was worried because there was no one to help me with this. Caishu's wrists are clumsy and he can't do this properly. Now I have a perfect chance to try you out, though I'm afraid you may not have the patience. First let me separate the yarn."

So one stretched the yarn in both hands, while the other wound it into separate balls. Even when they said nothing to each other, the yarn maintained a continual contact between them and spared them the trouble of looking for things to say. When two or three balls of yarn had been wound, Manqian, afraid that Tianjian might have become bored, suggested he quit, but he refused and continued helping her until all the yarn on the table had been wound up. At this point he rose, commenting that he hoped his wrists and patience had passed her test. He said he must leave and couldn't wait for Caishu to come home.

With great sincerity, Manqian apologized. "I've put you through too much! I'm afraid you'll be scared to come back again after this punishment."

Tianjian only smiled.

After that time, Tianjian would come to sit for a while every three or four days. Manqian noticed that, except for one Sunday when he invited her and her husband out to a restaurant, Tianjian had never come on a Sunday. When Tianjian came, Caishu was usually at work. She knew that Tianjian enjoyed her company, and his affection for her subconsciously improved her own self-image. Besides adding a bit of mild excitement to her humdrum existence, his interest also restored her shaky self-confidence—proving that she had not passed her prime and that life had not completely eroded her charms.

To prove to a woman that she is attractive, there is no better way than wooing her. For single girls in their prime, this type of proof is due recognition of their desirableness. For those who are married and approaching middle age, this poof is not only solace but also must be considered a compliment. Those women who, when young, set the highest standards in selecting their beaux frequently lower their standards when they find themselves at the twilight of their emotions. Persons who never could have become their husbands now have a chance to be just that.

Manqian had already reached a stage in life when she needed proof and compliments. She was certain that she and Tianjian would never fall in love—at least she would not love him with any passion. She was not worried about the future. She had a husband—that was her best security, her best defense against Tianjian. Her own marriage marked a line in her friendship with Tianjian that neither was to cross. Tianjian was a truly likable person. She kept that knowledge to herself, unwilling to give him any more definite signs of her liking by calling him "lovable." No wonder Caishu said Tianjian was a lady's man. When Manqian thought of Tianjian's girlfriends, an inexplicable annoyance surfaced. Maybe he considered her one of his many girlfriends. No, she would never consent to be that type of girlfriend, and he would not treat her like that. He had never treated her flippantly, in a materialistic manner. His frequent visits with her fully showed his capacity for quietness. After Tianjian had visited her a number of times, she was often tempted to ask him if what her husband had said of him, that he was really "madly in love," was true, but she was afraid to betray her secret, her vague sense of jealousy, by her tone of voice or choice of words. So she held herself back. This was also a secret she wanted to keep from her husband. Hence she never breathed a word to Caishu about Tianjian's frequent visits. Gradually she developed a routine. Every other day she prepared (never admitting she hoped) for him to visit her. After lunch she would apply light makeup to her face. Despite their familiarity with each other, whenever she heard him come in she became excited, and it required tremendous effort on her part to dispel the involuntary flush on her face before she came in.

In this way a new meaning seemed to enter her life. A month or so later it was winter, the best season in the mountain-ringed city. Day after day of brilliant sunshine dazzled newcomers, who could not believe that the weather could be so beautiful, particularly those who had been used to dramatic seasonal changes. Daylight emerged in tender, rosy morning rays and disappeared in the rich yellow of evening, completely different from the winter in the north, which brought chilly gusts of wind. Because the city was located at a high altitude, it was said that a thin layer of fog surrounded it in winter and thus diminished the possibility of its being attacked by enemy planes. The streets, as a result, were thronged with more shoppers than before.

One day Tianjian came to visit Manqian as usual. After sitting for a while, he said he had to leave. When she asked him why he was in a hurry, since it was still early, he replied, "The weather is too nice to be true. How can you stay home doing nothing? Why don't you take a walk with me."

The question put Manqian in a dilemma. If she said she was willing to be bored at home, she would be telling an obvious lie. There wasn't even enough truth in it to fool herself. On the other hand, to stroll with Tianjian in public, she felt, would be improper and might cause gossip. Wary of this, but unable to tell him her true feelings, she replied weakly, "If you're bored, please suit yourself."

Tianjian seemed to understand her. In a half-serious and half-joking tone he said, "It's not me. It's you who must be feeling bored sitting her all the time. I have lots of activities. What's wrong with going out together? Would Caishu think I've abducted you?"

Manqian was in more of a dilemma. Ambiguously she murmured, "It's not like that. You just go ahead. I won't keep you."

Knowing that he could not force her, Tianjian left. After he left Manqian felt disappointed for a while, with the knowledge that she had really wanted him to stay. It was only a little after three o'clock, a long time before evening—a stretch of time lay in front of her as impassable as a desert. At first, time had passed in blocks, but once Tianjian had left, the hours, minutes, and seconds, as if removed from their spines, loosened into countless tiny bits and pieces. No event could serve as a thread to string them together. She was used to lonely afternoons, but she couldn't bear this one. She thought she really should have gone out with Tianjian because she needed small items like toothpaste and a toothbrush. Though he was not her husband, she could justify the trip as business, which would soothe her conscience and provide an excuse to anyone who asked. No one could say she had asked him to accompany her, nor gone along just for the sake of accompanying him.

The next day the weather became even more beautiful. The events of the previous day had left a residue powerful enough to vibrate in her heart, and Manqian could not sit still at home. In the morning there were some household chores for her to do, and because of the air raids, stores and shops would not be open until three in the afternoon. Not having been out for a few days, she noticed some new stores that copied the style of the stores in Shanghai and Hong Kong. Standing before a new drugstore and looking at the sample goods advertised in the windows, she pondered what to buy. Suddenly she heard a man's voice behind her. It was Tianjian's. Eyes fixed on the windows, she blushed. Her vision blurring, she could not tell what she was looking at. Her heart felt as if it were being pummeled, and for a moment she hadn't the nerve to turn and call to him. Then as she began to turn, she heard a woman talking and laughing with him. Involuntarily she stopped herself. After the footsteps had passed her, she turned around and saw him and the woman enter the drugstore. Though the woman's face was partly blocked by him, she did get a rear view of the woman, a woman shapely enough to make an onlooker want to run ahead and catch the front view. Manqian, awakening from a dream, realized the woman must be the "aircraft carrier." All of a sudden she lost her courage to enter the drugstore and quickly left the place as if she were avoiding them. She no longer had any desire to buy sundries. Her heart and feet were as heavy as lead, and she could not walk home, so she hired a rickshaw.

Once she settled down, she fully comprehended how much anguish she had felt. She knew she had no reason to feel that way, but who could argue with a person's heart? She didn't hate Tianjian, but she felt uneasy, as if she realized the happiness of the past month really amounted to nothing. No, it did not amount to nothing. If it had, she wouldn't be feeling the way she did. She yearned to see him at once to calm her much-confused soul. What she had witnessed that day she could not fully accept, and she wanted him to prove to her that what she had seen was an illusion. All in all, she felt he must explain things to her. Would he come that day? Probably not. The next day? The next day seemed so far away. She really could not wait that long. Also at the same time she felt conscience stricken, afraid that her husband might notice her agitated state.

That evening when Caishu came home, she was an unusually attentive wife, and she asked him this and that. Meanwhile, she valiantly tried to prevent her vexations from intruding into her consciousness and from making her answers to her husband appear incoherent. After they went to bed, dreading insomnia, she concentrated with all her might on removing thoughts of Tianjian, or at least on putting them aside. She did not want to think of them now. It was like putting fish and meat in a refrigerator overnight in hot weather.

The next day when she awoke, the agony of the evening before had slipped away with sleep, and she felt silly for having exaggerated matters. What did it matter to her that Tianjian had gone out with some woman? After all, he would be coming to see her soon, and she could subtly tease him about it. But as soon as noon passed, her heart fluttered, and she became fidgety, eagerly awaiting him.

Tianjian did not appear that afternoon, nor the next day. In fact, he didn't come even on the fifth day. He had never stayed away for this length of time since they had come to know each other. Then a thought occurred to Manqian: "Maybe, through some uncanny telepathy, he has become aware of my attitude toward him and is afraid to come anymore. But how could he know my mind?" In any case, it was better to abandon hope, never to expect to see him again. Having tasted the ironic paradoxes that life offers, she knew how God fools everyone. To turn hope into reality, she concluded, the first thing to do was to stop yearning and prepare herself for a surprise later. This "abandoning of hope" lasted three days, during which period there was no trace of Tianjian. It seemed that God did not care to correct any error that had been made, pretending not to know that her "abandoning of hope" was only a debased form of hope and allowing her to be confirmed in her disappointment.

During those eight days Manqian seemed gravely ill and aged mentally ten years. All the emotions that accompany love she tasted in a double dose. Her weary body and mind were as tense as ever. Like an insomniac, the more exhausted she was, the tauter her nerves became. Several times she wanted to write Tianjian, having drafted the letter many times in her mind, but her pride prevented her from doing so. The thought "maybe he'll show up today or tomorrow" stopped her from writing. In her husband's presence, she tried her best to appear normal, but this required a lot of energy and effort. Therefore, she wanted her husband to stay out of the house so that she would not have to expend energy on him. But once he left the house, alone with herself, she felt defenseless and besieged by vexations. It was literally impossible for her not to think of the matter. Whatever she was doing, she inevitably thought of Tianjian—she was like an ox turning a grindstone. In these eight days the physical separation between her and Tianjian enhanced their mental affinity. Previously she had been unwilling to think of him and forbade herself to think of him. Now she not only missed him, she also hated him. The last time he said good-bye to her, they had been on speaking terms, but during these eight days it was as if her heart had been fermenting, intensifying her feelings for him. Her attempt to turn despair into hope had failed. It was so unfair that he had obtained her affection without wooing her. She blamed herself for being weak. She must discipline herself into not wanting to see him. At the most she'd see him once more. She'd have to be cool to him, and so let him know that she didn't care whether he came or not.

Another day passed. After lunch Manqian was washing her silk stockings, which could not withstand the maid's crude hands—a conclusion Manqian had drawn from past experience. At this time the maid told her she was going out. Her hands covered in soapy water, Manqian did not rise to latch the door, merely telling the maid to close it. Meanwhile, Manqian thought that Christmas would come in a few days, followed by New Year's, and she wondered if she should send Tianjian a Christmas card—just a card with nothing else in it. Then she hated herself for being a fool, for not being able to forget him, for wanting to retain some contact with him. A little later, after washing the stockings and drying her hands, she was about to latch the door.

Then the door creaked open. When she saw it was Tianjian she felt so weak that she almost could not stand still. Dazed, she watched him close the door behind him and heard him laugh on his way in, yelling, "Why was the door left open? Are you home alone? I haven't seen you for a few days. How have you been?"

The tension she had been under the last eight days was suddenly released. She discovered that the bitter tears she had stored up within her were now threatening to pour out. Her intention of giving him a perfunctory smile failed to materialize. Lowering her head she said in a hoarse voice, "What a rare visitor!"

Tianjian sensed something unusual in the situation. Stupefied for a moment, he kept staring at her. Suddenly a smile emerged, and he walked toward her, whispering, "You seem unhappy today. Who are you mad at?"

For some reason none of the vituperative words she had prepared for him could come out. She felt the weight of silence on her increasing every second. With considerable effort she finally blurted out, "Why did you bother to come? Such beautiful weather! Why didn't you go out with your girlfriend?" After she said these words, she felt as if she had suffered many grievances, and it became even more difficult for her to hold back her tears. She thought to herself, "What a disaster! Now he sees through me!"

In her confusion, she discovered Tianjian's cradling her neck with his hands and gently kissing her eyes. "Silly child! Silly child!" he murmured.

Instinctively Manqian struggled free of his hands and ran to her room, saying repeatedly, "Go away! I don't want to see you today. Leave this instant!"

Tianjian left. But what happened that day completely changed his attitude toward Manqian. In his recollections of his dealings with her over the past month or so, he saw a fresh meaning that had wholly escaped him before. Looking back, he understood what had always made him come to see her. Like a lamp on a ship's stern, his reflection suddenly lit up the path it had sailed. At the same time, he thought he had the right to request something of her and even the obligation to conquer her. Though he had no idea how far he wanted to go with her, his male ego told him he must pursue his course until she frankly and uninhibitedly admitted that he was her lover.

As for Manqian, she knew her secret had been compromised. There was no retreat. Her only regret was that she had allowed him so much leeway, allowed him to think everything would come so easily. Therefore, she decided she must be cool to him, to discount the degree of intimacy between them, so that he would not take her for granted or at face value. She hoped this strategy of reverse psychology would lead him to beg sincerely for her love. Only in this manner could she have vengeance for what had happened today and so even the score with him. Her only worry was that he wouldn't come the next day. And when he did show up the next day, she had told her maid in advance that she was not well and so forced him to come some other time.

Tianjian assumed that Manqian was truly ill, and in his concern, immediately bought two small baskets of Chongqing tangerines and had a special messenger deliver them. Since it would not be appropriate to write a note, he attached his name card to the gift. A day later he sent a Christmas card and an invitation asking Manqian and her husband to Christmas dinner.

The reply was in Caishu's name, but the writing was apparently Manqian's. It said simply, "We dare not refuse your dinner invitation. Let us thank you in advance. See you on that day."

Tianjian though about this carefully and concluded that Manqian had implied she did not want him to see her. People who are capable of defending themselves don't shut their doors to callers. He thought he must behave with the magnanimity of a victor, as there was no present need to impose himself on her.

On Christmas evening Tianjian and Manqian met. Maybe it was because her passion toward him had cooled, or maybe she was emboldened by the presence of her husband. To his surprise, she was very calm. Many a time he had hoped to discover their mutual secret revealed either in her face or in her eyes, but he couldn't find any indication of it. The dinner went smoothly, but he was nonetheless disappointed. Then the New Year holidays came around and Caishu remained at home. Tianjian went to visit Manqian once, but he had no chance to talk to her. Moreover, she seemed rather distant toward him and left the room a few times under false pretenses. At first he thought her behavior was due to her bashfulness and was a little pleased. But then, when she seemed to be totally indifferent to him, he felt uneasy.

Caishu went back to work after the holidays. Tianjian visited Manqian again. Like severed silk, their earlier friendship could not be rejoined. Her stern looks made him feel restrained, and he experienced the vexation of having something slip through his fingers. He could not decide what approach to use with her: to remain cool and detached or to be rude and passionate. Watching her knit a sweater with her head bent, the uncontrollable slight blush on her face, her long eyelashes covering her eyes like a lampshade over a lamp, he was tempted to kiss her. He even walked toward her. Her bent face appeared even more flushed.

"You shouldn't be mad at me anymore," he said half questioningly.

"Me mad at you? No such thing," she replied, trying to appear calm.

"We get along quite well. Why must we hide our secrets and not say what's in our hearts?"

She was silent, mechanically knitting with increased speed. Edging toward her, he put his hands on her shoulders. She struggled free and knit at a furious pace. In a low but commanding voice she said, "Go away. There'll be a scandal if the maid sees us."

He had no choice but to release her. In an aggrieved tone, he said, "I know I'm not welcome anymore. I've come too often and become a pest. Please forgive me this time. I won't be a nuisance anymore." As he was saying that, he realized he had been extreme in his choice of words. If she did not respond to what he said, he had allowed himself no room for other maneuvers, and he must consider the whole matter a complete fiasco. But Manqian continued to knit, giving no response. The few minutes that went by in total silence were nearly as painfully long as several lifetimes. Knowing he could not force anything from her, he was so exasperated that the following exploded from his throat: "Okay, I'm going now. I'll never come again . . . and you just leave me alone too."

As soon as that was said, he went to fetch his hat. Suddenly, Manqian raised her head. With a bashful smile she looked at the fiery-tempered Tianjian and said, with her head lowered again, "See you tomorrow then. I plan to go shopping. Would you have time to come with me tomorrow after lunch?"

Tianjian was bewildered for a moment before he realized that he had won. He was so ecstatic that he wanted to jump up and down. He felt he must kiss her to mark this moment of triumph. Then he realized she wouldn't dare to do such a thing, and he must be wary of the maid. As he left her, he was elated, thinking another romance of his had borne fruit, except he had not celebrated this victory with a kiss, as was his custom. And that must be considered the only flaw in an otherwise perfect victory.

This feeling of something less than perfection persisted and increased in the three or four weeks that followed. Even though Tianjian and Manqian became closer, he discovered that she was always evasive about physical intimacy. Not only did she seem to make few demands on him, but also she would not try to please him. Even when there were opportunities for embraces, he had to struggle with her in order to kiss her. Their kisses were never passionate, full, or harmonious.

Not endowed by nature with stimulating or intoxicating sexual charm, Manqian was not easily aroused or carried away. During courtship she was always a cool and reserved woman. Her low-key approach, ironically, stimulated Tianjian greatly. Her indifference seemed to imply a contemptuous challenge to his passion. It stirred up even greater desire in him and intensified his temper. The situation was like the spilling of a drop of cold water on a coal-burning stove, creating a *shee* sound and giving off steam. Every time she rejected him, he invariably lost his temper and was on the verge of asking her if she ever allowed her husband to be intimate with her. But he thought such a question would only imply that he was obsessed with sex and too vulgar. He firmly believed that just as there was a code of honor among thieves, there were ethical rules governing extramarital relations. It seemed to him that a husband had the right to question his wife about her relationship with a lover, but never vice versa—the lover inquiring into his mistress's relationship with her husband.

After several rejections, Tianjian gradually realized that his time and energy had been wasted. His efforts in keeping up appearances and his careful calculations to prevent suspicion by Caishu and others had all come to naught. He had, in fact, obtained nothing. It was like wrapping up an empty box and sending it by registered mail. This type of romance he could not drop and yet it was exasperating and boring. Something must come of it! He must find or make an opportunity to capture her body and soul. A few days after the Lantern Festival, his landlady's family would be going to the country for a few days, and, taking the initiative, he told the landlady he would watch the house for her. He planned to invite Manqian over, and if he failed in this attempt, he decided that he'd end all dealings with her. It would be far better to break off the relationship than to keep it going in a lukewarm and noncommittal manner.

Who could have known that he would break the ice today? His passion temporarily weakened Manqian's stubborn resistance. As if affected by his passion, she seemed to warm to him considerably. Their romance could be considered complete and concluded at this point. Nonetheless, Tianjian experienced the emptiness one usually feels after having achieved a goal. The restraint that Manqian exercised during her indiscretion seemed to suggest that she had not treated him fairly. So, in a way his success could be viewed as another failure. Because he was not happy with this outcome, he ended up feeling guilty for having cheated Manqian and grievously wronged Caishu. Since there were attractive women available, why must he dally with his *biaosao*? However, her abrupt departure afterward and her unwillingness to listen to his explanations and apologies made it easier for him to get out of this mess. He could now cast her aside completely on the pretext that he had affronted her and felt too ashamed to see her. And if she should seek him out in the future, he would think of some way to handle her then.

Without giving any thought to the future, Manqian ran home in one breath and collapsed on the bed. As sober as if she had just been splashed with ice water, she knew that she did not love Tianjian. She had desired him before because of her pride, which had now vanished without a trace. The romantic tryst of a moment ago left its ghostly shadows, which seemed imprinted with a thin impression of

Tianjian. Those disgusting, lingering sentiments! When would they completely fade away? When Caishu comes home in a while, how can I face him? she wondered. That night, Caishu did not detect anything strange about his wife.

Manqian was worried that Tianjian would come back to her, like a bad habit that was difficult to break. But fortunately he didn't show up for several weeks. Since he had had her once, he had obtained the right to have her again. If she were alone with him, she simply would not be able to cope with him. She knew he was a gentleman who would not betray her and would help her keep their secret. But what if the secret bore some kind of fruit that would be impossible to cover up? No, absolutely impossible! Could such a coincidence happen in this world? She was sorry she had been foolish, and she hated Tianjian for his impudence. She did not dare think about the matter any further.

The weather continued to be unbearably pleasant. It was as if Manqian's heart were a tree hollowed out with worms and unable to show any sign of growth. But also for this reason she was spared the usual vexations that came to her each spring.

One day right after lunch, Caishu was about to take a nap when suddenly air raid sirens sounded, destroying the calm of that pleasant day. The streets filled with commotion. Because the city had not heard any sirens in three months, everyone panicked. Chinese fighter planes climbed into the sky, and the clouds were filled with the sounds of their engines as they flew away toward the city's outskirts. The old maid, carrying a satchel on her back, demanded a few dollars from Manqian and breathlessly ran to the air shelter trench behind the alley for protection. Before she left, she said, "Madam, you and the master had better get going."

Lazily lounging in bed, Caishu told his wife that it was most likely a false alarm and he saw no need to fight the crowd and dust in any air shelter trench. Like many people, Manqian had the peculiar notion that even though many had died in the bombings, she herself would never be among the victims. Her husband had often quoted her as saying, "The chance of being bombed to death are as slim as winning the first prize in the aviation lottery drawings." A while later the second air raid warning siren sounded. The siren, with its long wails, was like a huge iron throat spewing cold air toward the blue sky. When the neighborhood sank into an eerie silence, Caishu and his wife became terrified. At first they had been too lazy to move; now they were too scared to move. Manqian stayed in the courtyard by herself. Holding her breath, she gazed at the enemy planes entering the air space above the city with contemptuous ease, as if taunting the antiaircraft guns.

The sound of the machine guns was like that of a stutterer, unable to express his meaning to the sky; or like phlegm stuck in the throat, unable to come out. Suddenly Manqian felt weak all over and did not dare to stand or look anymore. Quickly, she ran toward her bedroom. As she was about to step into the house, a noise constricted her heart and dragged it along into the abyss. As her heart began to sink, another explosion followed, lifting her heart from its depths and leaving her eardrums ringing with sound. The windows shook uneasily within their frames. The lidded cups on the tea tray clanked against one another, making their own music. So frightened was she that she fell into a chair and held her husband's hand. Whatever resentments she felt against him all vanished so long as he was close by her now. Her head seemed to have been packed with the commotions of the whole sky. The noises of machine guns and of bombs, distinct from those of the airplanes, wreaked havoc in her mind. She could not dispel them.

No one knows how long it was before calm was restored. The birds in the trees, after what seemed a long period of silence, began to chirp again. The blue sky acted as if nothing had happened, and one lone Chinese fighter plane suddenly flew overhead. Everything was over. Sometime later, the warning was lifted. Though there were no immediate stirrings in the neighborhood, the city seemed to be coming back to life. The old maid returned with her satchel, and Caishu and his wife went to the main street to find out what had happened.

There was more activity than usual in the streets, people gathering to read the notice written on a strip of red cloth that had just been posted by the Air Raid Prevention Committee: "Six enemy aircraft bombed the city at random. Our casualties were extremely light. After a crushing counterattack from our planes, one enemy plane was shot down, and the rest fled the province. Another enemy plane was seriously damaged and was forced to land somewhere in the outlying area. We are still searching for it." Caishu and his wife read the notice and simultaneously said they would be able to get more definitive information if they saw Tianjian. Then Caishu rather casually asked his wife why Tianjian hadn't come to see them for some time.

At that point Tianjian and his plane had gone down in the rubble some forty miles from the city. He had obtained his cruel peace. A man who had been active in the air all his life could find rest only underground.

The news came to Caishu and his wife three days later. He shed some tears, which were mingled with pride for being a relative of the dead. For the first time Manqian felt Tianjian was truly pitiable. Her feelings were exactly those an adult had toward a naughty child who was sound asleep. Tianjian's good looks, his ability, decisiveness, and smoothness were terribly attractive to women when he was alive, but in death all his qualities had now been shrunken, softened, jabbed through by death, as if they were those of a child and couldn't be taken seriously. At the same time she felt the relief of having been set free. What about the secret she had had with him? At first she did not want to think about it, something she'd like to keep a secret even from herself. Now, the secret, having suddenly lost some of its repugnancy, was transformed into a souvenir worthy of being kept and preserved. It was like a maple leaf or lotus petal to be folded in a book, to be allowed to fade in color with time; but every time you open the book it's still there, and it makes you shiver unintentionally. It was as if a part of Manqian's body had been contaminated by death, as if a part of her body had been snatched away by Tianjian and had died also. Fortunately, that part of the body was far away from her, like skin that has been shed, or hair or nails that have been cut and no longer hurt or itch.

Soon, various city groups sponsored a memorial service for Tianjian, at which the remains of one enemy plane were displayed. Caishu and his wife attended the service. The sponsors had asked Caishu to give a talk or be responsible for some program, as was appropriate for the relative of the deceased. But Caishu staunchly refused to do anything. He did not care to appear in public on account of the deceased and was unwilling to cheapen his private grief by making a public exhibition of it. This attitude increased Manqian's respect for him. After some hullabaloo, Tianjian's name, along with his corpse, went cold and was forgotten. It was only after two or three weeks that Tianjian's name was mentioned again between husband and wife. It was right after dinner, and they were chatting in the bedroom.

Caishu said, "All the symptoms are unmistakable. Since we're destined to have a child, there's no way to run away from it. We should have a child, and you shouldn't hate having one. We can afford a child at the moment. Maybe the war will be over before your delivery date. If that's the case, all the more reason for us not to worry about it. I say, if you have a boy, we should call him Tianjian, in memory of our friendship with him during those few months. What do you say?"

Manqian was looking for something. She walked to the window, pulled open the desk drawer, and, with her head lowered, fingered through all the items in it. Meanwhile she said, "I don't want to. Didn't you see the 'Aircraft Carrier' during the service? She was all tears and mucus, and she was dressed like Tianjian's widow. You know what kind of person Tianjian was. The two must have known each other very well. Who knows if she hasn't borne a child for him? Let her have a kid to honor him. I wouldn't want to. And let me tell you something else. I won't love this baby, because I never wanted it."

As usual, Caishu made no comment on what his wife had said. His wife's last sentence increased his alarm, as if he were responsible for the child. Leaning against the back of the chair, he yawned and said, "I'm tired. Oh well, we'll see. What are you looking for?"

"Nothing in particular," Manqian answered ambivalently. Closing the drawer, she said, "I'm tired too. I've got a slight temperature, but I haven't done anything today, have I?"

Indolently Caishu looked at his wife's still slim figure, and his eyes filled with infinite tenderness and affection.

Translated by Nathan K. Mao

NOTES

∾

GOD'S DREAM

1. "Accretionism" (literally, "the theory of successive change" [*cenghua lun* 層化論]) is Qian's term for a historiographical approach promoted by the revisionist historian Gu Jiegang 顧頡剛 (1893–1980), who sought to destroy the myth of a Chinese golden age of high antiquity (which he called "spurious history" [*weishi* 偽史]) in favor of "an ancient Chinese history that was created in stages" (*cenglei di zaocheng de Zhongguo gushi* 層累地造成的中國古史) through the legends of successive ages. Gu elaborated these views in vol. 1 of *Debates on Ancient History* (*Gushi bian* 古史辨), which is analyzed in Laurence A. Schneider, "From Textual Criticism to Social Criticism: The Historiography of Ku Chieh-kang," *Journal of Asian Studies* 28, no. 4 (1969): 771–88. *Gushi bian* was reprinted in seven volumes by the Hong Kong publisher Taiping shuju in 1962. The "New Life Movement" was a quasi-fascist cultural movement launched by the Kuomintang (KMT, or Guomindang 國民黨) government in February 1934 at the behest of Chiang Kai-shek (Jiang Jieshi 蔣介石 [1887–1975]) and his wife, Soong Mei-ling (Song Meiling 宋美齡 [ca. 1897–2003]). The movement, designed as an ideological alternative to Communism, called on citizens to embrace Confucian precepts of loyalty, self-cultivation, and obedience while practicing good hygiene and rejecting such "bourgeois" habits as dancing and gambling.

2. This phrase reverses the classical Chinese idiom "to run fifty steps and laugh at someone who has run one hundred," which derives from a parable in the classical Confucian text *Mencius* (*Mengzi* 孟子, ca. fourth–third centuries B.C.E.). In the story, Mencius relates to King Hui of the Liang kingdom how a soldier who had run fifty steps in retreat from battle mocked a companion who had run one hundred. The phrase has subsequently been used to refer to a hypocrite who is guilty, to a lesser degree, of the same fault she or he condemns in others. In the 1946 edition, Qian had fifty steps laughing at one hundred.

3. A harmonious and inseparable conjugal couple (or pair of lovers) was said to "nest together and fly together" (*shuangsu shuangfei* 雙宿雙飛) like a pair of swallows or mandarin ducks. "Nest together," as Qian's use of the phrase in the next paragraph implies, is also a euphemism for sex. One anonymous Tang poem contains the couplet "Better to be a pair of mandarin ducks in a pond / Nesting together and flying together for a lifetime" (*Buru chishang yuanyang niao, shuangsu shuangfei guo yisheng* 不如池上鴛鴦鳥，雙宿雙飛過一生).

4. This title seems to mock autobiographers who claim that their works cannot cover the entirety of their lives. The precise target is obscure.

5. A semimythical figure, Lao-tzu (Laozi 老子 [fl. fourth century B.C.E.]) is the putative author of the *Tao te ching* (*Daodejing* 道德經), the foundational philosophical text of Daoism. Here, Qian puns on the name Lao-tzu, which means "old master" but which—turning on the meaning of the character for *tzu*—can also be interpreted literally as "old son." The stories about both Lao-tzu and the Yellow Emperor (Huangdi 黃帝) spending a long time in utero are obscure to me but likely date to Daoist texts of the Han dynasty (206 B.C.E.–220 C.E.), which saw a revival of interest in both mythical figures.

6. The 1946 edition reads: ". . . or a supreme dictator (like Hitler) . . ." Qian added "uni-testicled" in the 1983 edition.

7. In the 1946 edition, this sentence is slightly different and is followed by an additional sentence: "Savage man, suspecting that divinities exist everywhere, submits to and worships them. Not even a shade of this thought had occurred to God."

8. The 1946 edition reads: "He wanted a companion to worship and praise him, so as to dispel the present silence."

9. The 1946 edition has an additional sentence here: "In pinching together a man out of a dream, he was just like those people who can slip into a dream while pinching their noses" (that is, indulge in impossible fantasies).

10. The 1946 edition reads: "His creation of man would have been a great topic for a war of words."

11. Lin Daiyu 林黛玉, the melancholy female protagonist of *Dream of the Red Chamber*, is given to poetically pathetic gestures, the most famous of which is her burying of flower petals in the Grand View Garden after witnessing an apparent betrayal by her bosom friend, Jia Baoyu.

12. The 1946 edition reads: ". . . appearance-conscious men always put on effeminate airs, such that fashionable women have to think of ways to be even more original and appear sexy."

13. This sentence is in the 1946 and 2001 editions but not in the 1983 edition.

14. Here Qian applies to the story of Genesis the famous injunction from the Confucian *Analects* (book 6, chap. 20) that humans should "respect ghosts and divinities, but keep them at a distance" (*jing guishen er yuan zhi* 敬鬼神而遠之).

15. The Chinese idea that women are waterlike probably dates back to Ming dynasty vernacular fiction. Because water changes its shape to fit any vessel, it has traditionally been taken as a metaphor for inconstancy and moral relativism. Additionally, because water always flows from high ground to low, the phrase "flow downward" (*xialiu* 下流) has come to refer to moral degeneration and indecency.

16. The 1983 edition (but not the 1946 or 2001 editions) reads: "The more God thought about it, the angrier he became."

17. In the 1983 edition, the last sentence reads simply: "Okay?"

18. Darkie brand toothpaste (Heiren yagao 黑人牙膏 [literally, "Black Man Toothpaste"]) was founded in Shanghai in 1933 and became famous for its logo featuring a black man in a black top hat with gleaming white teeth. The company moved to Taiwan with the Nationalists in 1949 and, in 1990, removed the racial slur from the brand's English name by modifying it to Darlie. The logo and Chinese brand remain unchanged.

19. The 1946 edition reads: "Luckily he hadn't made man beautiful, otherwise he wouldn't have had to bring a gift either! He then ordered man to explain his request."

20. Parallel prose and regulated verse are two Chinese poetic forms governed by strict rules about symmetry, parallelism, and tonal balance.

21. The 1983 edition reads: "Once again, he couldn't help admiring the exquisiteness of his art. As a result, God felt at peace."

22. The Chinese idiom "Humans beseech Heaven when in dire straits" (*ren qiong ze hutian* 人窮則呼天) captures the tendency of humans to seek divine intervention when compelled by circumstance.

23. This Buddhist-sounding line is an excellent example of Qian's fondness for mixing allusions, one ancient and one modern in this case, as a way of obliquely making fun of his contemporaries. The phrase parodies a famous line attributed to Cao Cao 曹操 (155–220), a military leader and chancellor of the Eastern Han dynasty (25–220). In the historical novel *Romance of the Three Kingdoms* (*Sanguo yanyi* 三國演義), which is largely responsible for Cao Cao's subsequent reputation as an archvillain, Cao justifies his backstabbing of a sworn brother by remarking that "I would rather wrong the world than have the world wrong me" (*Ningke wo fu tianxia ren, buke tianxia ren fu wo* 寧可我負天下人，不可天下人負我). The reference to eating grass likely alludes to Lu Xun's 魯迅 (1881–1936) self-mocking remark that "I'm like a cow, eating grass and squeezing out milk and blood" (*Wo haoxiang yizhi niu, chide shi cao, jichulaide shi niunai, xue* 我好像一隻牛，吃的是草，擠出來的是牛奶、血). Lu Xun also likens himself to a humble beast of burden elsewhere in his works, most notably in the poem "Self-Mockery" (Zichao 自嘲), which contains the famous line "Brow arched, I coolly defy a thousand pointing fingers / Head bowed, I serve as the children's willing ox" (*Hengmei lengdui qian fuzhi, fushou ganwei ruzi niu* 橫眉冷對千夫指，俯首甘爲孺子牛). The "milk and blood" comment appears in his common-law wife Xu Guangping's 許廣平 (1898–1968) dedication to her book *Xinwei de jinian* 欣慰的紀念 (*A Memento of Consolation*) (Beijing: Renmin wenxue chubanshe, 1953).

24. Tripitaka is the Buddhist monk protagonist in the famous Ming dynasty vernacular novel *Journey to the West*. Accompanied by three anthropomorphic beasts with magical powers (Monkey, Piggy, and Sandy), Tripitaka travels to India to obtain Buddhist sutras and along the way experiences a series of adventures, including encounters with carnivorous monsters.

25. This expression refers to a situation in which one not only fails to gain any benefit but ends up inconveniencing oneself to boot. The proverb appears in slightly different form in chap. 12 of the Qing vernacular novel *The Scholars* (*Rulin waishi* 儒林外史): "be unable to taste lamb meat and end up reeking of mutton for nothing" (*yangrou bu ceng chi, kong re yishen shan* 羊肉不曾喫，空惹一身羶).

26. The 1946 edition has an additional sentence here: "His protruding stomach made him look like a patient suffering from goiter or a country suffering from inflation. But the goat's horns . . ."

27. "Offering to a Crocodile" (Ji e'yu wen 祭鱷魚文) is a celebrated parodic essay by the Tang dynasty (618–907) essayist, poet, and courtier Han Changli 韓昌黎 (768–824), better known as Han Yu 韓愈. In the piece, addressed to a crocodile that has been terrorizing a nearby village, Han, the newly arrived district magistrate, threatens the crocodile with death if he does not cease eating humans and accept banishment to the ocean. An English translation of this work is in David Pollard, trans. and ed., *The Chinese Essay* (New York: Columbia University Press, 2000), 33.

28. In Chinese folklore, dragons are serpent shaped, and black dragons carry a pearl under their chins. The terms "black dragon pearls" (*lizhu* 驪珠) and "pearls from below the chin" (*lingxia zhi zhu* 領下之珠) came to refer generally to anything precious, or to the essence of something, such as a piece of writing. An early parable about black dragon pearls occurs in the "Lie Yukou" 列禦寇 section of the Daoist philosophical text *Zhuangzi* 莊子.

29. A prevalent belief in traditional Chinese medicine is that consuming the "essence" of a wild beast endows the consumer with that animal's qualities, such as fierceness or virility.

30. This cliché appears in traditional Chinese literary romances, as well as a vow of brotherhood made by the bandits in the vernacular novel *The Water Margin*.

CAT

Translation revised from Yiran Mao, *Cat, by Qian Zhongshu: A Translation and Critical Introduction* (Hong Kong: Joint Publishing, 2001).

1. The Forbidden City is located in the center of Beijing, opposite what is now Tiananmen Square. First constructed in the period 1406 to 1420, the complex served as the seat of imperial rule from the mid-Ming through the Qing dynasty.

2. Les Pléiades (The Pleiades) refers to a number of "star" poets of the sixteenth-century French Renaissance. While the exact makeup of this canon varies by source, its core members include Joachim du Bellay (1522–1560), "prince of poets" Pierre de Ronsard (1524–1585), and Jean-Antoine de Baïf (1532–1589).

3. Shakespeare, *Sonnets* 127–52. In the 1946 edition, this and the following sentence read: "This cat is beautiful and dark, so we might as well follow Shakespeare and call her 'Dark Lady.' "

4. Daji 妲己 was the favored concubine of the reputedly tyrannical King Zhou of the Shang dynasty (sixteenth–eleventh centuries B.C.E.). She was the daughter of Yousushi 有蘇氏, the chief of an ancient tribe. When King Zhou defeated Yousushi, Yousushi presented Zhou with his daughter, who is said to have aided Zhou in his tyrannical rule. Ever since, Daji has been a classic Chinese symbol of beauty and viciousness.

5. Posthumous names and honorary titles were conferred on deceased emperors, aristocrats, and distinguished ministers to immortalize their deeds.

6. The League of Nations, the precursor to the United Nations, was formed to preserve peace and foster international cooperation through pledges by member states to eschew aggression and take united action in applying economic and military sanctions. In 1937, however, the league condemned Japan's Manchurian policy but failed to take forceful action against its aggression in China.

7. Tang Ruoshi 湯若士 (Tang Xianzu 湯顯祖 [1550–1617]) was a playwright born in Zhangle, Jiangxi. For his most famous work, see Tang Ruoshi, *The Peony Pavilion: Mudan ting*, trans. Cyril Birch, 2nd ed. (Bloomington: Indiana University Press, 2002). Xie Zaihang 謝在杭 (Xie Zhaozhe 謝肇淛 [1567–1624]) was a Ming dynasty writer born in Linchuan, Fujian.

8. Yuan (1271–1368); Ming (1368–1644); Qing (1644–1911).

9. Beijing (Northern Capital) was renamed Beiping (Northern Peace) in 1928, when the Nationalist government moved the capital to Nanjing (Southern Capital, or Nanking). The name reverted to Beijing in 1949 when the Communists took over and declared Beijing the capital of the People's Republic of China.

10. Over forty specimens of *Homo erectus*, who lived approximately 500,000 years ago, were unearthed at Zhoukoudian (thirty miles southwest of Beijing) in the 1920s and 1930s and came to be known as Peking (Beijing) man. In addition to fossil remains, many stone tools were found, along with evidence that *Homo erectus pekinensis* had mastered the art of fire making.

11. The 1930s saw ongoing disputes between writers and critics associated with the Beijing school (Capital school) and the Shanghai school. Lu Xun ridiculed the bickering between these schools in his essay "The Beijing School and the Shanghai School" (Jingpai yu haipai 京派與海派).

12. With the abduction of the last emperor of the Qing dynasty on February 12, 1912, the feudal system that had prevailed in China for more than two thousand years ended. In this story, the two old men are branded as old-fashioned remnants of a bygone age.

13. The Chinese democratic revolution led by Dr. Sun Zhongshan 孫中山 (Sun Yat-sen [1866–1925]) overthrew the Qing dynasty and established the Republic of China.

14. During the latter years of the Qing dynasty, certain official titles could be purchased. Unscrupulous purchasers exploited their newly acquired prestige for graft and other forms of self-aggrandizement, a practice chronicled in highly popular exposé novels such as Wu Jianren's (1866–1910) *Ershi nian mudu zhi guai xianzhuang* 二十年目睹之怪現狀 (serialized 1903–1910) and Li Boyuan's (1867–1906) *Guanchang xianxing ji* 官場現形記 (1903), both available in partial English translation as Wu Wo-yao, *Vignettes from the Late Ch'ing: Bizarre Happenings Eyewitnessed over Two Decades*, trans. Shih Shun-Liu (Hong Kong: Chinese University of Hong Kong, 1975), and *Officialdom Unmasked*, trans. T. L. Yang (Hong Kong: Hong Kong University Press, 2001), respectively.

15. Wuchang, the capital of Hubei province, was the site of a military uprising launched on October 10, 1911, by anti-Qing soldiers of the New Army, aided by members of the Tongmeng hui 同盟會, a group founded by Sun Yat-sen that later evolved into the Nationalist Party. This uprising was followed by the new military government's declaration of independence from the Qing dynasty.

16. The Westernization Movement was initiated and promoted by bureaucrats such as Yi Xin, Zen Guofan, Li Hongzhang, Zuo Zongtang, and Zhang Zhidong in the latter half of the nineteenth century to introduce Western military and industrial technology in order to preserve the rule of the Qing government. See Bai Shouyi, *Zhongguo tongshi gangyao* 中國通史綱要 (*Essentials of General Chinese History*) (Shanghai: Shanghai renmin, 1980).

17. In the 1946 edition, this sentence ends: ". . . which looked like rose petals floating in milk."

18. In both Chinese and Japanese, "Japan" means "origin of the sun." Japan's national flag is called the "sun flag." The allusion likely refers to Japan's imperialist expansion across Asia, during which Japan substituted its own authorities in place of local governments.

19. "Demon seductress" (*yaojing* 妖精), an evil spirit or witch, is a derogatory term for an attractive woman.

20. "The three hundred and sixty trades" is a Chinese expression used to refer collectively to all professions.

21. In Chinese, *zhangfu* 丈夫 (husband), *daifu* 大夫 (doctor), and *tiaofu* 挑夫 (porter) all contain the character *fu* 夫, which can refer to (among other things) "laborer" or "intellectual," depending on context. Qian purposefully juxtaposes *fu* representing different social classes. The 1946 edition has *chefu* 車夫 (chauffeur) instead of *tiaofu*.

22. The Chinese term that Qian uses is literally "sitting bottom" (*zuotun* 坐臀). In the 1946 edition, the German reads: "*Sitzfleisch haben.*" *Haben* is cut from the 1983 and later editions.

23. French lawyer, politician, and epicure Jean Anthelme Brillat-Savarin (1755–1826) was the author of *La Physiologie du goût* (*The Physiology of Taste*, 1825).

24. The 1946 edition reads: ". . . modern man, unlike those court tasters of the past who held official title."

25. In the 1946 edition, the second title is *Scattered Notes on My Journey to the West* (*Xiyou sanji* 西遊散記).

26. Qian humorously transliterates the titles of these two popular travel guides as "a must see" (*bi deguo* 必得過) and "never visited" (*mei lai* 沒來).

27. Grandview Garden is a garden of the Rongguo Mansion. Lin Daiyu is the niece of the master of the Rongguo Mansion and comes from a less-prominent, less-wealthy family, whereas Grandma Liu is from the countryside. Her entrance into the garden is considered the quintessential comedic "country bumpkin" scene in premodern Chinese fiction.

28. In the old days, female characters in Beijing opera were played by males, who tended to be larger than women. This likely alludes to Mei Lanfang 梅蘭芳 (1894–1961), Beijing opera's most famous female impersonator, who, by the 1940s, when Qian wrote "Cat," was in his forties and had put on weight.

29. In the 1946 edition, the second title is *Scattered Notes on the Return of a Native* (*Huanxiang sanji* 還鄉散記).

30. The 1946 edition reads: ". . . just as when a car is pulling out of a garage the nose is the last to emerge."

31. Tianqiao was a market area in southeastern Beijing that, by the end of the Qing dynasty, had become a gathering place for folk performances, including traditional operas, ballad singing, storytelling, comic dialogues, clapper ballads, acrobatics, puppet shows, and martial arts.

32. The 1946 edition reads: "French symbolist poets."

33. The 1946 edition reads: ". . . and encouragement, which served the same purpose as a grown-up's ruffling a child's hair or patting his shoulder to tell him not to be afraid. As such, it was a pity that Yigu still . . ."

34. This passage alludes to the Tang poet Li Bai's 李白 (701–762) poem "A Banquet Held in Xie Tiao's Tower in Xuanzhou, to Bid Farewell to Archivist Shu Yun" (Xuancheng Xie Tiao lou jianbie jiaoshu Shu Yun 宣城謝朓樓餞別校書叔雲). The opening lines are "Ah, my betrayer! / Yesterday's day that never will return. / Ah, my dismayer! / This day today that makes me this day mourn" (棄我去者，昨日之日不可留，亂我心者，今日之日多煩憂).

35. The Boxer Rebellion was a quasi-religious, antiforeign, and anti-Christian armed struggle waged by Chinese peasants in 1900, with the eventual support of the Qing government. It started out in the provinces of Shandong and Hebei. Churches were sacked and missionaries as well as their Chinese converts were killed. Foreign legations in Beijing were besieged before a relief force of foreign powers attacked the Forbidden City and defeated the Qing troops.

36. The 1946 edition has an additional sentence here: "Thanks to clever advertising, these essays were said to be like the eight-legged essays Kuang Chaoren wrote in *The Scholars*: everyone was reading them in the Western world." In chap. 19 of *The Scholars* (*Rulin waishi* 儒林外史), Kuang Chaoren 匡超人 takes a civil service examination on behalf of an imbecile candidate, so Qian seems to be suggesting that Yuan Youchun (a stand-in for Lin Yutang) was pulling a similar sleight of hand as a cultural interpreter.

37. The 1946 edition has additional sentences here: "Otherwise, we'd have to say that the black circles under his eyes were marks of libertinism or insomnia, and that his red nose was a sign of hard drinking or constipation. Malicious speculation of this sort would be dishonest, however, and would furthermore contain too many hypotheses to accord with the scientific method."

38. In Chinese, the abbreviation for "Japan" also means "sun."

39. Cixi (1835–1908) was the dowager empress of the late Qing dynasty.

40. Bonsai is the creation of miniaturized landscapes in containers by carefully controlling the growth of trees over a period of years. Haiku is a concise form of Japanese poetry consisting of seventeen syllables divided into units of five, seven, and five syllables. The creation of bonsai, the writing of haiku verse, and the practice of the elaborate tea ceremony are distinctive Japanese traditional arts.

41. This is a satiric reference to Japan's grandiose plan for the Greater East Asia Co-Prosperity Sphere (*Da dongya gongrong quan* 大東亞共榮圈), a scheme by which Japan would dominate Asia economically, culturally, and militarily.

42. This term was promoted by the German scholar of Shakespeare and Goethe, Friedrich Gundolf (1880–1931), a close associate of the scholar-poet Stefan George.

43. The 1946 edition has an additional sentence here: "His discussion of 'crystallization' was akin to Stendhal's philosophy of love, and his discourse on 'selective affinity' was at one with Goethe's famous novel [*The Sorrows of Young Werther*]."

44. This term is associated with the self-deceptive behavior of Lu Xun's fictional protagonist, Ah Q, from his famous novella *The True Story of Ah Q* (1922).

45. The Qingyun Song was a classical song said to have been composed by Shun 舜, a legendary monarch of antiquity, which was used as the national anthem by the Northern Warlord government. On noise and thinkers, see "A Prejudice."

46. The 1946 edition reads: "Since too many of the dishes were steamed in clear soup, the colors were not well distributed." Expanded in the 1983 edition.

47. The 1946 edition reads: ". . . young men accustomed to living at home or at school would shake their heads and say, 'It really doesn't seem like him.'" Compare the Devil's comments on autobiography in "The Devil Pays a Nighttime Visit to Mr. Qian Zhongshu."

48. The 1946 edition reads: "His mind-set of fearing others and wanting to make others afraid of him must be likened to a cat when it sees a dog."

49. The 1946 edition has an additional sentence here: "He encouraged and guided them, subliminally shaping their outlooks on life and receiving their gifts of flowers."

50. Qian Ruoshui 錢若水 (960–1003), a high official of the Song dynasty, is said to have visited Mount Hua when he was young to get his fortune told by Chen Tuan 陳搏 (d. 989), a monk clad in a hempen robe. Later, when people wrote books on physiognomy, they often used "hempen robe physiognomy" in the title.

51. The 1946 edition has additional sentences here: "A man with such defining eyes was best suited for one of two paths: either become an optometrist and cure his own ocular malady by pledging to rid the world of all eye diseases, or to pair a bewitching smile with his contemptuous glances and get into ambush courtship by darting glances at girls on street corners. But Fu Juqing was a critic after all." Cut in the 1983 edition.

52. He Yimen 何義門 (He Zhuo 何焯 [1661–1722]) was a textual critic of the Qing dynasty born in Changzhuo, Jiangsu.

53. Jin Shengtan 金聖嘆 (1608–1661) was a literary critic who annotated editions of several

Chinese classics, including *Li sao*, *Zhuangzi*, *Book of Songs*, *Poetry of Du Fu*, *The West Wing*, and *The Water Margin*.

54. Joseph Addison (1672–1719) was, for a time, Alexander Pope's most important mentor. But in "Atticus," Pope portrays Addison as one who could "Damn with faint praise, assent with civil leer, / And without sneering, teach the rest to sneer" (quoted in Robert M. Otten, *Joseph Addison* [Boston: Twayne, 1982], 13).

55. This phrase appears in English in the original text. Qian's Chinese rendering, *piyan* 批眼, is a homophone for *piyan* 屁眼 (asshole), though it is not clear that a vulgar pun is intended. In the 1946 edition, the remainder of this sentence reads simply: "he was delighted."

56. The 1946 edition has an additional passage here: "When he had just returned to China, his eyes accidentally lost this special property. A nouveau riche Shanghai businessman felt that, from the car to the pug, his home possessed every foreign product out there except for a sufficiently Westernized person, so he made it his hobby to raise a foreign student and intended to marry Juqing to his only daughter. The daughter forced Juqing to see a doctor about getting a pair of glasses to fix his eyes. Juqing acquiesced, thinking to himself that getting a wife and a fortune wouldn't be a bad way to recoup his foreign study expenses. After two or three days of wearing glasses, however, he couldn't help but protest. He claimed that his habit of leering and sneering had already determined his life's course and ideals, and that if he got rid of them now, over a decade of effort would go to waste, leaving him hesitating at the crossroads of life, seeking a different calling. Fixing his eyes would be no big deal in itself, but it would force him to completely reinvent his entire persona, and this wasn't worth it. He'd prefer not to marry. This incident only elevated Juqing's reputation." Cut in the 1983 edition.

57. The 1946 edition has additional sentences here: "Humble women tend to be insecure about their bodies and are willing to suffer the indignity of having to asking for help with makeup and clothing. Women interested in culture seem to lack this virtue of modesty, however. They tend not to lack for filial piety, as they respectfully carry forward the exact same physical features of their parents, excepting perhaps the addition of a pair of gold-rimmed or tortoiseshell eyeglasses for nearsightedness." Cut in the 1983 edition.

58. The 1946 edition has additional sentences here: "Mrs. Li possessed a deep self-awareness, unlike some girls who regret that they don't have a second body so that they can see how sweet and adorable they look when they're asleep. She wasn't willing to put on powder and cold cream to hide a sleep-worn face. What Yigu was now seeing was what was most adorable about her." Cut in the 1983 edition.

59. The 1946 edition has an additional sentence here: "Not one of them was around his own age."

60. These scrolls were hung in the middle of the wall of the main room.

61. A collection of works by the Southern school of traditional Chinese painting. Also termed Literati Painting, the school was initiated by the Tang poet and painter Wang Wei 王維 (701–761). In depictions of mountains, rivers, flowers, and trees, this school emphasized the expression of the spirit over verisimilitude through freehand brushwork.

62. Dachi (1341–1367) was a Changshou artist.

63. The name Luo Lianfeng puns on that of the artist Luo Pin 羅聘 (1733–1799). In Chinese, the first characters in the words "lychee" (*lizhi* 荔枝) and "profit" (*lixi* 利息) are pronounced the same way.

64. Silly Sister, a maid, finds one day a perfumed embroidered purse in the garden, on one side of which is some writing and on the other two intertwined nude figures. Not knowing that it is a lover's gift, she thinks that they are a pair of fighting demons. In the 1946 edition, the following sentences appear between "the fight of the demons" and "Cold-shouldered in Shanghai . . .": "That wouldn't do! As such, rich businessmen with mistresses kept their distance. Xiajun felt so out of step with the times that when he saw a car kill a pedestrian he would vent that he couldn't even match the popularity of this wronged ghost, who became the center of attention for a crowd for a few minutes."

65. The 1946 edition has an additional phrase here: ". . . such that women had the sensation of a flirtatious man pinching their cheeks." Cut in the 1983 edition.

66. In China, the term of pregnancy is counted from conception, with the first partial month counting as a whole month. Thus ten months is considered to be a full term.

67. The "eight trigrams" (*bagua* 八卦) came from the eight combinations of three whole or broken lines in *The Book of Changes*. They are used in divination.

68. Glyphomancy is the practice of the art of taking characters apart and telling fortunes by reading meaning into the component parts.

69. The first line is from Lao-tzu's *Tao te ching* (*Daodejing* 道德經). See the translation annotated by Fang Juehui, *The Way and Its Virtue* (Taipei: Zhonghua, 1961), 62. The second and third lines are from *Mencius*, "Li lou shang."

70. In traditional Chinese novels, the chapters are headed by rhymed couplets that, in a slightly allusive way, summarize the action to come.

71. This was a practice popular in the Wei 魏 (220–266) and Jin 晉 (265–420) dynasties. It was started by He Yan 何晏 (ca. second–third centuries), Xia Houxuan 夏侯玄 (209–254), and Wang Bi 王弼 (226–249), who attempted to interpret Confucian classics using Daoist ideas. They were famous for paying no attention to worldly affairs and engaging only in profound theoretical discussions. At their leisurely gatherings, they drank, wrote poetry, and took pleasure in ignoring Confucian etiquette. Many intellectuals admired them and followed their example.

72. Vicente Blasco Ibáñez (1867–1928), *Los cuatro jinetes del Apocalipsis* (Valencia: Prometeo, 1916). See also Revelation 6:2–8.

73. Eating vinegar is a Chinese euphemism for jealousy, especially between lovers.

74. In Buddhism, acts of charity and compassion for living creatures help one achieve higher levels of spiritual attainment in future reincarnations.

75. In the 1946 edition, Qian explicitly mentions here William T. Preyer's (1841–1897) *Die Seele des Kindes* (*The Mind of the Child*, 1882). Cut in the 1983 edition.

76. This phrase was added in the 1983 edition.

77. Qian specifies the French spelling, Cléopâtre, in the 1946 edition, which follows this sentence with: "Didn't Old Uncle Lu say that during the Ming dynasty the empress and court ladies all loved having cats as pets?" Cut in the 1983 edition.

78. The 1946 edition has an additional sentence here: "At that moment he felt like a romantic youth committing suicide by swallowing sleeping pills, lacking the energy to save himself from certain death, but with enough lingering consciousness to reproach himself for having left this world too soon, resent everyone else for living on as if nothing had occurred, and anxiously wonder in vain what opinions or criticisms they had about his conduct." Cut in the 1983 edition.

79. The 1946 edition has additional sentences here: "He had always detested Saturday after-

noons and Sundays and envied his lucky classmates who got to spend this time in idle pursuits. Now he felt the loss of this day and a half of leisure even more acutely, like the raw gap left by a tooth that has fallen out." Cut in the 1983 edition.

80. The 1946 edition reads: "Aimo looked at her husband and said . . ." Changed in the 1983 edition.

81. The two sentences that follow were added in the 1983 edition.

82. As a *juedai jiaren* 絕代佳人 (peerless beauty), Aimo is both a beauty "for time immemorial," or to "end the ages" (*juedai* 絕代), and an "heirless" (*juedai* 絕代) beauty.

83. The 1946 edition has additional sentences here: "He knew what all romance led to, but he refused to admit that his love was the same as others'. 'Maybe that's all I'd want from other women, but that'd never be the case with *her*,' he'd tell himself. This was the stage Yigu was at." Cut in the 1983 edition.

84. The 1946 edition has an additional sentence here: "In contrast, the freshness of young girls struck him as abrasive." Cut in the 1983 edition.

85. The 1946 edition has an additional sentence here: "He didn't care about the future, having entrusted his entire being to an eternal present." Cut in the 1983 edition.

86. The 1946 edition has three different sentences instead of this one: "When he thought of her his heart beat as if it would burst into blossom. While alone, he would find himself suddenly blushing. Whenever he heard her voice, his face, for no reason, would be covered in red like a World War II map of the world." Cut in the 1983 edition.

87. The 1946 edition has an additional sentence here: "He became absurdly angry, thinking that Aimo shouldn't cry—that no beautiful woman should cry." Cut in the 1983 edition.

88. In the 1946 edition, the following sentences read: "Her wounded pride kept calling out for 'revenge.' Yigu saw her face harden with hatred. It was not a pretty sight. He realized that there would be no work today, and it was no fun watching someone else's domestic dispute, so it would be better if he went home. He got up. 'Mrs. Li . . . ,' he began."

89. The 1946 edition has an additional passage here: "If Yigu had been the type to speak impulsively and honestly, he would have said, 'I'm deeply in love with you, but what happened just now made you less lovable.' If Yigu had been of a more opportunistic disposition, he would have responded, 'Do you love me?' If Yigu had been too afraid to tell the truth, unwilling to lie, and also an old hand at dealing with women, he wouldn't have said anything but simply taken Aimo in his arms and kissed her. Worried that lovers would run into problems if they said too much, or even bigger problems if they had no response to such queries, God created the kiss as a type of all-purpose expressive first aid. At times, it meant 'That goes without saying'; at other times it meant 'Don't bring all that up again.' In short, it meant 'Actions speak louder than words.' Unfortunately, Yigu didn't know any of this and was taken aback . . ." Cut in the 1983 edition.

90. In the 1946 edition, the following sentences read: "Taoqi scurried in with a painful tail, and Yigu ran out to the street, filled with shame and anger. He didn't even wait for Old Whitey to open the gate. 'Big fool! Big fool!' The words resounded in his head like the sound of rice being husked with mortar and pestle. The gentle spring breeze made his cheeks burn where he had been slapped."

INSPIRATION

Translation adapted from Dennis T. Hu, trans., "The Inspiration, by Ch'ien Chung-shu," in *Modern Chinese Short Stories and Novellas, 1919–1949*, ed. Joseph S. M. Lau, C. T. Hsia, and Leo Ou-fan Lee (New York: Columbia University Press, 1981), 418–34.

1. Fei Ming 廢名 (literally, "abolished name") was the pen name of Feng Wenbing 馮文炳 (1901–1967), a fiction writer who emerged during the May Fourth period and specialized in pastoral lyricism.

2. Victor Marie Hugo (1802–1885).

3. Gabriele D'Annunzio (1863–1938).

4. In the 1946 edition, this sentence appears in parentheses: "(Regrettably, the 'Sinologist' had not yet begun his research on the semantics of Chinese, so this forceful essay had been written for nothing.)"

5. The 1946 edition has an additional sentence here: "There's no chance that Heaven will be stocked with all these innovations of modern medicine." Cut in the 1983 edition.

6. The 1946 edition has additional sentences here: "The playboy Don Juan boasted an unprecedented 2,594 mistresses, it's true, but such an impressive record has got to be the result of unremitting efforts of a lifetime, plucking flowers and accumulating experience in illicit love. Taking seventy-two females all at once is something even Don Juan couldn't have handled." Cut in the 1983 edition.

7. In the 1946 edition, the mustache and beard are described as follows: "The growth was so black and thick that his mouth could scarcely be seen even when he spoke. The words that came out through this curly grove seemed somehow dyed with the color of that beard, every one of them dark. They also appeared to have grown hair of their own, brushing the listener's ears until they itched."

8. The 1946 edition has additional sentences here: "To get there you've got to keep going for quite a while yet. You see, the Eastern Hemisphere is where you've fallen from, sir. Despite the weight of your genius, you haven't made it all the way through the earth, since the western half of the earth's crust is fortified by those American skyscrapers, structures of steel and reinforced concrete. But your works have had a tremendous impact on the center of the earth, I'm sure, and San Francisco and other places like it may very well have experienced earthquakes of several minutes' duration." Cut in the 1983 edition.

9. In the 1946 edition, the paragraph finishes: ". . . came the bearded one's quiet reply. The chill in his tone cooled the dark gloom of his words to the freezing point."

10. In isolation, Zhongguo dichan gongsi 中國地產公司 would be more aptly translated as "China Real Estate Company"; in this story, however, the current rendering helps preserve some of the wordplay that follows.

11. The 1946 edition reads: "This is the only way we can avoid letting down those who make comparisons of Eastern and Western civilization or disrupting their pet theories."

12. The 1946 edition has additional sentences here: "Anyway, you wanted to make me a roughneck, but I don't feel myself one at all. Swollen and bloated sounds more like it, and maybe that was what you had in mind. I might as well have been soaked in water, I was so completely lacking in strength." Cut from the 1983 edition.

13. The 1946 edition has an additional sentence here: "His only problem was that he was unfamiliar with the intricacies of Chinese tones as used in classical poetry; consequently, the verses he was capable of making up were not in quite as archaic a style as he would have liked."

14. The 1946 edition has four different sentences instead of the following three: "For crying out loud, I should have known better! Having such a murderous pen, I should have used it to produce propaganda for the war against Japan. It could have rivaled the atom bomb! Why an autobiography, of all things?" Changed in the 1983 edition.

15. This term from Hegelian philosophy is used to explain the interaction between thesis and antithesis.

16. The 1946 edition has an additional sentence preceding this sentence: "The Writer had long since tossed all of his thread-bound volumes into the toilet."

SOUVENIR

Translation adapted from Nathan K. Mao, trans., "Souvenir, by Ch'ien Chung-shu," in *Modern Chinese Short Stories and Novellas, 1919–1949*, ed. Joseph S. M. Lau, C. T. Hsia, and Leo Ou-fan Lee (New York: Columbia University Press, 1981), 435–53.

1. Presumably, the city is Chongqing 重慶 (Chunking), the Nationalists' base during the Second Sino-Japanese War (1937–1945).

2. The Lantern Festival was held on the fifteenth day of the first lunar month.

3. *Qipao* is a tight-fitting dress with a high mandarin collar and side slits.

4. In the 1946 edition, "modern women" put comfort first.

5. *Heroic Sons and Daughters* (*Ernü yingxiong zhuan* 兒女英雄傳) is a novel by Wen Kang 文康 (fl. 1821). Thirteenth Sister is among its major heroines.

6. Biaosao is polite title for an older cousin's wife.

7. In the 1946 edition, Tianjian adds here: "—That's right! On days I was off duty and came into town I had a place to stay. It was convenient to have friends by too."

8. "Flower vase" was a belittling term for any female employee who did not type and who did little work but who looked pretty.

EDITIONS

The translations in this volume either are based on or have been revised to match the editions published in Fujian renmin chubanshe's *Compendium of Shanghai Literature from the War Period* in 1983. Annotations in the endnotes call attention to differences between the 1983 editions and (1) the 1939 "Cold Room Jottings" editions of four *Margins* essays; (2) the 1941 Kaiming shuju edition of *Margins*; (3) the 1946 Kaiming shuju edition of *Human*; and (4) the 2001 Sanlian editions of both works. The generic numbered titles of the four "Cold Room Jottings" essays were changed when they were republished in the 1941 Kaiming edition.

WRITTEN IN THE MARGINS OF LIFE

1939. "Lengwu suibi zhi yi" 冷屋隨筆之一 (Cold Room Jottings No. 1). ["Lun wenren" 論文人.] *Jinri pinglun* 今日評論 (*Criticism Today*) (Kunming) 1, no. 3 (January 15).

1939. "Lengwu suibi zhi er" 冷屋隨筆之二 (Cold Room Jottings No. 2). ["Shi wenmang" 釋文盲.] *Jinri pinglun* 1, no. 6 (February 5).

1939. "Lengwu suibi zhi san" 冷屋隨筆之三 (Cold Room Jottings No. 3). ["Yige pianjian" 一個偏見.] *Jinri pinglun* 1, no. 14 (April 2).

1939. "Lengwu suibi zhi si" 冷屋隨筆之四 (Cold Room Jottings No. 4). ["Shuo xiao" 說笑.] *Jinri pinglun* 1, no. 22 (May 24).

1941. *Xie zai rensheng bianshang* 寫在人生邊上 (*Written in the Margins of Life*). Kaiming wenxue xinkan 開明文學新刊 (Kaiming New Literature Series). Shanghai: Kaiming shudian. Reprinted in 1946, 1947, 1948.

1950. *Xie zai rensheng bianshang*. Hong Kong: Yixin shudian / Wenchang shuju. Reprinted in 1973.

1982. *Xie zai rensheng bianshang*. Zhongguo xiandai wenxue congshu 中國現代文學叢書 (Modern Chinese Literature Compendium). Hong Kong: Wenjiao chubanshe.

1983. *Xie zai rensheng bianshang*. Shanghai kangzhan shiqi wenxue congshu, di er ji 上海抗戰時期文學叢書，第二輯 (Compendium of Shanghai Literature from the War Period, no. 2). Fuzhou: Fujian renmin chubanshe. Reprinted in the same compendium in a joint volume with *Ren, shou, gui* 人獸鬼, Fuzhou: Haixia wenyi chubanshe, 1991.

1990. *Xie zai rensheng bianshang*. Beijing: Zhongguo shehui kexue chubanshe.

1990. *Xie zai rensheng bianshang*. Vol. 4 of *Qian Zhongshu zuopinji* 錢鍾書作品集 (*Collected Works of Qian Zhongshu*). Taipei: Shulin chuban youxian gongsi.

2000. *Xie zai rensheng bianshang*. Shenyang: Liaoning renmin chubanshe / Liaohai chubanshe.

2001. *Xie zai rensheng bianshang, Rensheng bianshang de bianshang, Shi yu* 寫在人生邊上；人生邊上的邊上；石語 (*Written in the Margins of Life; In the Margins of the Margins of Life; Stone's Words*). Vol. 6 of *Qian Zhongshu ji* 錢鍾書集 (*The Qian Zhongshu Collection*). Beijing: Sanlian shudian. Simplified character edition published in 2002 and reprinted in 2003, 2007.

HUMAN, BEAST, GHOST

1946. *Ren, shou, gui* 人獸鬼 (*Human, Beast, Ghost*). Shanghai: Kaiming shudian. Reprinted in 1947.

1971. *Ren, shou, gui*. Hong Kong: Wanyou tushu gongsi.

1982. *Ren, shou, gui*. Zhongguo xiandai wenxue congshu. Hong Kong: Wenjiao chubanshe.

1983. *Ren, shou, gui*. Shanghai kangzhan shiqi wenxue congshu. Fuzhou: Fujian renmin chubanshe.

1987. *Ren, shou, gui*. Xinzhuang, Taiwan: Fuxin shuju.

1999. *Ren, shou, gui*. Beijing: Zhongguo huaqiao. Based on the 1983 edition.

2001. *Ren, shou, gui*. Vol. 5 of *Qian Zhongshu ji*. Beijing: Sanlian shudian. Simplified character edition published in 2002 and reprinted in 2003, 2007.

JOINT EDITIONS

1987. *Ren, shou, gui; fu: Xie zai rensheng bianshang* 人獸鬼，附：寫在人生邊上 (*Human, Beast, Ghost; Addendum: Written in the Margins of Life*). Xindian, Taiwan: Gufeng chubanshe.

1989. *Xie zai rensheng bianshang*. Vol. 3 of *Qian Zhongshu zuopinji*. Taipei: Shulin chuban gongsi. Includes *Human*.

1991. *Ren, shou, gui; Xie zai rensheng bianshang*. Shanghai kangzhan shiqi wenxue congshu. Fuzhou: Haixia wenyi chubanshe.

1994. *Xie zai rensheng bianshang; Ren, shou, gui*. Hong Kong: Tiandi tushu youxian gongsi. Reprinted in 1997.

1997. *Qian Zhongshu zuopinji*. Shenyang: Chunfeng wenyi chubanshe. Contains *Margins, Human,* and *Qi zhui ji* 七綴集 (*Seven Patches*).

1998. *Qian Zhongshu zuopinji*. Lanzhou: Gansu renmin chubanshe. Contains *Weicheng* 圍城 (*Fortress Besieged*), *Human, Margins, Guan zhui bian* 管錐編 (*The Tube and Awl Collection*), and *Qi zhui ji*.

FURTHER READING IN ENGLISH

WORKS BY QIAN ZHONGSHU

A Collection of Qian Zhongshu's English Essays. Beijing: Foreign Language Teaching and Research Press, 2005.

Fortress Besieged. Translated by Jeanne Kelly and Nathan K. Mao. New York: New Directions, 2004.

Limited Views: Essays on Ideas and Letters. Edited and translated by Ronald Egan. Cambridge, Mass.: Harvard University Press, 1998.

"Preface." In *Six Chapters from My Life "Downunder,"* by Yang Jiang. Translated by Howard Goldblatt. Seattle: University of Washington Press, 1984.

STUDIES

Chang, Sheng-Tai. "Reading Qian Zhongshu's 'God's Dream' as a Postmodern Text." *Chinese Literature: Essays, Articles, Reviews* 16 (1994): 93–110.

Egan, Ronald. "Introduction." In *Limited Views: Essays on Ideas and Letters*, by Qian Zhongshu. Edited and translated by Ronald Egan, 1–26. Cambridge, Mass.: Harvard University Press, 1998.

Gunn, Edward M., Jr. "Antiromanticism." In *Unwelcome Muse: Chinese Literature in Shanghai and Peking, 1937–1945*, chap. 5. New York: Columbia University Press, 1980.

Hsia, C. T. "Ch'ien Chung-shu." In *A History of Modern Chinese Fiction*, chap. 16. 3rd ed. Bloomington: Indiana University Press, 1999.

Hu, Dennis Ting-pong. "A Linguistic-Literary Study of Ch'ien Chung-shu's Three Creative Works." Ph.D. diss., University of Wisconsin–Madison, 1977.

——. "Ch'ien Chung-shu's Novel *Wei-ch'eng.*" *Journal of Asian Studies* 37, no. 3 (1978): 427–43.

Huters, Theodore. "Illumination of Chinese Fictional Conventions in Qian Zhongshu's *Weicheng.*" *Selected Papers in Asian Studies* 1 (1976): 50–60.

——. "In Search of Qian Zhongshu." *Modern Chinese Literature and Culture* 11, no. 1 (1999): 193–99.

——. *Qian Zhongshu.* World Authors 660. Boston: Twayne, 1982.

——. "Traditional Innovation: Qian Zhong-shu (Ch'ien Chung-shu) and Modern Chinese Letters." Ph.D. diss., Stanford University, 1977.

Linsley, Robert. "Qian Zhongshu and the Late, Late Modern." *Yishu: Journal of Contemporary Chinese Art* 1, no. 1 (2002): 60–67.

Mao, Nathan K. "Introduction." In *Fortress Besieged*, by Ch'ien Chung-shu [Qian Zhongshu]. Translated by Jeanne Kelly and Nathan K. Mao, xiii–xxix. Bloomington: Indiana University Press, 1979.

Mao, Yiran. "Introduction." In *Cat: A Translation and Critical Introduction*, 17–46. Hong Kong: Joint Publishing, 2001.

Zhang Longxi. "Qian Zhongshu on Philosophical and Mystical Paradoxes in the *Laozi*." In *Religious and Philosophical Aspects of the Laozi*, edited by Mark Csikszentmihalyi and Philip J. Ivanhoe, 97–126. Albany: State University of New York Press, 1999.

TRANSLATORS

CHRISTOPHER G. REA received his Ph.D. from Columbia University and is assistant professor of modern Chinese literature at the University of British Columbia.

DENNIS T. HU received his Ph.D. from the University of Madison–Wisconsin with a dissertation on Qian Zhongshu's creative works.

NATHAN K. MAO, cotranslator (with Jeanne Kelly) of *Fortress Besieged* (2004) and translator of *Cold Nights* (2002), was educated at New Asia College, Chinese University of Hong Kong; Yale University; and the University of Wisconsin. He now teaches English at Shippensburg University of Pennsylvania.

A full-time mother, a part-time businesswoman, and a sometime translator, YIRAN MAO received her B.A. in English from Beijing Foreign Languages Institute and dual M.A.'s in comparative literature and art history from the University of Iowa. Selena, Arianna, and Apollo are her best achievements.

PHILIP F. WILLIAMS was professor of Chinese literature and culture at Arizona State University and Massey University and is currently teaching at the University of Montana. His ninth and most recent book is *From Marginal to Mainstream: Asian Literary Voices* (2010).

CPSIA information can be obtained
at www.ICGtesting.com
Printed in the USA
JSHW030813140922
30440JS00011B/26

9 780231 152754